Ethnography

KT-477-848

Ethnography

Principles in practice

Second edition

Martyn Hammersley and
Paul Atkinson

London and New York

First edition published in 1983 by
Tavistock Publications Ltd
Reprinted in 1986 and 1987

Reprinted 1989, 1990, 1991, 1992, 1993
by Routledge

Second edition first published 1995
by Routledge
11 New Fetter Lane, London EC4P 4EE

Simultaneously published in the USA and Canada
by Routledge
29 West 35th Street, New York, NY 10001

Reprinted 1996, 1997, 2000, 2001, 2002

Routledge is an imprint of the Taylor & Francis Group

© 1995 Martyn Hammersley and Paul Atkinson

Typeset in Palatino by Intype, London
Printed and bound in Great Britain by
Biddles Ltd, Guildford and King's Lynn

All rights reserved. No part of this book may be reprinted or
reproduced or utilized in any form or by any electronic,
mechanical, or other means, now known or hereafter
invented, including photocopying and recording, or in any
information storage or retrieval system, without permission in
writing from the publishers.

British Library Cataloguing in Publication Data
A catalogue record for this book is available from the British Library

Library of Congress Cataloging in Publication Data
Hammersley, Martyn.
    Ethnography: principles in practice / Martyn Hammersley and
Paul Atkinson.—2nd ed.
        p. cm.
    Includes bibliographical references and index.
    1. Ethnology—Methodology. 2. Ethnology—Field work.
3. Social sciences—Field work. I. Atkinson, Paul. II. Title.
GN345.H35 1995
306´01´8—dc20   94–30136
                                                                   CIP

ISBN 0–415–08664–7

The more ancient of the Greeks (whose writings are lost) took up ... a position ... between the presumption of pronouncing on everything, and the despair of comprehending anything; and though frequently and bitterly complaining of the difficulty of inquiry and the obscurity of things, and like impatient horses champing at the bit, they did not the less follow up their object and engage with nature, thinking (it seems) that this very question – viz., whether or not anything can be known – was to be settled not by arguing, but by trying. And yet they too, trusting entirely to the force of their understanding, applied no rule, but made everything turn upon hard thinking and perpetual working and exercise of the mind.

(Francis Bacon 1620)

Contents

Acknowledgements

We thank the following colleagues for much help in clarifying our ideas over the long period during which the first and second editions of this book were produced: Sara Delamont, Anne Murcott, and other members of the School of Social and Administrative Studies, University of Wales College of Cardiff; Andy Hargreaves, Phil Strong, Peter Woods, John Scarth, Peter Foster, and Roger Gomm. We must also express our thanks to Meryl Baker, Stella Riches, Myrtle Robins, Lilian Walsh, Aileen Lodge, and June Evison for typing various drafts of the manuscript.

Preface to the second edition

In preparing a new edition of this book we have not altered its basic structure. We have, however, made substantial changes throughout, clarifying and developing the discussion where it seemed to need this, and updating it where this has been made necessary by subsequent developments. Chapter 1 has undergone considerable rewriting, for both of these reasons. Extensive new material has also been introduced into Chapter 7, dealing with the use of microcomputers in handling data, and also in Chapter 9, concerned with ethnographic writing. Finally, a chapter has been added on the ethics of ethnography, a topic which was not given sufficient attention in the first edition.

The central theme of the book remains the importance of a reflexive approach to ethnographic work. As we explained in the Preface to the first edition, we have sought to steer a course between an abstract, methodological treatise and a practical 'cookbook'. This is because for us methodology and method, like social theory and empirical research, feed into one another. Neither can be discussed effectively in isolation. The first chapter is devoted to spelling out what we mean by a reflexive approach, and locating this in relation to the other methodological ideas that have influenced ethnography, from naturalism to post-structuralism. Subsequent chapters focus on more concrete aspects of the research process, advocating and illustrating the reflexive point of view. We have tried to make this new edition more accessible than the first, even though the issues it deals with are not always easy or straightforward. How successful we have been in this and other respects only our readers can judge.

Chapter 1

What is ethnography?

In recent decades ethnography has become a popular approach to social research, along with other kinds of qualitative work. This stems in part from disillusionment with the quantitative methods that for long held the dominant position in most of the social sciences, and in most areas of applied social research. Indeed, the popularity of qualitative research is now such that in some areas it has itself become the dominant approach. At the same time, though, this success has brought diversification and disagreement: there is considerable variety in prescription and practice, and along with this some dissensus about the proper nature of qualitative research and its purposes. This diversity in perspective and practice has been formalized in attempts to identify multiple paradigms. Thus, Marshall and Rossman (1989) list six forms of qualitative research, while in the field of education Jacob finds seven or eight distinct qualitative paradigms in the United States (Jacob 1987), and similar diversity is to be found in British work in that field (Atkinson *et al.* 1988).

For the purposes of this book we shall interpret the term 'ethnography' in a liberal way, not worrying much about what does and does not count as examples of it. We see the term as referring primarily to a particular method or set of methods. In its most characteristic form it involves the ethnographer participating, overtly or covertly, in people's daily lives for an extended period of time, watching what happens, listening to what is said, asking questions – in fact, collecting whatever data are available to throw light on the issues that are the focus of the research. Equally, though, as we shall suggest later, there is a sense in which all social researchers are participant observers;

and, as a result, the boundaries around ethnography are necessarily unclear. In particular, we would not want to make any hard-and-fast distinction between ethnography and other sorts of qualitative inquiry.

In many respects ethnography is the most basic form of social research. Not only does it have a very long history (Wax 1971), it also bears a close resemblance to the routine ways in which people make sense of the world in everyday life. Some commentators regard this as its basic strength; others see it as a fundamental weakness. In the past it was more commonly seen as a weakness, but recently it has increasingly come to be regarded more positively. As a result, the case for qualitative work is now more widely accepted than before, and this has led to a growth of interest in the combination of qualitative and quantitative techniques (Bryman 1988; Brannen 1992). However, there has been a countervailing tendency on the part of some ethnographers to distinguish their approach more sharply from quantitative method, and in the process to reject the very notion of a *science* of social life devoted to understanding human behaviour (see, for example, Smith 1989; Guba 1990; Lather 1991).

Social researchers have long felt the tension between conceptions of scientific method modelled on the practices of the natural sciences, on the one hand, and ideas about the distinctiveness of the social world and the implications of this for how it should be studied, on the other. But in recent years this has been exacerbated by increased questioning of the value and character of natural science. It no longer represents the prestigious model it once did. In part this arises from recognition that its fruits are a mixed blessing. In addition, there has been much emphasis on the fact that it is a social product; so stress has been placed on what it shares with other sorts of human activity, and also on parallels with scholarship in the humanities and the arts. Furthermore, such scholarship has itself become an increasingly important influence on social research, especially among ethnographers.

The purpose of this chapter is to explore and assess these changes in ideas about ethnographic methodology. We shall begin by looking at the conflict between quantitative and qualitative method as competing models of social research, which raged across many fields in the past and continues in some even today. This was often seen as a clash between competing philosophical positions. Following much precedent we shall call these 'positivism' and 'naturalism': the former privileging quantitative methods, the latter promoting ethnography as the central, if not the only legitimate, social research method. ('Naturalism' is a term which is used in a variety of different, even contradictory, ways in the literature: see Matza 1969. Here we have simply adopted the conventional meaning within the ethnographic literature.)

POSITIVISM VERSUS NATURALISM

Positivism has a long history in philosophy, but it reached its high point in the 'logical positivism' of the 1930s and 1940s (Kolakowski 1972). This movement had a considerable influence upon social scientists, notably in promoting the status of experimental and survey research and the quantitative forms of analysis associated with them. Before this, in both sociology and social psychology, qualitative and quantitative techniques had generally been used side by side, often by the same researchers. Nineteenth-century investigators, such as Mayhew (1861), LePlay (1879), and Booth (1902–3), treated quantitative and qualitative data as complementary. Even the sociologists of the Chicago School, often represented as exponents of participant observation, employed both 'case-study' and 'statistical' methods. While there were recurrent debates among them regarding the relative advantages and uses of the two approaches, there was general agreement on the value of both (Bulmer, 1984; Harvey 1985; Hammersley 1989b). It was only later, with the rapid development of statistical methods and the growing influence of positivist philosophy, that survey research came to be regarded by some of its practitioners as a self-sufficient methodological tradition. (In social psychology this process started rather earlier, and it was the experiment which became the dominant method.)

Today, the term 'positivism' has become little more than a term of abuse among social scientists, and as a result its meaning has become obscured. For present purposes the major tenets of positivism can be outlined as follows (for more detailed discussions see Keat and Urry 1975; Giddens 1979; Cohen 1980):

1 *Physical science, conceived in terms of the logic of the experiment, is the model for social research.* While positivists do not claim that the methods of all the physical sciences are the same, they do argue that these share a common logic. This is the logic of the experiment, where quantitatively measured variables are manipulated in order to identify the relationships among them. This logic is taken to be the defining feature of science.

2 *Universal laws.* Positivists adopt a characteristic conception of explanation, usually termed the 'covering law' model. Here events are explained in deductive fashion by appeal to universal laws that state regular relationships between variables which hold across all relevant circumstances. However, it is the statistical version of this model, whereby the relationships have only a high probability of applying across relevant circumstances, that has generally been adopted by social scientists; and this has encouraged great concern with sampling procedures, especially in survey research. Given this model of explanation, a premium is placed on the generalizability of findings.

3 *Neutral observation language.* Finally, positivists give priority to phenomena that are directly observable; any appeal to intangibles runs the risk of being dismissed as metaphysical speculation. It is argued that scientific theories must be founded upon, or tested by appeal to, descriptions that simply correspond to the state of the world, involving no theoretical assumptions and thus being beyond doubt. This foundation could be sense data, as in traditional empiricism, or it may be the realm of the 'publicly observable': for example, the movement of physical objects, such as mercury in a thermometer, which can be easily agreed upon by all observers. Great emphasis is therefore given to the standardization of procedures of data collection, which is intended to facilitate the achievement of measurements that are stable across observers. If measurement is reliable in this sense, it is argued, it provides a sound, theoretically neutral base upon which to build.

Central to positivism, then, is a certain conception of scientific method, modelled on the natural sciences, and in particular on physics (Toulmin 1972). Method here is concerned with the testing of theories. A sharp distinction is drawn between the context of discovery and the context of justification (Reichenbach 1938 and 1951). The question of how theoretical ideas are generated belongs to the former and is outside the realm of scientific method. It is the procedures employed in the context of justification that are held to mark science off from common sense, since they involve the rigorous assessment of alternative theories from an objective point of view.

Thus, for positivists, the most important feature of scientific theories is that they are open to, and are subjected to, test: they can be confirmed, or at least falsified, with certainty. This requires the exercise of control over variables, which can be achieved through physical control, as in experiments, or through statistical analysis of a large number of cases, as in survey research. Without any control over variables, it is argued, one can do no more than speculate about causal relationships, since no basis for testing hypotheses is available. So, the process of testing involves comparing what the theory says should occur under certain circumstances with what actually does occur – in short, comparing it with 'the facts'. These facts are collected by means of methods that, like the facts they collect, are regarded as theory-neutral; otherwise, it is assumed, they could not provide a conclusive test of the theory. In particular, every attempt is made to eliminate the effect of the observer by developing an explicit, standardized set of data elicitation procedures. This allows replication by others so that an assessment of the reliability of the findings can be made. In survey research, for example, the behaviour of interviewers is typically specified down to the wording of questions and the order in which they are asked. In experiments the behaviour of the experimenter and the instructions he or she gives to subjects are closely defined. It is argued that if it can be ensured that each survey respondent or experimental subject in a study and its replications is faced with the same set of stimuli, then their responses will be commensurable. Where such explicit and standardized procedures are not employed, as in participant observation, so the argument goes, it is impossible to know how to interpret the responses since one has no idea what they are responses to. In short, it is only through the exercise of physical or statistical control of variables and their rigorous measurement, positivists argue, that science is able to produce a body of knowledge whose validity is conclusive, which can replace the myths and dogma of common sense.

Qualitative research does not match these positivist canons, and as a result it came under criticism as lacking scientific rigour. It was sometimes dismissed as quite inappropriate to social *science*, on the grounds that the data and findings it produces are 'subjective', mere idiosyncratic impressions of one or two cases that cannot provide a solid foundation for rigorous scientific analysis. In reaction, ethnographers developed an alternative view of the proper nature of social research, often termed 'naturalism' (Lofland 1967; Blumer 1969; Matza 1969; Denzin 1971; Schatzman and Strauss 1973; Guba 1978). They too sometimes appealed to natural science as a model, but their conception of its method was different to that of the positivists, and the exemplar was usually nineteenth-century biology rather than twentieth-century physics.

Naturalism proposes that, as far as possible, the social world should be studied in its 'natural' state, undisturbed by the researcher. Hence, 'natural' not 'artificial' settings, like experiments or formal interviews, should be the primary source of data. Furthermore, the research must be carried out in ways that are sensitive to the nature of the setting. The primary aim should be to describe what happens in the setting, how the people involved see their own actions and those of others, and the contexts in which the action takes place.

A key element of naturalism is the demand that the social researcher should adopt an attitude of 'respect' or 'appreciation' towards the social world. In Matza's words, naturalism is 'the philosophical view that remains true to the nature of the phenomenon under study' (1969:5). This is counterposed to the positivists' primary and prior commitment to a conception of scientific method reconstructed from the experience of natural scientists:

> Reality exists in the empirical world and not in the methods used to study that world; it is to be discovered in the examination of that world. Methods are mere instruments designed to identify and analyze the obdurate character of the empirical world, and as such their value exists only in their suitability in enabling this task to be done. In this fundamental sense the procedures employed in each part of the act of scientific

inquiry should and must be assessed in terms of whether they respect the nature of the empirical world under study – whether what they signify or imply to be the nature of the empirical world is actually the case.

(Blumer 1969:27–8)

A first requirement of social research according to naturalism, then, is fidelity to the phenomena under study, not to any particular set of methodological principles, however strongly supported by philosophical arguments.

Moreover, naturalists regard social phenomena as quite distinct in character from physical phenomena. In this respect, naturalism drew on a wide range of philosophical and sociological ideas, but especially on symbolic interactionism, phenomenology, and hermeneutics. From different starting points these traditions all argue that the social world cannot be understood in terms of simple causal relationships or by the subsumption of social events under universal laws. This is because human actions are based upon, or infused by, social meanings: that is, by intentions, motives, beliefs, rules, and values. Thus, for example, at the heart of symbolic interactionism is a rejection of the stimulus-response model of human behaviour which is built into the methodological arguments of positivism. In the view of interactionists, people *interpret* stimuli, and these interpretations, continually under revision as events unfold, shape their actions. As a result, the same physical stimulus can mean different things to different people – and, indeed, to the same person at different times. Mehan provides a striking example that relates directly to the sort of data collection method supported by positivism:

A question from [a] language development test instructs the child to choose 'the animal that can fly' from a bird, an elephant, and a dog. The correct answer (obviously) is the bird. Many first grade children, though, chose the elephant along with the bird as a response to that question. When I later asked them why they chose that answer they replied: 'That's Dumbo'. Dumbo (of course) is Walt Disney's flying elephant, well known to children who watch television and read children's books as an animal that flies.

(Mehan 1974:249)

Such indeterminacy of interpretation undermines attempts to develop standard measures of human behaviour. Interpretations of the same set of experimental instructions or interview questions will undoubtedly vary among people and across occasions.

Equally important, naturalists argue that because people's behaviour is not caused in a mechanical way, it is not amenable to the sort of causal analysis and manipulation of variables that are characteristic of the quantitative research inspired by positivism. Any hope of discovering 'laws' of human behaviour is misplaced, it is suggested, since human behaviour is continually constructed, and reconstructed, on the basis of people's interpretations of the situations they are in.

According to naturalism, in order to understand people's behaviour we must use an approach that gives us access to the meanings that guide that behaviour. Fortunately, the capacities we have developed as social actors can give us such access. As participant observers we can learn the culture or subculture of the people we are studying. We can come to interpret the world in the same way as they do, and thereby learn to understand their behaviour in a different way to that in which natural scientists set about understanding the behaviour of physical phenomena. (This form of understanding social phenomena is often referred to as *Verstehen*. See Truzzi 1974 for a discussion and illustrations of the history of this concept.)

The need to learn the culture of those we are studying is most obvious in the case of societies other than our own. Here, not only may we not know *why* people do what they do, often we do not even know *what* they are doing. We are in much the same position as Schutz's (1964) stranger. Schutz notes how in the weeks and months following an immigrant's arrival in the host society, what he or she previously took for granted as knowledge about that society turns out to be unreliable, if not obviously false. In addition, areas of ignorance previously of no importance come to take on great significance; and overcoming them is necessary for the pursuit of important goals, perhaps even for the stranger's very survival in the new environment. In the process of learning how to participate in the host society, the stranger gradually acquires an inside knowledge of it, which supplants his or her previous 'external' knowledge. Schutz argues that by virtue of being forced to come to understand a culture in this way, the stranger acquires a certain objectivity not normally available to culture members. The latter live inside the culture, and tend to see it as simply a reflection of 'how the world is'. They are often not conscious of the fundamental presuppositions that shape their vision, many of which are distinctive to their culture.

Schutz's account of the experience of the stranger matches most closely the work of anthropologists, who typically study societies very different to their own. However, the experience of the stranger is not restricted to those moving to live in a different society. Movement among groups within a single society can produce the same effects, though generally in a milder form. There are many different layers or circles of cultural knowledge within any society. Indeed, this is particularly true of modern industrial societies with their complex divisions of labour, multifarious life-styles, ethnic diversity, and deviant communities – and the subcultures and perspectives that maintain, and are generated by, these social divisions. This was, of course, one of the major rationales for the research of the Chicago School sociologists. Drawing on the analogy of plant and animal ecology, they set out to document the very different patterns of life to be found in different parts of the city of Chicago, from the 'high society' of the so-called 'gold coast' to slum ghettos such as Little Sicily. Later, the same kind of approach came to be applied to the cultures of occupations, organizations, and deviant groups, as well as to even more diffuse 'social worlds' (Strauss 1978 and 1993) such as those of art (Becker 1974), racing (Scott 1968), or organized drug dealing (Adler 1993).

According to the naturalist account, the value of ethnography as a social research method is founded upon the existence of such variations in cultural patterns across and within societies, and their significance for understanding social processes. Ethnography exploits the capacity that any social actor possesses for learning new cultures, and the objectivity to which this process gives rise. Even where he or she is researching a familiar group or setting, the participant observer is required to treat this as 'anthropologically strange', in an effort to make explicit the presuppositions he or she takes for granted as a culture member. In this way, it is hoped, the culture is turned into an object available for study. Naturalism proposes that through marginality, in social position and perspective, it is possible to construct an account of the culture under investigation that both understands it from within and captures it as external to, and independent of, the researcher: in other words, as a natural phenomenon. Thus, the *description* of cultures becomes the primary goal. The search for universal laws is downplayed in favour of detailed accounts of the concrete experience of life within a particular culture and of the beliefs and social rules that are used as resources within it. Indeed, attempts to go beyond this, for instance to *explain* particular cultural forms, are sometimes discouraged. Certainly, as Denzin (1971:168) notes, 'the naturalist resists schemes or models which over-simplify the complexity of everyday life'; though some forms of theory, those which are believed to be capable of capturing social complexity, are often recommended, most notably the grounded theory of Glaser and Strauss (Glaser and Strauss 1968; Strauss and Corbin 1990; but see also Williams 1976).

In recent years, the influence of positivism has waned and with it, in many areas, the dominance of quantitative method. However, at the same time naturalism has come under attack from within the ranks of qualitative researchers. In the next section we shall explore these more recent developments.

ANTI-REALIST AND POLITICAL CRITIQUES OF NATURALISM

As we noted earlier, in the past decade or so there have been conflicting trends of development in social research methodology. On the one hand, there has been growing acceptance of ethnography and qualitative method, and attempts to combine them with quantitative techniques. On the other hand, there have been criticisms of such moves for neglecting the conflicting philosophical and political presuppositions built into qualitative and quantitative approaches (Smith and Heshusius 1986; Smith 1989; Guba 1990). There has also been criticism of older forms of ethnographic work and thinking on the grounds that they still betray the influence of positivism and scientism. What is pointed to here is that, despite their differences, positivism and naturalism share much in common. They each appeal to the model of natural science, albeit interpreting it in different ways. As a result, they are both committed to the attempt to understand social phenomena as objects existing independently of the researcher. Similarly, they both regard practical and political commitments on the part of the researcher as, for the most part, extraneous to the research process – indeed, as a source of distortion whose effects have to be guarded against to preserve objectivity. Many ethnographers have begun to question the commitment of qualitative research to naturalism, challenging one or both of these assumptions. Doubts have been raised about the capacity of ethnography to portray the social world in the way that naturalism claims it does. Equally, the commitment of the older kinds of ethnography to some sort of value neutrality has been questioned, and politically interventionist forms of ethnography have been recommended. We shall look at these aspects of the critique of naturalism separately, though they are often closely related.

Questioning realism

Many critics of positivism and naturalism today reject them on the grounds that they both assume that the task of social research is to represent social phenomena in some literal fashion: to document their features and explain their occurrence. What is being questioned here is sometimes referred to as realism. In part, criticism of realism stems from a tension within ethnography between the naturalism characteristic of ethnographers' methodological thinking and the constructivism and cultural relativism that shape their understanding of the perspectives and behaviour of the people they study. As we saw, ethnographers portray people as *constructing* the social world, both through their interpretations of it and through actions based on those interpretations. Furthermore, those interpretations sometimes reflect different cultures, so that there is a sense in which through their actions people create different social worlds (Blumer 1969:11). But constructivism and relativism are compatible with naturalism only so long as they are not applied to ethnographic research itself. Once we come to see ethnographers as themselves constructing the social world through their interpretations of it, there is a conflict with the naturalistic realism built into ethnographic methodology.

This internal source of doubts about realism was reinforced by the impact of various external developments. One of these was changes in the field of the philosophy of science. Whereas until the early 1950s positivism had dominated this field, at that time its dominance began to be undermined, eventually producing a range of alternative positions, some of which rejected realism. A sign of this change was the enormous impact of Thomas Kuhn's book *The Structure of Scientific Revolutions* (Kuhn 1970; first published in 1962). Kuhn argued against views of the history of science that portray it as a process of cumulative development towards the truth, achieved by rational investigation founded on evidence. He, and others, showed that the work of the scientists involved in the major developments of scientific knowledge in the past was shaped by theoretical presuppositions about the world that were not themselves based on empirical research, and many of which are now judged to be false. Kuhn further claimed that the history of science, rather than displaying the gradual build-up of knowledge, is punctuated by periods of revolution when the theoretical presuppositions forming the 'paradigm' in terms of which scientists in a particular field have previously operated are challenged and replaced. An example is the shift from Newtonian physics to relativity theory and quantum mechanics in the early part of the twentieth century. The replacement of one paradigm by another, according to Kuhn, does not occur on the basis simply of the rational assessment of evidence. Paradigms are incommensurable, they picture the world in incompatible ways, so that the data themselves are interpreted differently by those working in different paradigms. This implies that the validity of scientific claims is always relative to the paradigm within which they are judged; they are never simply a reflection of some independent domain of reality.

Kuhn's work embodied most of the arguments against positivism that had become influential: that there is no theory-neutral observational foundation against which theories can be tested, and that judgments about the validity of theories are never fully determined by any evidence. He also proposed an alternative conception of science that contrasted sharply with the positivist model. However, his critique counted as much against naturalism, against the idea of the researcher getting into direct contact with reality, as it did against positivism: on his account all knowledge of the world is mediated by paradigmatic presuppositions. Furthermore, the alternative view he offered made even natural scientists look very much like the people constructing their social worlds that ethnographers had long portrayed in their accounts. And sociologists of science have subsequently produced ethnographies of the work of natural scientists along these lines (Latour and Woolgar 1979; Knorr-Cetina 1981). In this way, natural science moved from being primarily a methodological model for social research to being an object of sociological investigation; and for ethnographers this brought the conflict between naturalism and constructivism to a head.

As important as developments within the philosophy of science for the generation of doubts about realism was the influence of various continental European philosophical trends. Naturalism had been influenced by nineteenth-century ideas about hermeneutics, about the interpretation of historical texts, notably the work of Dilthey. This was the source of the idea, mentioned earlier, that socio-cultural understanding takes a different form to the understanding of physical phenomena. In the twentieth century, however, this earlier hermeneutic tradition came to be challenged by a new form of 'philosophical hermeneutics'. Where previously understanding human texts had been presented as a rigorous process of recovering the meaning intended by the author and locating it within relevant cultural settings, philosophical hermeneutics viewed the process of understanding as inevitably reflecting the 'prejudices', the pre-understandings, of the interpreter. Interpretation of texts, and by extension understanding of the social world too, could no longer be seen as a matter of capturing social meanings in their own terms; the accounts produced were regarded as inevitably reflecting the socio-historical position of the researcher (Warnke 1987).

Another powerful influence on ethnography in recent years has been post-structuralism. This is a diverse movement, but we shall mention just two of its most influential strands: Derrida's 'deconstruction' and the work of Foucault. Like philosophical hermeneutics, deconstruction also led to questioning of the idea that ethnographers can capture the meanings on the basis of which people act, and it did this on related grounds: that meanings are not stable; nor are they properties of individuals, but rather reflect the constitution of subjectivities through language. Also important has been deconstruction's undermining of the distinctions between different genres of writing: between those of 'writers' and critics, between fiction and non-fiction, indeed between literary and technical writing generally. This has led to recognition of the fact that the language used by ethnographers in their writing is not a transparent medium allowing us to see reality through it, but rather a construction that draws on many of the rhetorical strategies used by journalists or even novelists. Some have drawn the conclusion from this that the phenomena described in ethnographic accounts are created through the rhetorical strategies employed, rather than being external to the text; in short, this concern with rhetoric has often been associated with forms of anti-realism (see, for example, Tyler 1986).

Foucault's work is also based on a rejection of realism. He stresses the fact that social research is a socio-historical phenomenon, one which functions as part of the process of surveillance and control, which he sees as the central feature of modern society. Its products reflect its social character, rather than *representing* some world that is independent of it. Foucault argues that different 'regimes of truth' are established in different contexts, reflecting the play of diverse sources of power and resistance. Thus, what is treated as true and false, in social research as elsewhere, is constituted through the exercise of power. (For a discussion of the implications of Foucault's work for ethnography, see Gubrium and Silverman 1989.)

While realism has not been completely abandoned by most ethnographers, the idea that ethnographic accounts can represent social reality in a relatively unproblematic way has been rejected; and doubt has been thrown on the claims to scientific authority associated with realism. Moreover, in the work of Foucault we have a direct link with the second criticism of naturalism: its neglect of the politics of social research.

The politics of ethnography

Naturalists shared with positivists a commitment to producing accounts of factual matters that reflected the nature of the phenomena studied rather than the values or political commitments of the researcher. Of course, both recognized that in practice research is affected by the researcher's values, but the naturalist's aim was to limit the influence of those values as far as possible, so as to produce findings that were true independently of any particular value stance. In recent years, any such striving after value neutrality and objectivity has been questioned, sometimes being replaced by advocacy of 'openly ideological' research (Lather 1986).

In part this has resulted from the continuing influence of Marxism and 'critical' theory, but equally important has been the impact of feminism. From a traditional Marxist point of view the very distinction between facts and values is a historical product, and one that can be overcome through the future development of society. Values refer to the human potential that is built into the unfolding of history. In this sense values are facts even though they may not yet have been *realized* in the social world. Moreover, they provide the key to any understanding of the nature of current social conditions, their past and their future. The science of society thus provides not just abstract knowledge but the basis for action to transform the world to achieve human self-realization. From this point of view ethnography, like other forms of social research, cannot but be concerned simultaneously with factual and value matters, and its role inevitably involves political intervention (whether researchers are aware of this or not).

A similar conclusion about the political character of social research has been reached in other ways, for example by those arguing that the fact that research is always affected by values, and always has political consequences, means that researchers ought to take responsibility for their value commitments and for the effects of their work. It has also been suggested that ethnography and other forms of social research have had too *little* impact, that their products simply lie on library shelves gathering dust, and that as a result they are worthless. To be of value, it is suggested, ethnographic research should be concerned not simply with understanding the world but with applying its findings to bring about change.

There are differences in view about the nature of the change that should be aimed at. Sometimes the concern is with rendering research more relevant to national policy-making or to one or another form of professional practice, as with some versions of the teacher-as-researcher movement (see, for example, Hustler *et al.* 1986). Alternatively, it may be argued that research should be emancipatory. This has been proposed by feminists, where the goal is the emancipation of women (and men) from patriarchy (Lather 1991; Fonow and Cook 1991); but it is also to be found in the writings of critical ethnographers and advocates of emancipatory action research, where the goal of research is taken to be the transformation of Western societies so as to realize the ideals of freedom, equality, and justice (Carr and Kemmis 1986; Kemmis 1988; Gitlin *et al.* 1989).

Of course, to the extent that the very possibility of producing knowledge is undermined by the sort of anti-realist arguments we outlined earlier, a concern with the effects of research may come to seem an appropriate alternative goal to the traditional concern with truth. This too has led to the growth of more interventionist conceptions of ethnography. In this way post-structuralism has contributed to the politicization of social research, despite the fact that it seems simultaneously to undermine all political ideals (Dews 1987).

REFLEXIVITY

The criticisms of naturalism we have outlined are sometimes seen as arising from the reflexive character of social research. It is argued that what both positivism and naturalism fail to take into account is the fact that social researchers are part of the social world they study. The distinction between science and common sense, between the activities and knowledge of the researcher and those of the researched, lies at the heart of both these positions. It is this that leads to their joint concern with eliminating the effects of the researcher on the data. For one, the solution is the standardization of research procedures; for the other, it is direct experience of the social world, in extreme form the requirement that ethnographers 'surrender' themselves to the cultures they wish to study (Wolff 1964; Jules-Rosette 1978a and b). Both positions assume that it is possible, in principle at least, to isolate a body of data uncontaminated by the researcher, by turning him or her either into an automaton or into a neutral vessel of cultural experience. However, searches for empirical bedrock of this kind are futile; all data involve theoretical pre-suppositions (Hanson 1958).

Reflexivity thus implies that the orientations of researchers will be shaped by their socio-historical locations, including the values and interests that these locations confer upon them. What this represents is a rejection of the idea that social research is, or can be, carried out in some autonomous realm that is insulated from the wider society and from the particular biography of the researcher, in such a way that its findings can be unaffected by social processes and personal characteristics. Also, it is emphasized that the production of knowledge by researchers has consequences. At the very least, the publication of research findings can shape the climate in which political and practical decisions are made, and it may even directly stimulate particular sorts of action. Nor are the consequences of research neutral or necessarily desirable. Indeed, some commentators see social research as playing an undesirable role in supporting one or another aspect of the political status quo in Western societies.

There is no doubt that reflexivity is a significant feature of social research. Indeed, there is a sense in which all social research takes the form of participant observation: it involves participating in the social world, in whatever role, and reflecting on the products of that participation. However, we do not draw the same conclusions from the reflexivity of social research as many of the critics of naturalism. For us, recognition of reflexivity implies that there are elements of positivism and naturalism which must be abandoned; but it does not require rejection of all of the ideas associated with those two lines of thinking. Thus, we do not see reflexivity as undermining researchers' commitment to realism. In our view it only undermines naive forms of realism which assume that knowledge must be based on some absolutely secure foundation. Similarly, we do not believe that reflexivity implies that research is necessarily political, or that it should be political, in the sense of serving particular political causes or practical ends. For us, the primary goal of research is, and must remain, the production of knowledge.

Reflexivity and realism

It is true that we cannot avoid relying on 'common-sense' knowledge nor, often, can we avoid having an effect on the social phenomena we study. In other words, there is no way in which we can escape the social world in order to study it. Fortunately, though, this is not necessary even from a realist point of view. There is as little justification for rejecting all common-sense knowledge out of hand as there is for treating it as all 'valid in its own terms': we have no external, absolutely conclusive standard by which to judge it. But we can work with what 'knowledge' we have, while recognizing that it may be erroneous and engaging in systematic inquiry where doubt seems justified; and in so doing we can still make the reasonable assumption that we are trying to describe phenomena as they are, and not merely how we perceive them or how we would like them to be (Hammersley 1992:ch.3). In our everyday activities we rely on presuppositions about the world, few of which we have subjected to test, and none of which we could fully test. Most of the time this does not and should not trouble us, and social research is no different from other activities in this respect. We need to reflect only on what seems problematic, while leaving open the possibility that what currently is not problematic may in the future become so.

It is also important to recognize that research is an active process, in which accounts of the world are produced through selective observation and theoretical interpretation of what is seen, through asking particular questions and interpreting what is said in reply, through writing fieldnotes and transcribing audio- and video-recordings, as well as through writing research reports. And it is true that some aspects of this process have not been given the attention they deserve until recently. However, to say that our findings, and even our data, are constructed does not automatically imply that they do not or cannot represent social phenomena. To believe that they do is to assume that the only true form of representation would involve the world imprinting its characteristics on our senses, a highly implausible account of the process of perception (Gregory 1970).

Similarly, the fact that as researchers we are likely to have an effect on the people we study does not mean that the validity of our findings is restricted to the data elicitation situations on which we relied. We can minimize reactivity and/or monitor it. But we can also exploit it: how people respond to the presence of the researcher may be as informative as how they react to other situations. Indeed, rather than engaging in futile attempts to eliminate the effects of the researcher completely, we should set about understanding them, a point that Schuman has made in relation to social surveys:

> The basic position I will take is simple: artifacts are in the mind of the beholder. Barring one or two exceptions, the problems that occur in surveys are opportunities for understanding once we take them seriously as facts of life. Let us distinguish here between the simple survey and the scientific survey. . . . The simple approach to survey research takes

responses literally, ignores interviewers as sources of influence, and treats sampling as unproblematic. A person who proceeds in this way is quite likely to trip and fall right on his artifact. The scientific survey, on the other hand, treats survey research as a search for meaning, and ambiguities of language and of interviewing, discrepancies between attitude and behaviour, even problems of non-response, provide an important part of the data, rather than being ignored or simply regarded as obstacles to efficient research.

(Schuman 1982:23)

In short, 'what is an artifact if treated naively reflects a fact of life if taken seriously' (1982:24). In order to understand the effects of the research and of research procedures, we need to compare data in which the level and direction of reactivity vary. Once we abandon the idea that the social character of research can be standardized out or avoided by becoming a 'fly on the wall' or a 'full participant', the role of the researcher as active participant in the research process becomes clear. He or she is the research instrument *par excellence*. The fact that behaviour and attitudes are often not stable across contexts and that the researcher may influence the context becomes central to the analysis. Indeed, it can be exploited for all it is worth. Data should not be taken at face value, but treated as a field of inferences in which hypothetical patterns can be identified and their validity tested. Different research strategies can be explored and their effects compared with a view to drawing theoretical conclusions. Interpretations need to be made explicit and full advantage should be taken of any opportunities to test their limits and to assess alternatives. Such a view contrasts sharply with the image of social research projected by naturalism, though it is closer to other models of ethnographic research such as 'grounded theorizing' (Glaser and Strauss 1967), 'analytic induction' (Cressey 1950; Denzin 1978), and the strategy model to be found alongside naturalism in the work of Schatzman and Strauss (1973). And in this way the image of the researcher is brought into parallel with that of the people studied, as actively making sense of the world, yet without undermining the commitment of research to realism.

Reflexivity and the political character of research

Positivism and naturalism, in the forms we have discussed them, tend to present research as an activity that is done for its own sake and in its own terms. By contrast, as we have seen, some critics insist that research has a social function, for instance serving to legitimate and preserve the status quo. And on this basis they argue that researchers must try to make their research serve a different function, such as challenging the status quo. Often, this point of view is organized around the question: whose side is the researcher on? (Becker 1967a; Troyna and Carrington 1989).

As we saw earlier, others argue that what is wrong with ethnography is its lack of impact on policy-making and practice, its limited payoff in the everyday worlds of politics and work. Here it is dismissed as an idle pastime, a case of fiddling while the world burns, or one engaged in by intellectual dilettantes who live off the taxes paid by hard-working citizens.

These criticisms of naturalist ethnography seem to us to involve an overestimation of the actual and potential contribution of research to policy and practice, and an associated failure to value the more modest contributions it offers. It is also worth pointing out that one may believe that the only justification for research is its contribution to policy and practice, and recognize that it inevitably has effects on these, without concluding that it should be directed towards the achievement of particular political or practical goals. Indeed, there are good reasons for research not being directed towards such goals. The most important is that this would increase the chances of the findings being distorted by ideas about how the world ought to be, or by what it would be politic for others to believe. When we are engaged in political or practical action, the truth of what we say is often not our principal concern, even though we may prefer to be honest. We are more concerned with the practical effects of our actions, and sometimes this may lead us to be 'economical' with the truth, at the very least. Moreover, even where the truth of our beliefs is the main issue, in practical activities judgment of factual and value claims as more or less reliable will be based on somewhat different considerations than in research directed towards producing knowledge: we will probably be concerned above all with whether the information is sufficiently reliable for our current purposes. Of course, if one believes, as Marx and others did and do, that (ultimately at least) the true and the good are identical, one might deny the significance of this difference in orientation between research and other practical activities. But this view relies on an elaborate and unconvincing philosophical infrastructure (Hammersley 1992:ch.6 and 1993).

It is worth emphasizing that to deny that research should be directed towards political goals is not to suggest that researchers could, or should, abandon their political convictions. It is to insist that as researchers their primary goal must always be to produce knowledge, and that they should try to minimize any distortion of their findings by their political convictions or practical interests. Nor are we suggesting that researchers should be unconcerned about the effects of their work on the world. The point is that acknowledging the reflexivity of research does not imply that it must be primarily directed towards changing (or for that matter preserving) the world in some way or other. And, as we have indicated, there are good reasons why it should not be so directed.

CONCLUSION

We began this chapter by examining two contrasting reconstructions of the logic of social research and their implications for ethnography. Neither positivism nor naturalism provides an adequate framework. Both neglect its fundamental reflexivity: the fact that we are part of the social world we study, and that there is no escape from reliance on common-sense knowledge and methods of investigation. All social research is founded on the human capacity for participant observation. We act in the social world and yet are able to reflect upon ourselves and our actions as objects in that world. However, rather than leading to doubts about whether social research can produce knowledge, or to its transformation into a political enterprise, for us this reflexivity provides the basis for a reconstructed logic of inquiry that shares much with positivism and naturalism but goes beyond them in important respects. By including our own role within the research focus, and perhaps even systematically exploiting our participation in the settings under study as researchers, we can produce accounts of the social world and

justify them without placing reliance on futile appeals to empiricism, of either positivist or naturalist varieties.

Reconstructing our understanding of social research in line
with the implications of its reflexivity also throws light on the
relationship between quantitative and qualitative approaches.
Certainly there is little justification for the view, associated with
naturalism, that ethnography represents a superior, alternative
paradigm to quantitative research. On the other hand, it has a
much more powerful contribution to make to social science than
positivism allows.

Reflexivity is an aspect of all social research. It is one that has
been given increasing attention by ethnographers and others in
recent years, notably in the production of 'natural histories'
of their research. (For examples of such natural histories, see
Hammond 1964; Freilich 1970b; Bell and Newby 1977; Shaffir *et
al.* 1980; Hammersley 1983a; Bell and Roberts 1984; Burgess
1984b, 1985a and b, 1988a, 1989, 1990 and 1992; Golde 1986;
Whitehead and Conaway 1986; McKeganey and Cunningham-
Burley 1987; Walford 1987 and 1991b; Shaffir and Stebbins 1991;
Okely and Gallaway 1992.) The remainder of this book is
devoted to spelling out what we take to be the implications of
reflexivity for ethnographic practice.

Chapter 2

Research design: problems, cases, and samples

At first blush, the conduct of ethnography can seem deceptively simple. Indeed, some authors have reported being given little or no research advice before they set out on their fieldwork. Nader, for example, relates how at one time this had become a tradition among North American anthropologists:

> Before leaving Harvard I went to see Kluckhohn. In spite of the confidence I had gained from some of my training at Harvard, this last session left me frustrated. When I asked Kluckhohn if he had any advice, he told the story of a graduate student who had asked Kroeber the same question. In response Kroeber was said to have taken the largest, fattest ethnography book off his shelf, and said, 'Go forth and do likewise.'
>
> (Nader 1986:98)

Such non-advice seems to rest on the assumption that the conduct of ethnography is unproblematic, and requires little preparation and no special expertise.

One of the reasons for this reluctance to give advice about how to do ethnographic research is awareness of the fact that such research cannot be programmed, that its practice is replete with the unexpected, as any reading of the many published research biographies now available will confirm. More than this, all research is a practical activity requiring the exercise of judgment in context; it is not a matter of simply following methodological rules.

There is, however, another, less legitimate reason why the advice given to those about to embark upon ethnography is often simply to 'go and do it'. This is the idea, associated with naturalism, that ethnography consists of open-ended observation and description, so that 'research design' is almost superfluous. Here, one useful research strategy is inflated into a paradigmatic approach. Speaking of the study of animal behaviour, Tinbergen (1972:23) remarks that periods of exploratory, intuitive observation are of particular value 'when one feels in danger of getting out of touch with the natural phenomena, of narrowing one's field of vision'. Naturalists in sociology have sometimes appealed to natural history and ethology to legitimate their recommendation of exploratory observation and description (Lofland 1967; Blumer 1969; Speier 1973). It is important to remember, though, that observation in ethology is guided by a relatively well-defined set of assumptions derived from evolutionary theory. Darwin (quoted in Selltiz *et al.* 1959:200) himself remarks at one point: 'How odd it is that anyone should not see that observation must be for or against some view, if it is to be of any service.'

Certainly we must recognize that, even less than other forms of social research, the course of ethnography cannot be predetermined. But this neither eliminates the need for pre-fieldwork preparation nor means that the researcher's behaviour in the field can be haphazard, merely adjusting to events by taking 'the line of least resistance'. Indeed, we shall argue that research design should be a reflexive process which operates throughout every stage of a project.

FORESHADOWED PROBLEMS

Research always begins with some problem or set of issues, from what Malinowski refers to as 'foreshadowed problems':

> Good training in theory, and acquaintance with its latest results, is not identical with being burdened with 'preconceived ideas'. If a man sets out on an expedition, determined to prove certain hypotheses, if he is incapable of changing his views constantly and casting them off ungrudgingly under the pressure of evidence, needless to say his work will be worthless. But the more problems he brings with him into the field, the more he is in the habit of moulding his theories according to facts, and of seeing facts in their bearing upon theory, the better he is equipped for the work. Preconceived

ideas are pernicious in any scientific work, but foreshadowed problems are the main endowment of a scientific thinker, and these problems are first revealed to the observer by his theoretical studies.

(Malinowski 1922:8–9)

Sometimes the starting point for research is a well-developed theory from which a set of hypotheses can be derived. Such theories are relatively rare in sociology and anthropology, but perhaps more frequent in social psychology. An example of a participant observation study in this mould is the work of Festinger *et al.* (1956). They tested cognitive dissonance theory by investigating the reaction of members of an apocalyptic religious group to the fact that the world did not end on the day predicted by their leader.

Most ethnographic research, however, has been concerned with producing descriptions and explanations of particular phenomena, or with developing theories rather than with testing existing hypotheses. A number of authors, most notably Glaser and Strauss (1967), have pointed to the advantages to be gained from developing theory through systematic data collection rather than by reliance on 'armchair theorizing'. Nevertheless, as Strauss (1970) himself has shown, considerable progress can sometimes be made in clarifying and developing research problems before fieldwork begins. As an illustration he examines Davis's (1961a) research on 'the management of strained interaction by the visibly handicapped':

Davis's theory is about (1) *strained* (2) *sociable* interaction (3) in *face-to-face* contact between (4) *two persons*, one of whom has a (5) *visible handicap* and the other of whom is (6) *normal* (no visible handicap). . . . The underlined terms in the above sentence begin to suggest what is explicitly or implicitly omitted from Davis's theoretical formulation. The theory is concerned with the visibly (physically) handicapped, not with people whose handicaps are not immediately visible, if at all, to other interactants. The theory is concerned with interaction between two people (not with more than two). . . . The interaction occurs in situations termed 'sociable'; that is, the relations between interactants are neither impersonal nor intimate. Sociable also means interaction prolonged enough to permit more than a fleeting exchange but not so prolonged that close familiarity ensues.

(Strauss 1970:47–8)

Strauss goes on to show that by varying these different elements of the theory new research questions can be generated.

Often the relevant literature is less developed even than in the case referred to by Strauss. However, the absence of detailed knowledge of a phenomenon or process itself represents a useful starting point for research. MacIntyre (1977) provides an example in her study of the 'pregnancy careers' of single women:

> Approximately one fifth of all conceptions, and an even higher proportion of first conceptions, in Britain in the early 1970s were to single women. There were four common outcomes of pregnancy for single women: marriage to the putative father; induced abortion; remaining single and keeping the baby; and remaining single and giving the baby up for adoption. It is known that the incidence of these outcomes has changed from time to time, as have, of course, the relevant social attitudes, social policy and legislation, and these have been the subject of demographic and historical studies. *Yet little is known about how these outcomes are reached, or how these may be affected by social attitudes, policies and legislation.*
>
> (MacIntyre, 1977:9; our emphasis)

Alternatively, the stimulus may be a surprising fact or set of facts. Thus, Measor (1983) noted that not only did girls tend to fare worse than boys in science examinations, but that the gap was even greater in the case of the Nuffield science course, a course emphasizing discovery learning. She set out to investigate why this was the case through participant observation in Nuffield science lessons and by interviewing both boys and girls about their attitudes to these lessons.

As this example illustrates, the significance of the initial problem may be not so much theoretical as political or practical. Even where the starting point is not current social theory, however, elaboration of the problem soon draws such theory in, as Freilich's work on 'Mohawk heroes' indicates:

> New Yorkers sometimes read in their newspapers about a unique phenomenon in their midst: the Mohawk Indians who

work on the steel structures of various buildings in and around their city. Articles, at times accompanied by pictures of smiling Indians, discuss these 'brave' and 'sure-footed' Mohawks. The question of why so many Mohawks work in structural steel is one that is often researched by students enrolled in colleges located in and around New York. In 1956, this problem was, in fact, my first professional research assignment. I used A.F.C. Wallace's paper 'Some Psychological Determinants of Culture Change in an Iroquoian Community' as the foil in my proposal for research support. Wallace's paper suggested that Mohawks lack a fear of heights, and that this lack of fear explains their involvement with the steel industry. I argued that a negative trait (lack of fear) cannot have specific positive consequences (lead a tribe into steel work). I argued further that there is no functional value in a lack of fear of heights for steel work, and that in actuality the opposite is true: a normal fear of high places leads to caution that saves lives. A more plausible argument seemed to be that Mohawks frequently act as if they have no fear of heights. In presenting a subsidiary problem, 'Why these acts of dare-devilry?', I put forth my theoretical belief that socio-cultural factors explain social and cultural phenomena better than do psychological factors. I had a vague notion that Mohawks in steel work represented some kind of cultural continuity. Thus, the questions I posed were (1) why is it good, culturally, for a Mohawk male to be a structural steel worker? and (2) How does such a cultural 'goodness' relate to Mohawk cultural history?

(Freilich 1970a:185–6)

Social events themselves may also stimulate research, providing an opportunity to explore some unusual occurrence or to test a theory. Notable here are what are sometimes called 'natural experiments': organizational innovations, natural disasters, or political crises that promise to reveal what happens when the limiting factors that normally constrain a particular element of social life are breached. At such times social phenomena that are otherwise taken for granted become visibly problematic for the participants themselves, and thus for the observer. Schatzman and Strauss (1955) provide an example in their discussion of the problems of inter-class communication arising subsequent

to a tornado. Studying the origins and consequences of organizational innovations is even more common. An example is Walford and Miller's study of Kingshurst School, the first City
Technology College in Britain, established as part of the educational reforms of the late 1980s (Walford 1991a; Walford and
Miller 1991).

Even chance encounters or personal experiences may provide
motive and opportunity for research. Henslin came to do research
on the homeless as a result of meeting someone for whom the
problem of homelessness had become a consuming passion:

> When [he] found out that I was a sociologist and that I
> was writing a textbook on social problems, he asked me to
> collaborate on a book about the homeless. He felt that my
> background might provide an organizing framework that
> would help sort out his many experiences and observations
> into a unified whole. During our attempt at collaboration, he
> kept insisting that as a sociologist I owed it to myself to gain
> first-hand experience with the homeless. Although I found
> that idea somewhat appealing, because of my heavy involve-
> ment in writing projects I did not care to pursue the possi-
> bility. As he constantly brought up the topic, however, I must
> admit that he touched a sensitive spot, rubbing in more than
> a little sociological guilt. After all, I was an instructor of social
> problems, and I did not *really* know about the homeless. . . .
> With the continued onslaught, I became more open to the
> idea. (Or perhaps I should say that I eventually wore down.)
> When he invited me on an expense-paid trip to Washington,
> DC, and promised that I would see sights hitherto unbe-
> knownst to me – such as homeless people sleeping on the
> sidewalks in full view of the White House – firing my imagin-
> ation, he had pierced my armor through. With the allure of
> such an intriguing juxtaposition of power and powerlessness,
> of wealth and poverty, how could I resist such an offer?
>
> (Henslin 1990:52)

By contrast, Currer (1992:4–5) began her research on Pathan
mothers in Britain as a result of her own experience as an
English mother in Peshawar, Pakistan. Her research questions
arose initially from what she saw as the parallels between her
own former position and that of the people she chose to study,
and from her sympathy for them. It is also common for research

to be stimulated by previous experience in temporary or permanent jobs. Thus Olesen traces the origins of her research on temporary clerical workers to her own experience supporting herself as a student by working in a typing pool (Olesen 1990:214). Of course, research interest may equally arise from difference, conflict, and negative feelings. Van Maanen (1991:33) reports that his long career investigating police culture began in part because he had been 'subject to what I regarded as more than my fair share of police attention and hence viewed the police with a little loathing, some fear, and considerable curiosity'.

Stimuli such as these are not usually sufficient in themselves for the formulation of a research problem. For this to occur, experiences prior to entering the field must be subjected to analytic reflection. Experiences are rendered interesting or significant by theoretical ideas: the stimulus is not intrinsic to the experiences themselves. However, there are no hard-and-fast rules for deciding how far the initial research problem can be elaborated before the collection of data begins. Exploring the components and implications of a general foreshadowed problem with the help of whatever secondary literature is available is certainly a wise first step. Relevant here are not only research monographs and journal articles but also official reports, journalistic exposés, autobiographies, diaries, and 'non-fiction novels' (see Chapter 6). There comes a point, however, when little more progress can be made without beginning the collection of primary data – though reflection and the use of secondary literature should of course continue beyond that point.

THE DEVELOPMENT OF RESEARCH PROBLEMS

The aim in the pre-fieldwork phase and in the early stages of data collection is to turn the foreshadowed problems into a set of questions to which an answer can be given, whether this be a narrative description of a sequence of events, a generalized account of the perspectives and practices of a particular group of actors, or a more abstract theoretical formulation. Sometimes in this process the original problems are transformed or even completely abandoned in favour of others, as Dollard illustrates:

My original plan was to study the personality of Negroes in

the South, to get a few life histories, and to learn something about the manner in which the Negro person grows up. It was far from my wish to make a study of a community, to consider the intricate problem of the cultural heritage of the Negro, or to deal with the emotional structure of a specific small town in the deep South. I was compelled, however, to study the community, for the individual life is rooted in it. Only a few days of five months in Southerntown had passed before I realized that whites and whiteness form an inseparable part of the mental life of the Negro. He has a white employer, often white ancestors, sometimes white playmates, and he lives by a set of rules which are imposed by white society. The lives of white and Negro people are so dynamically joined and fixed in one system that neither can be understood without the other. This insight put an end to the plan of collecting Negro life histories in a social void. Negro life histories refer at every point to a total situation, i.e. to Southerntown itself, the surrounding county, the southeastern culture area, and in a strict sense the whole region which is bound to American cotton economy. This observation came as a very unwelcome perception, since it necessitated getting a perspective on the community and the county, and informing myself incidentally on many apparently remote matters. Study of the social context of the lives of Negroes has crowded out the original objective of the research, as least so far as the publication of specific life histories is concerned.

(Dollard 1957:1–2)

Change in research problems stems from several different sources. As with Dollard, it may be discovered that the original formulation of the problem was founded on erroneous assumptions. Equally, it may be concluded that, given the current state of knowledge, the problem is not soluble. Medawar comments:

Good scientists study the more important problems they think they can solve. It is, after all, their professional business to solve problems, not merely to grapple with them. The spectacle of a scientist locked in combat with the forces of ignorance is not an inspiring one if, in the outcome, the scientist is routed. That is why some of the most important biological problems have not yet appeared on the agenda of practical research.

(Medawar 1967:7)

Periodically, methodologists rediscover the truth of the old adage that finding the right question to ask is more difficult than answering it (Merton 1959). Much of the effort that goes into data analysis is concerned with formulating and reformulating the research problem in ways that make it more amenable to investigation.

Problems vary in their degree of abstractness. Some, especially those deriving from practical or political concerns, will be 'topical' (Lofland 1976), being concerned with types of people and situations readily identified in everyday language. Others have a more 'generic' cast. Here the researcher is asking questions such as 'Of what abstract sociologically conceived class of situation is this particular situation an instance?' and 'What are the abstract features of this kind of situation?' This distinction between topical and generic research problems is closely related to the distinction between substantive and formal analyses outlined by Glaser and Strauss:

> By substantive theory, we mean that developed for a substantive, or empirical, area of sociological inquiry, such as patient care, race relations, professional education, delinquency, or research organizations. By formal theory, we mean that developed for a formal, or conceptual, area of sociological inquiry, such as stigma, deviant behaviour, formal organization, socialization, status incongruency, authority and power, reward systems, or social mobility.
>
> (Glaser and Strauss 1967:32)

In ethnographic research there is frequently a constant interplay between the topical and the generic, or the substantive and the formal. One may begin with some formal analytic notion and seek to extend or refine its range of application in the context of a particular new substantive application. This can be illustrated by reference to the work of Hargreaves *et al.* (1975) on deviance in school classrooms. Starting from the formal concepts of 'labelling theory', Hargreaves and his colleagues sought to extend the use of this analytic framework to, and examine its value for, the study of student deviance in secondary schools. They were able to derive from it a sort of 'shopping list' of issues. This list of topics moves the focus of concern from the formal towards the substantive, from the generic towards the topical. Their list reads:

Rules. What are the rules in schools and classrooms? Which rules are allegedly broken in imputations of deviance? Who makes the rules? Are the rules ever negotiated? How are the rules communicated to members? What justifications are given for the rules, by whom, to whom, and on what occasions? Do teachers and pupils view the rules in the same way? Are some rules perceived as legitimate by some teachers and some pupils? How do members know that certain rules are relevant to (i.e. are 'in play' in) a given situation? How do members classify the rules? What differences do members see between different rules? For example, do rules vary in importance?

Deviant acts. How do members link an act to a rule to permit the imputation of deviance? How do teachers know that a pupil has broken a rule? That is, what is the interpretive work undertaken by teachers to permit the categorization of an act as deviant? Similarly, how do pupils know that their acts are deviant? . . .

Deviant persons. How do teachers link deviant acts to persons so that persons are defined as deviant? What is the relationship between different labels? Why is one label used rather than another? . . .

Treatment. What treatments are made by teachers in relation to acts or persons defined as deviants? On what grounds and with what justifications do teachers decide on one treatment rather than another? . . .

Career of the deviant. What is the structure of the career of the deviant pupil? What are the contingencies of such careers? How are such careers initiated and terminated?

(Hargreaves *et al.* 1975:23–4)

Such a list of problems clearly draws on the authors' prior knowledge of sociological work on schools and deviance, and reflects an interplay between formal and substantive interests. Of course, these questions do not constitute a research design as such. Similarly, one would not expect such a list to be a definitive one: in some ways it would probably prove to be over-ambitious, and in others it would undoubtedly omit unforeseen problems.

One can also develop research problems by extending the use of an analytic framework from one substantive area to another.

This is one feature of the classic study of the Kansas medical school by Becker *et al.* (1961). They adopted a perspective from industrial sociology – that industrial workers attempt to set their own 'level and direction of effort' – and applied it to the topical situation of the medical students, who, faced with overwhelming academic demands, likewise attempt to negotiate manageable levels of effort, and to establish appropriate directions for their efforts.

Just as one can formulate problems by moving from the formal to the substantive, so one can move from the substantive to the formal or generic. This can be illustrated in part from a research project in which one of us was involved (Atkinson 1981b). It was concerned with the investigation of 'industrial training units' designed to ease the transition from school to working life for 'slow learners'. The research included a number of strands, including participant observation in two such industrial units, interviews with a range of officials, documentary sources, and so on. The project was not simply a 'one-off' case-study, but one of a number of similar pieces of research being undertaken in Britain. These other projects were also investigating innovative interventions to facilitate the transition from school to work.

The formulation of the interests of the research began with foreshadowed problems that were primarily substantive or topical in origin. In an exploratory orientation, the research team began the fieldwork phase with general interests of this sort: How is the day-to-day work of the unit organized? How are the students selected and evaluated? What sort of work do they do, and what sort of work are they being prepared for?

During the course of the fieldwork a number of issues were identified with more precision, and new categories were developed. At the same time, it became apparent that there was a need to formulate these ideas in terms that were more general than their local manifestations in our own project. A more pressing reason for this was the desirability of generating concepts that would permit of principles for, and systematic comparison between, the different research projects in Britain. A research memorandum put the issue in this way:

> During our last meeting ... we talked about the possibility of developing and working with some general analytic

categories. The idea I was putting forward . . . was that evaluation projects were doomed to be little more than one-off, local affairs, unless we were able to work with ideas and frameworks of more general applicability. Such 'generalization' would not imply that all projects should work within 'the same' research design, or collect 'the same' data by 'the same' technique. Clearly, particular evaluations must remain sensitive to local conditions and responsive to changing circumstances. Nor should such a suggestion be interpreted as a plea for a straitjacket of predetermined questions and categories. Such categories should only be thought of as 'sensitizing' concepts – indicating some broad dimensions for comparison between projects, and for the development of general frameworks to tie together disparate projects and evaluation.

(Atkinson 1981b)

The issues of comparison and generalization touched on in this memorandum will be developed elsewhere. For the time being we simply wish to illustrate the general rationale for attempting to move from the local to the more generic, in so far as it directs attention towards comparison, and draws on the work of other analysts. We shall not attempt to detail all the ideas drawn on and alluded to in this particular project. The following extracts from the same research memorandum are illustrative of how these ideas were used to categorize some key issues in the research, and to stimulate the posing of further topical questions:

Gatekeepers. By gatekeepers I mean actors with control over key sources and avenues of opportunity. Such gatekeepers exercise control at and during key phases of the youngster's status passage(s). Such gatekeepers' functions would actually be carried out by different personnel in the different organization settings. . . .

The identification of the general class of 'gatekeepers' would then allow us to go on to ask some pertinent questions of a general nature. For instance: What resources do gatekeepers have at their disposal? What perceptions and expectations do gatekeepers have of 'clients'? Are these perceptions mutually compatible or are there systematic differences of opinion? Do gatekeepers believe that their expectations of clients are met or not? Do they have an implicit (or even an explicit) model of the 'ideal client'?

What is the information-state of gatekeepers? For example, what sort of model of the labour market are they operating with? What views of working life do they bring to bear? How accurate are their assessments of the state of local labour markets?

What sort of routines and strategies do gatekeepers employ? For instance, what criteria (formal and informal) are used to assess and categorize 'clients'? What bureaucratic routines are used (if any)? What record-keeping procedures are used, and how are such data interpreted in practice?

(Atkinson 1981b)

Closely allied with this outline of 'gatekeepers' as a general sensitizing device, the memorandum also included the following:

Labelling. This general category clearly overlaps with the gate-keepers' practical reasoning, and with some issues in definitions of client populations. To what extent is there a danger of self-fulfilling prophecies, as a result of the identification of target populations? To what extent do projects themselves help to crystallize racial, gender or ability categorizations and stereotypes?

Do employers and potential employers operate with stigmatizing stereotypes? Do projects overcome, or do they help to confirm, such stereotypes? What particular aspects of projects and the youngsters do 'gatekeepers' such as employers seize on and react to?

Do the youngsters label themselves and each other in accordance with formal or informal labels attached to them? Are the professionals involved in projects themselves subject to stigma in the views of other professionals and agencies?

(Atkinson 1981b)

Obviously, these extracts from a research memorandum do not constitute more than the beginning of an exhaustive analysis of projects aimed at easing the transition to work, or at coping with the problem of youth unemployment. Our reference to it here is an attempt to exemplify one stage in the process whereby ideas are formulated. While many of the questions that are posed here are fairly concrete or topical in content, the general tenor of the document draws attention to generic concepts such as gatekeepers, labelling, stigma, routines, strategies, practical reasoning, and self-fulfilling prophecies.

This research memorandum, then, helps to 'freeze' the process of problem formulation during an intermediate stage in a research project. The initial fieldwork has suggested a number of potentially important aspects to be identified more thoroughly, and some potentially useful analytic ideas. Thus, research problems are identified more precisely. At the same time, such identifications permit new research questions to be posed, or for them to be posed more systematically. Hence guidelines for further data collection are also laid down.

One must beware of over-simplifying the distinction between topical and generic levels of analysis. One does not simply progress in a uni-directional way from one to the other. In the conduct of an actual project, one would not expect simply to progress from a series of substantive issues, and end up with one's formal categories, or vice versa. There will normally be a constant shuttling back and forth between the two analytic modes. Particular substantive issues may suggest affinities with some formal concept that will, in turn, indicate substantive issues as deserving new or further attention, and so on.

SELECTING SETTINGS AND CASES

There is another factor that often plays a significant role in shaping the way in which research problems are developed in ethnography: the nature of the setting or settings chosen for study. Sometimes the setting itself comes first – an opportunity arises to investigate an interesting setting; and foreshadowed problems spring from the nature of that setting. This is true, for example, in the case of research on 'natural experiments' and other kinds of 'opportunistic research' (Riemer 1977). Here, the selection of a setting for study hardly arises, and the research problem and the setting are closely bound together. The same is true in the case of professional practitioners doing research on the settings in which they work:

The decision of where to locate an ethnographic case study is normally a matter of careful consideration and assessment with the advantages and disadvantages of various locales being carefully considered. . . . Because of my circumstances, my choice reduced to a straightforward decision between doing my research at the school at which I worked or abandoning my desire to do an ethnographic study.

(Pollard 1985:218)

However, even where a setting is selected on the basis of foreshadowed problems, the nature of the setting may still shape the development of the research questions. This arises because, as we noted earlier, in ethnographic research the development of research problems is rarely completed before fieldwork begins; indeed, the collection of primary data often plays a key role in that process of development.

At the same time, it is often found that some of the questions into which the foreshadowed problems have become decomposed or transformed are not open to investigation in the setting selected. The researcher is then faced with the choice of either dropping these questions from the investigation or re-starting the research in a setting where they *can* be investigated. While on occasion the importance of a problem may lead to the latter course, generally researchers stay where they are and select problems that can be investigated there. After all, as in the case of Hargreaves *et al.* (1975), more questions are usually generated than can be tackled in a single study. Moreover, not only does moving to another setting involve further delay and renewed problems of access, but there is also no guarantee that the new setting will turn out to be an appropriate one in which to investigate the preferred problem. Everett Hughes is reported to have remarked, only half jokingly, that the researcher should select the research problem for which the setting chosen is the ideal site!

All this does not mean that the selection of settings for study is unimportant, simply that the ethnographer is rarely in a position to specify the precise nature of the setting required. It is a matter of identifying the sorts of setting that would be most appropriate for investigation of the research problem, as currently formulated. Moreover, when a type of setting has been decided on, it is advisable (if possible) to 'case' possible research sites with a view to assessing their suitability, the feasibility of carrying out research there, and how access might best be accomplished should they be selected (Schatzman and Strauss 1973:19). This involves collecting and subjecting to preliminary analysis any documentary evidence available about the setting, interviewing anyone who can be easily contacted who has experience or knowledge of the setting, and perhaps making brief visits to the setting, covertly or overtly.

'Casing the joint' in this fashion not only may provide information about settings in which the research might be carried out, but also feeds into the development and refinement of the research problem. It may be discovered that what had been assumed to be a homogeneous category of people must be broken down into a number of sub-types who have different characteristics and who are likely to be found in very different places. Warren provides an example:

> The first decision that must be made by a researcher who wishes to study the gay community – unless he has unlimited time and money to spend – is which gay community he wishes to study: the world of exclusive private gay clubs for businessmen and professionals? or the dope addict transvestites so vividly depicted in *Last Exist to Brooklyn*? or the sado-masochistic leather boys? Any extended preliminary observation will make it objectively obvious that 'the' gay community is divided – fairly loosely at the boundaries – into a hierarchy linked to some extent with status and class criteria in the 'real' world.
>
> (Warren 1972:144)

The role of pragmatic considerations must not be under-estimated in the choice of a setting. While by no means absent in hypothesis-testing research, they are likely to play an especially important role in research concerned with theory development. This is because here the criteria specifying suitability are usually much less determinate: there is generally a very wide range of relevant settings. As a result, contacts with personnel promising easy access, the scale of the travel costs likely to be involved, and the availability of documentary information, etc. are often major considerations in narrowing down the selection. (See, for example, Fox's 1964 discussion of her choice of Belgium as the site for a study of European medical research.)

Sometimes, the search for an appropriate setting can take

unpredictable turns, as Campbell's account of his research in Greece in the 1950s illustrates. He set out to study one of the villages in a mountain region north-east of Jannina. However, he found the populations of the villages much depleted as a result of civil war, and that his English background led to suspicions that he was a spy. A fortuitous event transformed his research plans. Sarakatsan transhumant shepherds lived on the hills above the village, and relations between them and the villagers were uneasy:

> Our own contacts with them had not gone beyond formal greetings when one day in the heat of summer a young shepherd-boy returning from school had stopped at the village spring to drink, and was there set upon by larger village boys. . . . At this point, the anthropologist's wife entered indignantly to rescue the victim. This small adventure had its consequences. We received an invitation to visit a Sarakatsan encampment and the relationship prospered. When some weeks afterwards the time arrived for the Sarakatsani to take their flocks and families down to the plains of Thesprotia for the winter, one family sent us a peremptory message. We were to accompany them and they would build us a hut.
>
> (Campbell 1992:152)

This example also illustrates how occasionally researchers find that they have effectively been chosen to research a setting by one or more of the people involved in it, though usually with rather more strings attached than in this case. In such circumstances, the ethnographer must balance the ease of initial access offered against the desirability of the site in other respects, as well as against any problems that such direct sponsorship by a gatekeeper might cause.

Usually ethnographers study only one or a small number of settings, and usually ones that are geographically close to where they are based. Often this is forced by the cost of using more remote sites and the limited resources available. This is not always the case, however. An exception is Henslin's study of the homeless. He decided to do a national study, but found that setting off with his family in a motor home to combine research with sight-seeing led to little fieldwork being done. Fortunately, an alternative arose:

I heard about a 'fly-anywhere-we-fly-as-often-as-you-want-for–21-days' sales gimmick from Eastern Airlines. I found their offer was legitimate, that for $750 I could pack in as many cities as I could stand – actually more than I could stand as it turned out. . . . It was the method itself, participant observation, that became the key for making this research affordable. Obviously, the homeless spend very little money, which dovetailed perfectly with my situation and desires. I was able to stay in the shelters at no financial cost. (The shelters, however, exacted a tremendous cost in terms of upsetting my basic orientational complacencies.) In addition to a free bed and a shower, the shelters usually provided morning and evening meals. Although those meals were not always edible, I was able to count on the noon meal being of quality, and that was already included in the price of my airline ticket. . . . I primarily focused on major cities in the Western part of the United States, later adding cities in other areas during subsequent travels. My purpose was to obtain as good a 'geographical spread' as I could.

(Henslin 1990:55)

Generally speaking, of course, the more settings studied the less time can be spent in each. The researcher must make a trade-off here between breadth and depth of investigation.

It is important not to confuse the choice of settings with the selection of cases for study. The vocabulary of studying 'fields' and 'settings' is widely used in talking and writing about ethnography. The main source of this tendency to regard natural settings as the object of study is of course naturalism, and it can be found, for example, in the work of the Chicago School:

[The sociological study of Chicago] was nursed as a carto-graphic exercise studying Little Sicily, the Jewish ghetto, Polonism, the Gold Coast, the slums, Hobohemia, rooming-house districts and the gangs of the city. Each of these areas was treated as a symbolic world which created and perpetu-ated a distinctive moral and social organization. Each was subjected to an interpretative analysis which attempted to reproduce the processes by which that organization was brought into being. They were collectively identified as natural areas: 'natural' because they were themselves part of the natural evolution and selection which shaped society;

because they were different from the structures produced by planning and science; and because they represented a unit which allegedly framed American thinking on social and political life.

(Rock 1979:92)

In other sociological contexts, too, similar appeals are made to models of relatively self-contained groups of 'communities'. In the past, the anthropological tradition, for instance, tended to lay stress on the investigation of small-scale 'face-to-face' societies and local collectivities (such as 'the village'). This, and the cognate tradition of 'community studies', has often rested on a *Gemeinschaft*-like view of the local society, emphasizing its internal stability and its relative discreteness.

However, settings are not naturally occurring phenomena, they are constituted and maintained through cultural definition and social strategies. Their boundaries are not fixed but shift across occasions, to one degree or another, through processes of redefinition and negotiation.

There is another reason too why it is potentially misleading to talk of 'studying a setting'. It is not possible to give an exhaustive account of any object. In producing descriptions we always rely on criteria of selection and inference. There is an important sense, then, in which even in the most descriptively oriented study the case investigated is not isomorphic with the setting in which it takes place. A setting is a named context in which phenomena occur that might be studied from any number of angles; a case is those phenomena seen from one particular angle. Some features of the setting will be given no attention at all, and even those phenomena that are the major focus will be looked at in a way that by no means exhausts their character-istics. Moreover, a setting may contain several cases. Thus, for example, in studying the effects of various kinds of external examinations on secondary school teaching, it will be particular examination courses within the school that constitute the cases under investigation rather than the school as a whole (Scarth and Hammersley 1988). Conversely, a case may not be contained within the boundaries of a setting; it may be necessary to go outside of the setting to collect information on important aspects of it. In studying gangs among male prisoners (Jacobs 1974), it may be necessary to explore their links with groups outside if the manner in which they came to be formed and in which they continue to recruit new members is to be understood. While it may seem innocent enough, then, the naturalistic conception of studying fields and settings discourages the systematic and explicit selection of aspects of a setting for study, as well as movement outside of it to follow up promising theoretical leads. And, of course, the process of identifying and defining the case under study must proceed side by side with the refinement of the research problem and the development of the analysis.

One of the limitations often raised in connection with ethnographic work is that because only a single case, or at any rate a small number of cases, is studied, the representativeness of the findings is always in doubt. This can be an important point, but it is not always so. Sometimes, ethnographic research is concerned with a case that has intrinsic interest, so that generalization is not the primary concern. This is most obviously true with action research and evaluation studies, where the target is the characteristics of particular situations. And, occasionally, ethnographic work involves the study of a relatively large number of cases, thereby often providing a substantial basis for generalization. For instance, Strong (1979) studied 1000 cases of paediatric consultation in three hospitals, two in Britain and one in the United States. However, even where generalization is a goal of ethnographic research but only a small number of cases is studied, various strategies can be used to deal with the problem, more or less adequately. How it should be dealt with depends on whether the research is directed towards the development and testing of a theory or whether the aim is generalization about a finite population of cases, whether actually existing or possible in the future (Schofield 1990).

Where the concern is theory development and testing, the strategic selection of cases is particularly important. This can take a variety of forms. One is what Glaser and Strauss (1967) call 'theoretical sampling'. The primary concern of these authors is the generation and elaboration of theory, and they argue that the selection of cases should be designed to produce as many categories and properties of categories as possible and to relate categories to one another. They recommend two complementary strategies: minimizing the differences between cases to highlight basic properties of a particular category; and then subsequently maximizing the differences between cases in order to increase the density of the properties relating to core categories, to integrate categories and to delimit the scope of the theory. As an illustration they cite their research on the awareness contexts surrounding patients dying in hospital:

> Visits to the various medical services were scheduled as follows: I wished first to look at services that minimized patient awareness (and so first looked at a premature baby service and then a neurosurgical service where patients were frequently comatose). I wished next to look at dying in a situation where expectancy of staff and often of patients was great and dying was quick, so I observed on an Intensive Care Unit. Then I wished to observe on a service where staff expectations of terminality were great but where the patient's might or might not be, and where dying tended to be slow. So I looked next at a cancer service. I wished then to look at conditions where death was unexpected and rapid, and so looked at an emergency service. While we were looking at some different types of services, we also observed the above types of services at other types of hospitals. So our scheduling of types of service was directed by a general conceptual scheme – which included hypotheses about awareness, expectedness and rate of dying – as well as by a developing conceptual structure including matters not at first envisioned. Sometimes we returned to services after the initial two or three or four weeks of continuous observation, in order to check upon items which needed checking or had been missed in the initial period.
>
> (Glaser and Strauss 1967:59)

Strategic selection of cases can also be employed in *testing* theoretical ideas. Here the aim is to select cases for investigation which subject theories to relatively severe test. An example is the sequence of studies by Hargreaves, Lacey, and Ball (Hargreaves 1967; Lacey 1970; Ball 1981; see also Abraham 1989a). They argue that the way in which schools differentiate students on academic and behavioural grounds, especially via streaming, tracking, and banding, polarizes them into pro- and anti-school subcultures. These subcultures, in turn, shape students' behaviour inside and outside school and affect their levels of academic achievement. This theory is tested in examples of three types of secondary school: secondary modern

(Hargreaves), grammar (Lacey), and comprehensive (Ball). Moreover, in the case of the grammar school, because the students entering the school have been strongly committed to school values at their junior schools, variables at the heart of competing explanations for the process of polarization – such as attitude to school, aspects of home background, etc. – are partially controlled. Similarly, in his study of Beachside Comprehensive, Ball examines the effects of a shift from banding to mixed ability grouping within a single case (some factors thereby remaining constant), this representing a weakening of differentiation. (For further discussion, see Hammersley 1985.)

Where the aim is generalization to some finite set of cases, rather than the development and testing of theory, it may be possible to assess the typicality of the case or cases studied by comparing their relevant characteristics with information about the target population, if this is available in official statistics or in other studies. Thus, in his investigation of religious intermarriage in Northern Ireland, Lee sought to check the representativeness of his snowball sample of couples by comparing some of their characteristics with a special tabulation of the census data. This revealed that his sample 'showed a sharp bias towards young, recently married couples, mostly without children and with relatively high levels of educational attainment' (Lee 1992:133). While he was not able to correct this sampling bias, because of the problem of gaining access to couples whose position was delicate in the Northern Ireland situation, he was able to allow for it in his analysis.

It may even sometimes be possible to carry out a small-scale survey on a larger sample of the population to gather information to assess the typicality of the cases being studied. Thus, in his study of students at Rutgers University, Moffatt used a survey to assess the extent to which they had a vocational orientation, and he was able to compare the results with those of a national study (Moffatt 1989:331). Another possibility is to combine in-depth study of a small number of cases with more superficial checks on other cases. For example, in his study of law enforcement agencies, Skolnick concentrated on those in one city, but he made a brief investigation of agencies in another to check the likely generalizability of his findings (Skolnick 1966).

The appropriate strategy to adopt in selecting cases may vary over the course of the research. In the early phases, which cases are chosen for investigation may not matter greatly. Later on, it may come to acquire considerable importance. Certainly, initial decisions may have to be revised. Klatch reports how in her research on women involved in right-wing political organizations she began with 'a neat fourfold table comparing four organizations: two Old Right groups and two New Right groups; two "religious" and two "secular organizations" '. However, she soon faced some problems. In particular, she discovered that:

> the chosen organizations for my original design did *not* in fact divide along secular versus religious lines.... Furthermore, I noticed a general pattern developing between the 'homemaker' type of woman active in many religious/pro-family groups... and the 'professional' type of women active in the more secular conservative groups.... The final design continued to rely on in-depth interviews, participant observation, and a textual analysis of right-wing literature, but I broadened the sample to include a much wider range of conservative groups in order to increase the variation among the female activists, thereby gaining a better understanding of the broader divisions within the Right.
>
> (Klatch 1988:75)

Research design in ethnography, both as it relates to the selection of cases for study and in other respects too, is a continuous process. The match between research problems and cases selected must be continually monitored.

SAMPLING WITHIN THE CASE

Selecting cases for investigation is not the only form of sampling involved in social research. Equally important, often, is sampling *within* cases. At least this is true where cases are not so small that they can be subjected to exhaustive investigation, as for example in Strong's study of paediatric consultations. Decisions must be made about where to observe and when, who to talk to and what to ask, as well as about what to record and how. In this process we are not only deciding what is and is not relevant to the case under study but also usually sampling from the data available in the case. Very often this sampling is not the result of conscious deliberation, but it is important to make the criteria employed as explicit and as systematic as possible, so as to try to ensure that data about the case have been adequately sampled. There are three major dimensions along which sampling within cases occurs: time, people, and context.

Time

Time may seem a dimension of obvious importance in social life, but it has often been neglected. Attitudes and activities often vary over time in ways that are highly significant for social theory. Berlak *et al.* provide an example from their research on 'progressive' primary schools in England:

> During our first weeks in the English schools we gradually began to understand that the images of the schools conveyed in the literature were to some extent distorted. The way in which this understanding developed is exemplified by our experience during the first weeks of our study of Mr Thomas's classroom. In his classroom, in a school in an affluent suburban area, we observed thirty children on a Wednesday morning who, after a brief discussion with the teacher, went about their work individually: some began to work on 'maths', others to study spelling or to write original stories in much the way [that the literature describes]. We observed no teacher behavior on that morning which appeared to direct the children to what they were to do. It appeared that the children were pursuing their own interests. However, during the following days, we observed events and patterns which appeared to account for the behavior observed on that Wednesday morning. On the following Monday morning we observed Mr Thomas set work minimums in each subject for the week. . . . On the following Friday morning we saw him collect the children's work 'diaries' where each child had recorded in detail the work he had completed during the week. Over the weekend, Mr Thomas and, as we were to later discover, sometimes the head, checked each record book and wrote comments in the diaries such as 'good', 'more maths', or the ominous 'see me'. Such items, which explained

some of the apparently spontaneous classroom behavior, had
not appeared in the literature.

(Berlak *et al*. 1975:218)

The general issue of the social construction and distribution
of time is quite beautifully demonstrated in Zerubavel's (1979)
study of time in hospitals. In Zerubavel's work, the organization
of time is not an incidental feature or a background to a substantive focus on other organizational matters. Rather, it is an exercise, in the tradition of Simmel, on the formal category of time
itself:

Following the methodological guidelines which I derived
from Simmel's formal sociology, I focused my observations on
only one aspect of hospital life, namely, its temporal structure,
deliberately ignoring – for analytical purposes – the history
of the hospital, its national reputation, the quality of its patient
care, its architectural design and spatial organization, its
finances, the religious and ethnic makeup of its staff, and
so on.

(Zerubavel 1979:xvii)

Zerubavel's is thus an unusually sparse ethnography. Yet the
single-mindedness of his observations and his formal analyses
enable him to reveal the complex patterning of temporal orders
within the organization of daily life in the hospital. He fore-
shadows their diversity in the introduction:

The list of sociological aspects of temporality which can be
discussed within the context of hospital life is almost endless:
the temporal structure of patients' hospital careers; the
relations between time and space; deadlines and strategies of
beating the schedule; the temporal relations among the various hospital units; the impact of organizational time on hospital personnel's life outside the hospital; and so on.

(Zerubavel 1979:xxi)

To follow Zerubavel's example, think hypothetically about the
casualty department of an urban general hospital. Any systematic study here would almost certainly reveal different patterns
of work and activity according to the time of day or night, and
according to the day of the week. The nature of the referrals
and emergency presentations would vary too. Saturday nights

would probably be characterized by very different rates and patterns of admission from Sunday nights, and so on. Time in our casualty department would also relate to changing shifts of nursing staff, rotations among junior doctors, and so forth. Very similar considerations would apply in many other settings: in factories, prisons, educational settings, and residential homes, for example.

It should be apparent, therefore, that any attempt to represent the entire range of persons and events in the case under study will have to be based on adequate coverage of the various temporal divisions. On the other hand, it is impossible to conduct fieldwork round the clock, and some degree of time sampling must be attempted. It may be possible to undertake the occasional period of extended fieldwork, but these are hard to sustain. (These remarks do not apply in quite the same way to anthropological fieldwork, or to practitioner research, where the ethnographer is in principle 'in play' all day, every day – though, even here, the fieldworker will need to 'escape' periodically in order to write up notes, file material, and simply relax.) In any event, long uninterrupted periods of fieldwork are not always to be encouraged. The production of decent fieldnotes, transcribing audio- or video-recordings, the indexing and filing of material, writing memoranda and reflexive notes are all time-consuming and demanding activities. Very long periods of observation will thus become quite unmanageable. The longer the time between observation and recording, the more troublesome will be the recall and recording of adequately detailed and concrete descriptions. Long bursts of observation, uninterrupted by periods of reflexive recording, will thus tend to result in data of poor quality.

Hence, all ethnographers have to resist the very ready temptation to try to see, hear, and participate in everything that goes on. A more selective approach will normally result in data of better quality, provided the periods of observation are complemented by periods of productive recording and reflection. Rather than attempting to cover the entire working day, for instance, one may be able to build up an adequate representation by following the sort of strategy outlined by Schatzman and Strauss:

If the researcher elects to observe work around the clock, he can first observe a day shift for several days, then evenings and then nights, for a period of consecutive days until he is reasonably familiar with all three shifts. Or he may cover events at any given sub-site by 'overlapping' time on consecutive dates – for example, 7:00 a.m. to 9:00 a.m., 8:00 a.m. to 10:00 a.m., 9:00 a.m. to 11:00 a.m. – and over a period of days cover the organization around the clock.

(Schatzman and Strauss 1973:39)

Over and above these procedures for establishing adequate coverage, the researcher will probably identify particularly salient periods and junctures: the change-over between shifts, for instance, might prove crucial in the organization of work, the sharing of information, and so on. Such crucial times should then come in for particular attention.

Similar considerations to those outlined above will also apply to larger-scale temporal dimensions, such as seasonal or annual cycles, and patterns of recruitment of new cohorts, although overall constraints of time and resource will obviously prove limiting here.

Hitherto we have referred primarily to issues relating to fieldwork in organizations and the like. It should also be apparent that similar considerations might apply to fieldwork in less formally defined settings. The patterns of urban life, 'relations in public', the use of public settings, and patterns of deviant activity all follow temporal dimensions: the seasons, the days of the week, and the time of day or night all play their part. Likewise, it may be important to pay some attention to special occasions, such as seasonal festivals and carnivals, ceremonies and rituals, rites of passage, and social markers of status passage.

In organizing the sampling of time, it is as important to sample the routine as it is to observe the extraordinary. The purpose of such systematic data collection procedures is to ensure as full and representative a range of coverage as possible, not just to identify and single out the superficially 'interesting' events.

People

No setting will prove socially homogeneous, and the adequate representation of the people involved in a particular case will normally require some sampling (unless the whole population of relevant actors can be studied adequately and in equal depth). The sampling of persons may be undertaken in terms of fairly standard 'face-sheet' demographic criteria. That is, depending on the particular context, one may sample persons by reference to categories of gender, 'race', ethnicity, age, occupation, educational qualifications, and so on. However, these face-sheet categories are of importance only as they are relevant to the emerging analysis or to rival theories, or to ensuring representation in terms of some larger population, and they will usually be complemented by other categories of analytic relevance. Such emergent categories may be either 'member-identified categories' or 'observer-identified categories'. The distinction is drawn from Lofland (1976): 'member-identified categories' refers to typifications that are employed by members themselves, that is, they are 'folk' categories that are normally encapsulated in the 'situated vocabularies' of a given culture; 'observer-identified categories' are types constructed by an observer.

Some cultures are particularly rich in member-generated categories. Spradley (1970), for instance, in his work on tramps, identifies the following taxonomy of terms that are used to identify major types: ding, bore car tramp, bindle stiff, working stiff, airedale, home guard tramp, mission stiff, and rubber. The taxonomy also includes the sub-types: harvest tramp, tramp miner, fruit tramp, construction tramp, sea tramp, nose diver, and professional nose diver. Similarly, in her study of a women's prison, Giallombardo (1966) documents the following collection of labels that the prisoners themselves use to categorize the inmates: snitchers, inmate cops, and lieutenants; squares, jive bitches; rap buddies, homeys; connects, boosters; pinners; penitentiary turnouts, lesbians, femmes, stud broads, tricks, commissary hustlers, chippies, kick partners, cherries, punks, and turnabouts. These labels are applied on the basis of 'the mode of response exhibited by the inmate to the prison situation and the quality of the inmates' interaction with other inmates and staff', including styles of sexual orientation (Giallambardo 1966:270).

On the other hand, the observer may construct hypothetical categories, on the basis of the fieldwork. In a study of waiting behaviour, for instance, Lofland identified the following key types:

1 *The Sweet Young Thing.* (Generally a female.) Once having taken a position, normally a seated one, she rarely leaves it. Her posture is straight; potentially suggestive or revealing 'slouching' is not dared.

2 *The Nester.* Having once established a position, such persons busy themselves with arranging and rearranging their props, much in the manner of a bird building a nest.

3 *The Investigator.* Having first reached a position, the investigator surveys his surroundings with some care. Then . . . he leaves his position to begin a minute investigation of every inanimate object in sight.

4 *The Seasoned Urbanite* . . . is easy and relaxed . . . within the confines of legitimate setting use and proper public behavior.

5 *The Maverick* . . . is a non-style. . . . Its users are those who either do not know, are not able, or do not care to protect themselves in public settings. . . . There are three types . . . : *children* . . . ; the *constantly stigmatised* . . . ; and *eccentrics*.

(Lofland 1966; cited in Lofland 1971:35)

Whether the sampling of persons takes place on the basis of member-identified or observer-identified categories (and often both are used), the process is inextricably linked with the development of analytical ideas and the collection of data.

Context

Taking account of variations in context is as important as sampling across time and people. Within any setting people may distinguish between a number of quite different contexts that require different kinds of behaviour. Some of these will be fairly obvious, others less so. In schools, for example, it is well known that the behaviour of teachers often differs sharply between classrooms and staffrooms (Woods 1979; Hammersley 1980). This contrast is an example of a more abstract distinction between frontstage and backstage regions developed by Goffman:

A back region or backstage may be defined as a place, relative to a given performance, where the impression fostered by the performance is knowingly contradicted as a matter of course. There are, of course, many characteristic functions of such places. It is here that the capacity of a performance to express something beyond itself may be painstakingly fabricated; it is here that illusions and impressions are openly constructed. Here stage props and items of personal front can be stored in a kind of compact collapsing of whole repertoires of actions and characters. Here grades of ceremonial equipment, such as different types of liquor or clothes, can be hidden so that the audience will not be able to see the treatment accorded them in comparison with the treatment that could have been accorded them. Here devices such as the telephone are seques-tered so that they can be used 'privately'. Here costumes and other parts of personal front may be adjusted and scrutinized for flaws. Here the team can run through its performance, checking for offending expressions when no audience is pres-ent to be affronted by them; here poor members of the team, who are expressively inept, can be schooled or dropped from the performance. Here the performer can relax; he can drop his front, forgo speaking his lines, and step out of character.

(Goffman 1959:114–15)

Goffman illustrates his argument by reference to a wide range of settings from hotel restaurants to shipyards.

It is important, however, not to mistake places for contexts. We must remember, again following Goffman (1963), that archi-tectural structures are merely props used in the social drama; they do not determine behaviour in a direct fashion. What we think of, for example, as 'staffroom behaviour' may also occur in other parts of a school where conditions are right, or even in the bar of a local public house. Conversely, behaviour typical of the staffroom may not occur while visitors, or even the head-teacher, are there. If we are to ensure that we are not led into false generalizations about attitudes and behaviour within a case through contextual variability, we must identify the contexts in terms of which people in the setting act, recognizing that these are social constructions not physical locations, and try to ensure that we sample across all those that are relevant.

Up to this point we have talked for the most part as though it were simply up to the researcher to select the settings and cases for study, and to sample them appropriately. But, of course, the cases we might wish to select may not be open to study, for one reason or another; and, even if they are, effective strategies for gaining access to the necessary data will need to be developed. Similarly, not all the people we wish to observe or talk to, nor all the contexts we wish to sample, may be accessible – certainly not at the times we want them to be. The problem of gaining access to data is particularly serious in ethnography since one is operating in settings where the researcher generally has little power, and people have pressing concerns of their own which often give them little reason to co-operate. It is to this problem that we turn in the next chapter.

Chapter 3

Access

The problem of obtaining access to the data one needs looms large in ethnography. It is often at its most acute in initial negotiations to enter a setting and during the 'first days in the field'; but the problem persists, to one degree or another, throughout the data collection process.

In many ways, gaining access is a thoroughly practical issue. As we shall see, it involves drawing on the interpersonal resources and strategies that we all tend to develop in dealing with everyday life. But the process of achieving access is not merely a practical matter. Not only does its achievement depend upon theoretical understanding, often disguised as 'native wit', but the discovery of obstacles to access, and perhaps of effective means of overcoming them, itself provides insights into the social organization of the setting.

The work of Barbera-Stein (1979) illustrates this. Her field-work was undertaken in several different therapeutic or day-care centres for pre-school children. The original research design foundered because access was denied to several settings. She writes in retrospect of her experience: 'The access negotiations can be construed as involving multiple views of what is profane and open to investigation vs what is sacred or taboo and closed to investigation unless the appropriate respectful stance or distance is assumed' (Barbera-Stein 1979:15). She ties this observation to particular settings and particular activities in them:

> I had requested the permission to observe what the psycho-analytic staff considered sacred. In their interactions with emotionally disturbed children, they attempted to establish effective bonds modelled after the parent–child bond. This

was the first step in their attempts to correct the child's faulty emotional development. This also was the principal work of the social workers at the day-care centre. Formal access to the day-care centre initially was made contingent upon my not observing on Tuesdays and Thursdays when the social workers engaged the children in puppet play sessions. Puppet play was used as a psychological projective technique in monitoring and fostering the emotional development of the children.

(Barbera-Stein 1979:15)

Even after eight months of fieldwork, and after some renegotiation, access to such 'sacred' puppet-play sessions was highly restricted. Barbera-Stein was allowed to observe only three sessions and was forbidden to take notes.

In contrast, Barbera-Stein herself assumed that interactional data on families in the home would be highly sacred, and did not initially request access to such information. In fact it turned out that this was not regarded as problematic by the social workers, as they viewed working with families as their stock-in-trade, and it was an area in which they were themselves interested. Her experience illustrates, incidentally, that while one must remain sensitive to issues of access to different domains, it is unwise to allow one's plans to be guided entirely by one's own presuppositions concerning what is and is not accessible.

Negotiating access, data collection and analysis are not, then, distinct phases of the research process. They overlap significantly. Much can be learned from the problems involved in making contact with people as well as from how they respond to the researcher's approaches.

ENTRY TO SETTINGS

Access is not simply a matter of physical presence or absence. It is far more than the granting or withholding of permission for research to be conducted. Perhaps this can be illustrated by reference to research where too literal a notion of access would be particularly misleading. It might be thought that problems of access could be avoided if one were to study 'public' settings only, such as streets, shops, public transport vehicles, bars, and similar locales. In one sense this is true. Anyone can, in principle, enter such public domains; that is what makes them public. No process of negotiation is required for that. On the other hand, things are not necessarily so straightforward. In many settings, while physical presence is not in itself problematic, appropriate activity may be so.

Among other things, public domains may be marked by styles of social interaction involving what Goffman (1971) terms 'civil inattention'. Anonymity in public settings is not a contingent feature of them, but is worked at by displays of a studied lack of interest in one's fellows, minimal eye contact, careful management of physical proximity, and so on. There is, therefore, the possibility that the fieldworker's attention and interest may lead to infringements of such delicate interaction rituals. Similarly, much activity in public settings is fleeting and transient. The fieldworker who wishes to engage in relatively protracted observations may therefore encounter the problem of managing 'loitering', or having to account for himself or herself in some way.

Some examples of these problems are provided in Karp's (1980) account of his investigation of the 'public sexual scene' in and around Times Square in New York, particularly in pornographic bookshops and cinemas. Admittedly, this is a very particular sort of public setting, in that a good deal of what goes on may be 'disreputable' and the behaviour in public correspondingly guarded. Karp tried various strategies for achieving access and initiating interaction. He tried to negotiate openly with some bookshop managers, but failed. Similarly, after a while, regulars on the street interpreted his hanging around in terms of his being a hustler, or a cop. He also reports failure to establish relationships with prostitutes, although his fieldnotes display what seems a rather clumsy and naive approach to this.

Karp resolved his problems to some extent by realizing that they directly paralleled the interactional concerns of the participants themselves, and he was able to draw on his access troubles for analytical purposes in that light. He quotes a research note to this effect:

> I can on the basis of my own experience substantiate, at least in part, the reality of impression-management problems for persons involved in the Times Square sexual scene. I have been frequenting pornographic bookstores and movie theatres

for some nine months. Despite my relatively long experience I have not been able to overcome my uneasiness during activity in these contexts. I feel, for example, nervous at the prospect of entering a theatre. This nervousness expresses itself in increased heartbeat. I consciously wait until few people are in the vicinity before entering; I take my money out well in advance of entering; I feel reticent to engage the female ticket seller in even the briefest eye contact.

(Karp 1980:94)

In the face of such interactional constraints, Karp decided to resort to observation alone, with minimal participation beyond casual conversation. He concludes by pointing out that such public settings may be as constraining for a researcher as any organizational setting.

To a considerable extent Karp's is an account of relative failure to establish and maintain working 'presence' and relationships, although he learns from his problems. One should not conclude from his experience, however, that 'loitering' can never lead to workable research conditions. West writes about the value of such apparently casual approaches: he 'met both ... referred delinquents and others by frequenting their hangouts, such as stores, pool halls, restaurants, and alleys, and by trying to strike up casual acquaintanceship'; though he comments that 'some boldness and a tough-skinned attitude to occasional personal rejection were helpful, in addition to skills in repartee, sports, empathy, and sensitivity'. He reports that 'after a few visits or perhaps a couple of weeks, I became recognized as something of a regular, and usually had managed to strike up conversations with a few youngsters' (West 1980:34).

As in the case of West's research, some individuals and groups who one might want to study may be available in public settings. However, they are not always welcoming to researchers, or indeed to outsiders of any kind. Sometimes very extensive 'hanging about', along with lucky breaks, is necessary before access is achieved, as Wolf's experience illustrates:

As a new graduate student in anthropology at the University of Alberta, Edmonton, I wanted to study the 'Harleytribe'. It was my intent to obtain an insider's perspective of the emotions and the mechanics that underlie outlaw bikers' creation of a subcultural alternative.... I customised my

Norton, donned some biker clothing, and set off to do some fieldwork. My first attempts at contacting an outlaw club were near-disasters. In Calgary I met several members of the Kings Crew MC in a motorcycle shop and expressed an interest in 'hanging around'. But I lacked patience and pushed the situation by asking too many questions. I found out quickly that outsiders, even bikers, do not rush into a club, and that anyone who doesn't show the proper restraint will be shut out.

Following this, Wolf bought himself a new bike, and approached a new group, the Rebels, in a 'final make-it-or-forget-it attempt'. He writes that he sat in a bar watching them and working out how to approach them:

> I discovered that I was a lot more apprehensive than I thought as I sat at the opposite end of the Kingsway Motor Inn and watched the Rebels down their drinks. The loud thunder of heavy-metal rock music would make initiating a delicate introduction difficult, if not impossible, and there were no individual faces or features to be made out in the smoky haze, only a series of Rebel skull patches draped over leather jackets in a corner of the bar that outsiders seemed to avoid warily. . . . I decided to go outside and devise an approach strategy, including how I would react if one of the Rebels turned to me and simply said 'Who invited you?'. I had thought through five different approaches when Wee Albert of the Rebels MC came out of the bar to do a security check on the 'Rebel iron' in the parking lot. He saw me leaning on my bike and came over to check me out. For some time Wee Albert and I stood in the parking lot and talked about motorcycles, riding in the wind, and the Harley tradition. He showed me some of the more impressive Rebel choppers and detailed the jobs of customizing that members of the club had done to their machines. He then checked out my 'hog', gave a grunt of approval, and invited me to come in and join the Rebels at their tables. Drinking at the club bar on a regular basis gave me the opportunity to get to know the Rebels and gave them an opportunity to size me up and check me out on neutral ground. I had made the first of a long sequence of border crossings that all bikers go through if they hope to get close to a club.

(Wolf 1991:212–15)

Making contact in public settings with people one wishes to study can be a difficult and protracted process, then; though Wolfe's experience is undoubtedly extreme.

Sometimes, initial contacts may completely transform research plans. Liebow (1967) reports that on his first day he fell into conversation with some of the onlookers present at a scuffle between a policeman and a woman. This led into several hours of talk with a young man. This he wrote up, and in retrospect he comments:

> I had not accomplished what I set out to do, but this was only the first day. And, anyway, when I wrote up this experience that evening, I felt that it presented a fairly good picture of this young man and that most of the material was to the point. Tomorrow, I decided, I would get back to my original plan – nothing had been lost. But tomorrow never came.
>
> (Liebow 1967:238)

The 'original plan' that Liebow was cherishing initially was to do several small studies, 'each covering a strategic part of the world of the low-income male': a neighbourhood study, a labour union, and a bootleg joint, perhaps supplemented by some life-histories and genealogies. In the event, however, in the first neighbourhood he tried,

> I went in so deep that I was completely submerged and any plan to do three or four separate studies, each with its own neat, clean boundaries, dropped forever out of sight. My initial excursions into the street – to poke around, get the feel of things, and to lay out the lines of any fieldwork – seldom carried me more than a block or two from the corner where I started. From the very first weeks, or even days, I found myself in the middle of things: the principal lines of my field work were laid out, almost without my being aware of it. For the next year or so, and intermittently thereafter, my base of operations was the corner carry-out across the street from my starting point.
>
> (Liebow 1967:236–7)

On the second day of his fieldwork, Liebow returned to the scene of his first encounter. Again he fell into conversation, with three 'winos' in their forties, and a younger man 'who looked as if he had just stepped out of a slick magazine advertisement' (1967, 238–9). This younger man was Tally Jackson, who acted as Liebow's sponsor and confidant, and on whose social circle the research came to be focused.

Now Liebow's study is an impressive and important contribution to urban ethnography, but there are danger signals in his account of the fieldwork. It may or may not have been a good idea to abandon his original intentions of conducting several small, related projects. On the other hand, it may not have been such a good idea to have, as it appears, surrendered himself so thoroughly to the chance meeting with Tally and its consequences. As Liebow himself remarks, 'the principal lines of my fieldwork, were laid out, *almost without my being aware of it*' (1967:237; our emphasis). Here, rather than the research problem being transformed in response to opportunities arising in the course of the research, and the research design being modified accordingly, Liebow seems to have abandoned systematic research design altogether.

Nevertheless, Liebow's research illustrates the significance of informal 'sponsorship'. Tally vouchsafed for him, introduced him to a circle of friends and acquaintances, and so provided access to data. The most famous of such 'sponsors' in the field is undoubtedly 'Doc' who helped in Whyte's study of 'corner boys' (Whyte 1981). Whyte's methodological appendix is a classic description of the serendipitous development of a research design, and the influence of Doc was a major determinant in its evolution. Doc agreed to offer Whyte the protection of friendship, and coached him in appropriate conduct and demeanour.

Liebow's and Whyte's contacts with their sponsors were quite fortuitous. However, sponsorship of a similar kind may be gained through the mobilization of existing social networks, based on acquaintanceship, kinship, occupational membership, and so on. This is not always straightforward, however. Cassell reports the difficulties she had in negotiating access in a study of surgeons, and her reliance on personal and occupational networks:

> When I decided to study surgeons, I negotiated for the better part of a year with a representative of the Department of Surgery, at a hospital where my ex-husband was an attending

physician, before the Chief of Surgery definitively refused to allow me access to his department.

At the same time, after spending six months obtaining an interview with a representative of the American College of Surgeons, I flew to Chicago to ask for advice and possible sponsorship from this prestigious group. After a charming Southern surgeon, in his sixties, indulged in an hour of small-talk, I broke in and asked if he thought my study was worth doing. Silence. 'Your husband is a doctor?' he finally inquired. When I assented, he said: 'Have you ever thought of... I mean, with your background, you'd be such an asset... has it ever occurred to you to become active in the Ladies Auxiliary of your husband's hospital?' This was the only advice I received.

Eventually, at almost the last minute, when a reviewer for the agency that eventually funded my study asked for proof that I had access to surgeons, a friend of my ex-husband said that I could do research in the hospital where he was Chief of Surgery (and wrote a letter to that effect).

(Cassell 1988:94)

Hoffman (1980) also provides insight into the way in which personal networks can be used, while drawing attention once more to the relationship between problems of access and the quality of the data subsequently collected. Her research was concerned with a locally influential elite – members of boards of hospital directors in Quebec. In the first place she notes a general problem of access to such an elite:

Introducing myself as a sociology graduate student, I had very limited success in getting by the gatekeepers of the executive world. Telephone follow-ups to letters sent requesting an interview repeatedly found Mr X 'tied up' or 'in conference'. When I did manage to get my foot in the door, interviews rarely exceeded a half hour, were continually interrupted by telephone calls (for 'important' conferences, secretaries are usually asked to take calls) and elicited only 'front work' (Goffman 1959), the public version of what hospital boards were all about.

(Hoffman 1980:46)

During one interview, however, Hoffman's informant

discovered that he knew members of her family. This gave rise to a very different sort of interview, and more illuminating data:

> The rest of the interview was dramatically different than all my previous data. I was presented with a very different picture of the nature of board work. I learned, for example, how board members used to be recruited, how the executive committee kept control over the rest of the board, how business was conducted and of what it consisted, and many other aspects of the informal social organization of board work.
>
> (Hoffman 1980:46–7)

Abandoning her original research design – based on interviewing a representative sample from different institutions – Hoffman therefore started to select informants on the basis of social ties. She began with direct personal contacts, and then asked those acquaintances to refer her to other informants, and so on. This strategy, she concludes, produced 'more informative and insightful data'.

Hoffman graphically juxtaposes typical responses to illustrate the point:

Response to an Unknown Sociologist	*Response to a Known Individual*
Board Member A	Board Member B

Q. *How do you feel in general about how the board has been organized?*

I think the basic idea of participation is good. We need better communication with the various groups. And I think they probably have a lot to offer.	This whole business is unworkable. It's all very nice and well to have these people on the board, they might be able to tell us something here and there, or describe a situation, but you're not going to run a hospital on that!

Q. *How is the new membership working out? Do they participate? Any problems?*

... oh yes, Mr. X (orderly) participates. He asked something today, now what was it? Sometimes they lack skill and experience, but they catch on. There is no problem with them. We get along very well.

Mr. X (orderly) hasn't opened his mouth except for a sandwich ... But what can he contribute? ... You could rely on the old type of board member ... you knew you could count on him to support you. You didn't have to check up all the time. But these new people, how do you know how they will react? Will they stick behind you? And there is the problem of confidentiality. Everything you say you know will be all over the hospital ten minutes after the meeting. You can't say the same things anymore. You have to be careful in case someone interprets you as being condescending or hoity-toity.
(Hoffman 1980:48–9)

Hoffman tends to portray the issue of access here in terms of 'penetrating informants' fronts', and clearly contrasts the two varieties of data in terms of aiming for 'better' and more truthful accounts. This can be problematic: 'frankness' may be as much a social accomplishment as 'discretion', and we shall return to the problem of the authenticity of accounts later. But Hoffman's discussion dramatically focuses attention on the relationships between 'access', the fieldworker's perceived identity, and the data that can be gathered.

GATEKEEPERS

Cassell's and Hoffman's accounts take us towards those 'formal', 'private' settings where boundaries are clearly marked, are not easily penetrated, and may be policed by 'gatekeepers'. In formal organizations, for example, initial access negotiations may be focused on official permission that can legitimately be granted or withheld by key personnel. Although not necessarily the case, such gatekeepers are often the ethnographer's initial point of contact with such research settings.

It should be said, though, that identifying the relevant gate-keepers is not always straightforward. Indeed, the distinction between sponsors and gatekeepers is by no means clear-cut. Even in formal bureaucratic organizations it is not always obvious whose permission needs to be obtained, or whose good offices it might be advisable to secure. Gouldner reports precisely this kind of problem in his research on the Oscar Center gypsum plant. He recounts that the research team

> made a 'double-entry' into the plant, coming in almost simul-taneously by way of the Company and the Union. But it soon became obvious that we had made a mistake, and that the problem had not been to make a double-entry, but a triple-entry; for we had left out, and failed to make independent contact with a distinct group – the management of that par-ticular plant. In a casual way, we had assumed that main office management also spoke for the local plant management and this, as a moment's reflection might have told us, was not the case. In consequence our relations with local manage-ment were never as good as they were with the workers or the main office management.
>
> (Gouldner 1954:255–6)

Knowing who has the power to open up or block off access, or who consider themselves and are considered by others to have the authority to grant or refuse access, is, of course, an important aspect of sociological knowledge about the setting. However, this is not the catch-22 situation it might appear. For one thing, as we argued in Chapter 1, research never starts from scratch; it always relies on common-sense knowledge to one degree or another. We may already know sufficient about the setting to be able to judge what the most effective strategy is likely to be for gaining entry. If we do not, we may be able to 'case' the setting beforehand, for example by contacting people with knowledge of it or of other settings of a similar type. This will often solve the problem, though as Whitten (1970) found out in his research on black communities in Nova Scotia, there is no guarantee that the information provided is sound. He was told by local people that he should phone the councillor for the largest settlement, that to try to meet him without phoning would be rude. He did so, 'with disastrous results':

I introduced myself as an anthropologist from the United States, interested in problems encountered by people in rural communities in different parts of the Americas. Following procedures common in the United States and supported by educated Nova Scotians, I said that I was particularly interested in Negro communities kept somewhat outside of the larger social and economic system. I was told, politely, but firmly, that the people of the rural Dartmouth region had had enough of outsiders who insulted and hurt them under the guise of research, that the people of the region were as human as I, and that I might turn my attention to other communities in the province. I was asked why I chose 'Negroes' and when I explained that Negroes, more than others, had been excluded from full participation, I was again told that the people of rural Nova Scotia were all alike, and that the colored people were tired of being regarded as somehow different, because there was no difference.

(Whitten 1970:371)

Whitten discovered that he had made two basic mistakes:

First, when Nova Scotians tell one to first call the official responsible for a community, they are paying due respect to the official, but they do not expect the investigator to take this advice. They expect that the investigator will establish an enduring contact with someone who can introduce him to the official. Crucial to this procedure is that the investigator be first known to the person who will make the introduction, for the middleman may be held responsible for the investigator's mistakes. The recommendation to call relieves anyone from the responsibility for the call, and hence it is not expected that a person will follow this advice. Second, it is not expected that one will use the term 'Negro' in referring to Nova Scotians ethnically identified as colored. The use of ethnic terminology (including the term 'colored') is reserved for those who are already a part of the system. . . .

The most effective way to approach an official, we found, is to recognize no ethnic distinctions whatsoever, thereby forcing the official to make the preliminary distinction (e.g.

between colored community and white community). By so doing the investigator is in a position to immediately inquire as to the significance of ethnicity. Had we acted a bit more slowly, and ignored ethnic differences, we might have succeeded in gaining early entrée, but we erred by assuming that we knew the best way to do things in Anglo-America. By talking too much, and not reflecting carefully on the possible connotations attached to our 'instructions', our work bogged down for a time.

(Whitten 1970:371–2)

Whether or not they grant entry to the setting, gatekeepers will generally, and understandably, be concerned as to the picture of the organization or community that the ethnographer will paint, and they will have practical interests in seeing themselves and their colleagues presented in a favourable light. At least, they will wish to safeguard what they perceive as their legitimate interests. Gatekeepers may therefore attempt to exercise some degree of surveillance and control, either by blocking off certain lines of inquiry, or by shepherding the fieldworker in one direction or another.

As an illustration of one way in which gatekeepers may try to influence things, Bogdan and Taylor report:

We know one novice who contacted a detention home in order to set up a time to begin his observation. The supervisor with whom he spoke told him that he wouldn't be interested in visiting the home that day or the next because the boys would just be making Hallowe'en decorations. He then suggested which times of the day would be best for the observer to 'see something going on'. The observer allowed himself to be forced to choose from a limited number of alternatives when he should have made it clear that he was interested in a variety of activities and times.

(Bogdan and Taylor 1975:44–5)

Although Bogdan and Taylor report this as happening to a novice, it often remains a problem for even the most experienced fieldworker. (In this instance, the ethnographer needs to explain that he or she is willing or even eager to sample the mundane, the routine, or perhaps the boring aspects of everyday life.)

One of the difficulties regularly faced in this context arises from the fact that it is often precisely the most sensitive things that are of most *prima facie* interest. Periods of change and transition, for example, may be perceived as troublesome by the participants themselves, and they may wish, therefore, to steer observers away from them: the conflict of interest arises from the fact that such disruptions can be particularly fruitful research opportunities for the fieldworker.

The issue of 'sensitive' periods is something that Ball (1980) explicitly remarks on in the context of a discussion of initial encounters in school classrooms. He notes that researchers have tended to devote attention to classrooms where patterns of interaction are already well established. Hence there is a tendency to portray classroom life in terms of fixed, static models. The pictures of classroom interaction with which we are familiar, Ball argues, may be artefacts of the preferred research strategy. He goes on to note:

> The problem is that most researchers, with limited time and money available to them, are forced to organise their classroom observations into short periods of time. This usually involves moving into already established classroom situations where teachers and pupils have considerably greater experience of their interactional encounters than does the observer. Even where the researcher is available to monitor the initial encounters between a teacher and pupils, the teacher is, not unreasonably, reluctant to be observed at this stage.
>
> But the reasons for the teacher's reluctance are exactly the reasons why the researcher should be there. These earlier encounters are of crucial significance not only for understanding what comes later but in actually providing for what comes later.
>
> (Ball 1980:143–4)

Here, then, Ball neatly draws attention to a particular problem of access, and shows how this is not simply a practical matter of organizing the fieldwork (though it is that too), but also bears on issues of descriptive accuracy and analytical adequacy.

TO DECEIVE OR NOT TO DECEIVE?

Sometimes, of course, it may be judged that the relevant gate-keepers will almost certainly block entry altogether. Here, resort may be made to secret research. (We discuss the ethical issues surrounding covert research in Chapter 10.) Holdaway (1982) provides an example from his work on the police. As a serving officer who was seconded to university to read sociology and returned to the force wishing to do research on it, he was faced with six options:

A Seek the permission of the chief officer to research, giving full details of method and intention.
B Seek permission as above, so phrasing the research description that it disguised my real intentions.
C Seek permission of lower ranks, later requesting more formal acceptance from senior officers.
D Do no research.
E Resign from the police service.
F Carry out covert research.

I chose the final option without much difficulty. From the available evidence, it seemed the only realistic option; alternatives were unrealistic or contained an element of the unethical which bore similarity to covert observation. I believe that my senior officers would have either refused permission to research or obstructed me. Option B is as dishonest a strategy as covert research, if the latter is thought dishonest. For example, if I were a Marxist and wanted to research the police and declared my Marxism, I know that I would be denied research access; yet to 'front' myself in a different research guise is surely dishonest. Option C could not have been managed. D denies the relevance of my studies, and Option E would have been its logical progression – yet I felt an obligation to return to the police who had financed my study.

(Holdaway 1982:63)

Holdaway was in the unusual position of knowing the setting he wanted to research, and the gatekeepers who could give him permission to do the research, very well indeed. Often, however, judgments that access to a setting is impossible are less well founded. There are some settings to which one might expect entry to be blocked but that have been shown to be accessible, at least to some degree. For example, Fielding (1982) approached an extreme right-wing political organization, the National Front, for permission to carry out research on their organization, and received it – though he felt it necessary to supplement official access with some covert observation.

Indeed, there is often a considerable amount of uncertainty and variation in the scope for negotiating access. Shaffir was told that the Tasher Hassidic community he was interested in studying would not agree to be researched. He was advised to get a job in the community and do covert research, which he did:

Since I suspected that members of the community would not sanction my sociological investigation, I did not inform the Tasher that I was collecting data about them. (Neither did I tell them about my connection with the Lubavitcher, a community they disapproved of because of the involvement of its members with non-Orthodox Jews.) I did, however, tell those who were interested that I was a sociology student at McGill University. Invariably, I was asked to explain the meaning of 'sociology', a term that was entirely foreign to the Tasher. . . . But I was able to define it sufficiently to use my interest in sociology to add legitimacy to the kinds of questions I regularly asked about the organization of the community. . . . Some people were surprised at my curiosity about topics unconnected with my clerical duties. However, others seemed convinced by my explanations and volunteered information about themselves which they believed might interest an outsider. But several members looked at me so oddly that I felt they considered me an intruder and were (quite rightly!) suspicious of my presence.

(Shaffir 1985:126)

Shaffir found his covert role a severe constraint on his research, and experienced great difficulty in combining a full-time clerical job with his university studies. He decided to reduce his hours of work, explaining this to his Tasher employers on the grounds that

my commitments at the university required me to conduct research and to write a thesis. That thesis, I explained, would probably be about pool halls. 'Pool hall, what is that?', asked the rabbi in Yiddish. The other man, who had graduated from university before becoming a Tasher Hassid, gave his version of a pool hall, 'It's a place where you play with balls on a table', and turning to me, he asked: 'How can I describe a pool hall to him? He's never been'. Then he elaborated: 'It's a dirty place that attracts the criminal element. It's suitable for Gentiles, not for Jews.'

They both quickly agreed that I ought to be discouraged from pursuing that research and suddenly the rabbi said, 'Look, you know us. Why don't you write about us and we could help you . . . I'm telling you, you'll win a prize. I'll help you and so will the others and you'll win an award . . . When do you want to start? Let's set a time.' The other man seemed to be of the same opinion. Stunned, I managed to say calmly that I would consider the suggestion and meet them the next day to pursue it further.

Of course, I intended to tell them that I would do as they advised. By the following afternoon, however, both men had changed their mind. . . . That was the end of my first attempt at fieldwork among the Tasher.

I was to be more successful a few years later in the same Tasher community. There were new administrators in charge of the community's day-to-day affairs who were quite receptive to my request to visit and chat about matters of community life that interested me. I candidly explained my research interests to them. . . . The chief administrator appeared to adopt a 'We have nothing to hide' attitude.

(Shaffir 1985:128–9)

Rather surprisingly, perhaps, Chambliss recounts a more straightforward process of gaining access to the world of organized crime, but once again one relying on an initial covert approach:

I went to the skid row, Japanese, Filipino, and Black sections of Seattle dressed in truck driver's clothes. . . . Sitting in the bar of a café one day I noticed several people going through a back door. I asked the waitress, Millie – a slight, fortyish ex-prostitute and sometime-drug-user with whom I had become friends – where these people were going:

MILLIE: To play cards.

ME: Back there?

MILLIE: Yes, that's where the poker games are.

ME: Can I play?

MILLIE: Sure. Just go in. But watch your wallet.

So I went, hesitantly, through the back door and into a large room which had seven octagonal, green felt covered tables. People were playing five card stud at five of the tables. I was immediately offered a seat by a hand gesture from the card-room manager. I played – all the time watching my wallet as I had been advised.

I went back every day for the next week. . . . In conversation with the cardroom manager and other players I came to realize (discover?) what any taxicab driver already knew: that pornography, gambling, prostitution, and drugs were avail-able on practically every street corner. So I began going to other cafés, card-rooms, and bars. I played in many games and developed a lot of information just from casual conversation.

Within a week I was convinced that the rackets were highly organized. The problem became one of discovering how, and by whom. I was sitting talking to Millie on the 30th of the month when a man I recognized as a policeman came through the door and went into the manager's office. I asked Millie what he was doing:

MILLIE: He's the bag man.

ME: The what?

MILLIE: The bag man. He collects the payoff for the people downstairs.

ME: Oh.

I spent the next two months talking informally to people I met at different games, in pornography shops, or on the streets. I soon began to feel that I was at a dead end. . . . I had discovered the broad outlines of organized crime in Seattle, but how it worked at the higher level was still a mystery. I decided it was time to 'blow my cover'.

I asked the manager of the cardroom I played in most to go to lunch with me. I took him to the faculty club at the University of Washington. This time when he saw me I was shaven and wore a shirt and tie. I told him of my 'purely

scientific' interests and experience and, as best I could, why I
had deceived him earlier. He agreed to help. Soon I began
receiving phone calls: 'I understand you are interested in
Seattle. Did you ever think to check Charles Carroll's brother
in law?' And there was one honest-to-God clandestine meeting in a deserted warehouse down at the wharf. . . .

Over the next ten years I pursued this inquiry, widening
my contacts and participating in an ever larger variety of
rackets. As my interest in these subjects and my reliability as
someone who could be trusted spread, I received more offers
to 'talk' than I had time to pursue.

(Chambliss 1975:36–8)

The work of Holdaway, Fielding, Shaffir, and Chambliss raises
the question of deception in negotiations over access. Where the
research is secret to all those under study, and to gatekeepers
too, the problem of access may be 'solved' at a stroke, providing
the deception is not discovered. Even when 'cover' is successfully maintained, though, the researcher engaging in covert
research has to live with the moral qualms, anxieties, and practical difficulties to which the use of this strategy may lead. However, research carried out without the knowledge of anyone in,
or associated with, the setting is quite rare. Much more common
is that some people are kept in the dark while others are taken
into the researcher's confidence, at least partly.

What is at issue here, though, is not just whether permission
to carry out the research is requested, and from whom, but also
what those concerned are told about it. Some commentators
recommend that an explicit research bargain, spelling out in full
the purposes of the research and the procedures to be employed,
be made with all those involved, right from the start. Often,
though, this is neither possible nor desirable. Given the way in
which research problems may change over the course of fieldwork, the demands likely to be made on people in the setting
and the policy implications and political consequences of the
research are often a matter for little more than speculation at
the outset. There is also the danger that the information provided will influence the behaviour of the people under study
in such a way as to invalidate the findings. While often it may
be judged that the chances of this are small, given the other
pressures operating on these people, there are instances where

it may be critical. Had Festinger *et al.* (1956) informed the apocalyptic religious group they were studying not only that the
research was taking place but also about the hypothesis under
investigation, that would almost certainly have undermined the
validity of their research.

The other argument for not always providing a full account
of one's purposes to gatekeepers and others at the beginning of
the research is that unless one can build up a trusting relationship with them relatively rapidly, they may refuse access in a
way that they would not do later on in the fieldwork. Wolf's
study of bikers, in which he spent three years hanging out with
them before he raised the question of doing research, is an
extreme but instructive example (Wolf 1991). Once people come
to know the researcher as a person who can be trusted to be
discreet in handling information within the setting, and who
will honour his or her promises of anonymity in publications,
access may be granted that earlier would have been refused
point blank. On this argument it is sometimes advisable not to
request at the outset the full access to data one will eventually
require but to leave negotiation of what seem to be the more
delicate forms of access till field relationships have been established – though we should perhaps reiterate that assumptions
about what is and is not delicate may not always prove reliable.

Nevertheless, while telling the 'whole truth' in negotiating
entry for research, as in most other social situations, may not
always be a wise or even a feasible strategy, deception should
be avoided wherever possible, not just for ethical reasons but
also because it can rebound badly later on in the fieldwork.
Indeed, sometimes it may be necessary to warn gatekeepers
or sponsors of possible consequences of the research to avoid
problems subsequently, as Geer notes from her research on
American colleges:

> In colleges of high prestige, the researcher may be hampered
> in his negotiations because the administrators cannot imagine
> that anything harmful to the college could be discovered. In
> this case, it is up to the researcher to explain the kinds of
> things that often turn up – homosexuality, for example, or
> poor teaching. The administrator can sometimes be drawn
> into a scientific partnership. By treating him as a broadminded
> and sophisticated academic, one gradually works him around

to a realization that although the study may be threatening, he and his college are big enough to take it. It may seem unnecessary to prepare administrators for the worst in this fashion, but it prepares the ground for the shock they may get when they see the manuscript at the end of a study. Administrators may attempt to prevent publication or feel that the college has been exploited and similar research should not be authorized. However, the administrator who has committed himself to a generous research bargain is more likely to be proud of the results.

(Geer 1970:83)

Negotiating access is a balancing act. Gains and losses now and later, as well as ethical and strategic considerations, must be traded off against one another in whatever manner is judged to be most appropriate, given the purposes of the research and the circumstances in which it is to be carried out.

OBSTRUCTIVE AND FACILITATIVE RELATIONSHIPS

Seeking the permission of gatekeepers or the support of sponsors is often an unavoidable first step in gaining access to the data. And the relationships established with such people can have important consequences for the subsequent course of the research. Berreman, discussing his research on a Pahari village in the Himalayas, reports:

We were introduced [to the villagers] by a note from a non-Pahari wholesaler of the nearest market town who had long bought the surplus agricultural produce of villagers and had, as it turned out, through sharp practices of an obscure nature, acquired land in the village. He asked that the villagers treat the strangers as 'our people' and extend all hospitality to them. As might have been expected, our benefactor was not beloved in the village and it was more in spite of his intercession than on account of it that we ultimately managed to do a year's research in the village.

(Berreman 1962:6)

Equally, though, one can be fortunate in one's associations with gatekeepers:

The impression I received of people's attitudes to me was that they were very curious and very friendly. As I walked along country paths I was constantly being bothered by inquisitive peasants who had no inhibitions in talking about their problems, especially in relation to the land. It took at least an hour to cross from one side of the village to the other due to the constant need to stop and converse. This contrasts markedly to reports I had received from anthropologists who have worked in Quechua-speaking areas of Peru and have found people dour and uncommunicative. I believe one reason for this is that my introductions into the area were exceptionally good. On the one hand, my official introductions through the Ministry of Agriculture had come through the one official who was not distrusted. He was referred to as 'a good person, he didn't try to cheat us like the other officials'. On the other hand, I had introductions through, and for a time lived in the same building as, members of the progressive Catholic Church. They also happened to be Europeans. Their identification with the peasants, and people's identification of me with them, was extremely valuable.

(Rainbird 1990:89)

However, even the most friendly and co-operative of gatekeepers or sponsors will shape the conduct and development of the research. To one degree or another, the ethnographer will be channelled in line with existing networks of friendship and enmity, territory and equivalent 'boundaries'. Having been 'taken up' by a sponsor, the ethnographer may find it difficult to achieve independence from such a person, discovering that his or her research is bounded by the social horizon of a sponsoring group or individual. Such social and personal commitments may, like gatekeepers' blocking tactics, close off certain avenues of inquiry. The fieldworker may well find him- or herself involved in varieties of 'patron–client' relationship with sponsors, and in so doing discover influence exerted in quite unforeseen ways. The ambiguities and contingencies of sponsorship and patronage are aptly illustrated by two similar studies from rural Spain (Barrett 1974; Hansen 1977).

Barrett reports that the members of his chosen village, Benabarre, were initially reserved. This was partially breached when a village baker started to take Barrett round and introduce him to others. However, the big breakthrough came when the village was visited by a Barcelona professor who was descended from a Benabarre family. The professor was interested in Barrett's work and spent a good deal of time with him:

> Nothing could have had a more beneficial effect on my relations with the community. Don Tomás enjoys immense respect and popularity among the villagers, and the fact that he found my work significant was a behavioural cue to a great many people. The reasoning was apparently that if I were someone to beware of, Don Tomás would not be fooled; if he believed I was the genuine article, then I must be! The response was immediate. Doors which until then had been closed to me opened up; new people greeted me on the streets and volunteered their services.
>
> (Barrett 1974:7)

Barrett realized that this was not simply a lucky breakthrough; it was also an important clue to social relationships in the village. Hierarchical relationships were of fundamental importance. Initially, Barrett had avoided close association with the 'upper crust' families:

> I thought that if there were polarization between the social strata this might make it more difficult later to win acceptance among the peasants. It was virtually the opposite! The fact that I was not associating with those who were considered my peers was simply confusing, and made it vastly more difficult to place me in the social order. Once Don Tomás extended his friendship, and introduced me to other families of similar social rank, this served almost as a certificate of respectability.
>
> (Barrett 1974:8)

Hansen's experiences in rural Catalonia are equally revealing about the hierarchical assumptions of village life:

> Initially, the interviewing process went very slowly because I was overly polite and solicitous about seeking interviews with people I hardly knew. I made the error of being too formal, which made these people suspicious of me. My mistake was brought home to me forcefully by one of the few nobles remaining in the Alto Panadés, whom I had interviewed by chance. He explained in no uncertain terms that I was behav-

ing like a servant or client to these individuals when my own wealth, looks and education meant that I was superior to them. He proceeded to accompany me to more than twenty bourgeois landholders, and ordered them to give me what I wanted, on the spot, including details of business scandals, etc. All complied, some with obeisance towards the Count, and all with both deference and expansiveness toward me. The Count checked all their answers to see if they were concealing vital information. Astonished and embarrassed as I was, the Count had a point. After these twenty interviews, I was swamped by volunteers. It had suddenly become fashionable to be interviewed by *el distinguido antropólogo norteamericano*.

(Hansen 1977:163–4)

Gatekeepers, sponsors, and the like (indeed, most of the people who act as hosts to the research) will operate in terms of expectations about the ethnographer's identity and intentions. As the examples of Hansen and Barrett make clear, these can have serious implications for the amount and nature of the data collected. Many hosts have highly inaccurate, and lurid, expectations of the research enterprise, especially of ethnographic work. Two closely related models of the researcher tend to predominate in this context, 'the expert' and 'the critic'. Both images can conspire to make the gatekeeper uneasy as to the likely consequences of the research, and the effects of its conduct.

The model of the 'expert' often seems to suggest that the social researcher is, or should be, a person who is extremely well informed as to 'problems' and their 'solutions'. The expectation may be set up that the ethnographer seeking access is claiming such expertise, and is expecting to 'sort out' the organization or community. This view therefore leads directly to the second image, that of the 'critic'. Gatekeepers may expect the ethnographer to try to act as an evaluator. (Sometimes, of course, the ethnographer may be officially engaged in evaluation: see Fetterman 1984; Fetterman and Pittman 1986. However, even in this situation, it may still be advisable to distance oneself from the roles of both expert and critic.)

Under some circumstances, these expectations may have favourable connotations. Evaluation by experts, leading to improvements in efficiency, interpersonal relations, planning, and so on, may have at least the overt support of those at the top (though not necessarily of those in subordinate positions). On the other hand, the expectation of expert critical surveillance may create anxieties, on the part of gatekeepers and others. Even if permission for the research is not withheld altogether, gatekeepers may, as we have suggested, attempt to guide the research in directions they prefer, or away from potentially sensitive areas.

On the other hand, it may be very difficult for the ethnographer to establish credibility if hosts expect some sort of 'expertise'. Such expectations may clash with the fieldworker's actual or cultivated ignorance and incompetence. Smigel (1958), for example, has commented on the propensity of lawyers to try to 'brush off' researchers who appear to be legally ill-informed, a point confirmed to some extent by Mungham and Thomas (1981). Ethnographers are sometimes conspicuous for an apparent lack of activity as well. This, too, can militate against their being treated seriously by their hosts.

From a variety of contexts researchers report hosts' suspicions and expectations often proving barriers to access. Such suspicions may be fuelled by the very activities of the fieldworker. Barrett (1974), for instance, remarks on how the inhabitants of his Spanish village interpreted his actions. He was not sensitive to the possibility that villagers might be frightened by someone making notes, when they did not know what was being written down. Rumours about him included beliefs that he was a communist spy, a CIA agent, a Protestant missionary, or a government tax agent. Relatedly, in her fieldwork in Brazil in the late 1930s, Landes was accused of seeking 'vigorous' men to do more than carry her luggage. She was labelled a prostitute during her research because she inadvertently broke the local rules about the proper behaviour of a woman (Landes 1986:137). As might be expected, this created problems for her research and for her personal relationships in the field.

At the same time, it is possible to misread the responses of gatekeepers and participants as more negative than they are. In the case of his research on Hasidic Jews, Shaffir comments:

My suspicion that I was not fully welcomed resulted from a basic misinterpretation: I mistook an indifferent reaction for a negative one. As much as I wished for people to be curious and enthusiastic about my research, the majority could not have cared less. My research did not affect them, and they had more important matters to which to attend.

(Shaffir 1991:76)

Such indifference is not uncommon, nor is a tendency towards paranoia on the part of the ethnographer!

As we noted early on in this chapter, the problem of access is not resolved once one has gained entry to a setting, since this by no means guarantees access to all the data available within it. Not all parts of the setting will be equally open to observation, and not everyone may be willing to talk. Moreover, even the most willing informant will not be prepared, or perhaps even able, to divulge all the information available to him or her. If the data required are to be obtained, negotiation of access is therefore likely to be a recurrent preoccupation for the ethnographer. Negotiation here takes two different but by no means unrelated forms. On the one hand, explicit discussion with those whose activities one wishes to study may take place, much along the lines of that with sponsors and gatekeepers. But the term 'negotiation' also refers to the much more wide-ranging and subtle process of manoeuvring oneself into a position from which the necessary data can be collected. Patience and diplomacy are at a premium here. The ethnographer's negotiation of a role in the setting, and the implications of different roles for the nature of the data collected, will be examined in the next chapter.

Chapter 4

Field relations

Ethnographic research can take place, and has taken place, in a wide variety of types of setting: villages, towns, inner-city neighbourhoods, factory shop floors, deep-shaft mines, farms, retail stores, business offices of various kinds, hospital wards, operating theatres, prisons, public bars, churches, schools, colleges, universities, welfare agencies, courts, morgues, funeral parlours, etc. These settings vary from one another in all manner of respects that are relevant to the nature of the relationships that are possible and desirable with the people who live and/or work in them. Furthermore, there is much variation within each type of setting. Generalizations about field relations are therefore always subject to multiple exceptions. No set of rules can be devised which will produce good field relations. All that can be offered is discussion of some of the main methodological and practical considerations surrounding ethnographers' relations in the field.

INITIAL RESPONSES

Like gatekeepers and sponsors, people in the field will seek to place or locate the ethnographer within their experience. This is necessary, of course, for them to know how to deal with him or her. Some individuals and groups have little or no knowledge of social research; and, partly as a result, field researchers are frequently suspected, initially at least, of being spies, tax inspectors, missionaries, etc., as we noted in the previous chapter. Thus, Kaplan reports that the New England fishermen she studied believed her to be either a government official or an insurance investigator (Kaplan 1991:233).

Generally, such suspicions quickly dissipate as contact increases; but this is not always the case. And, sometimes, given the nature of the research, it may be difficult to distance oneself from such labels. Hunt (1984:288) reports that the police officers she studied suspected that she was an undercover agent for the Internal Affairs Bureau or the FBI, a suspicion encouraged by officials in the police department in which she was working. But, over and above this, she was, and was known to be, a consultant hired by the city to evaluate the police, a role that could easily be seen as spying by those subject to the evaluation. Despite this, Hunt was able to build trust among the police officers she studied by proving herself reliable in emergencies on the street, and by explicitly criticizing the higher echelons of the police department.

By contrast, Den Hollander provides an example of an apparently more favourable initial identification that nevertheless proved to be an insurmountable obstacle to his research:

> In a town in southern Georgia (1932) it was rumoured after a few days that I was a scout for a rayon concern and might help to get a rayon industry established in the town. My denial reinforced the rumour, everyone tried to convince me of the excellent qualities of the town and its population – the observer had turned into a fairy godmother and serious work was no longer possible. Departure was the only solution.
>
> (Den Hollander 1967:13)

Even where people in a setting are familiar with research, there may be a serious mismatch between their expectations of the researcher and his or her intentions. Like gatekeepers, they too may view the researcher as expert or critic. Occasionally, they may be, or consider themselves to be, very sophisticated in their knowledge of research methodology, without being familiar with ethnography; and/or they may have a negative attitude towards it. This problem is especially acute, of course, where the people being studied are academics, even sociologists themselves (Platt 1981). Scott provides an example from research on the experience of postgraduate students in British universities. Along with her co-researcher, Scott was asked to present a paper at a graduate seminar in a sociology department in which they had conducted interviews:

Almost before we had finished speaking the professor leapt
to his feet and began a diatribe, during which he evinced not
simply disagreement with our presentation and methodology,
but anger. He took us to task for writing an article in the
British Sociological Association's magazine *Network*...,
because this 'made our research worthless' since we had published before completing the research.... We felt that we had
been set up as an example of the 'dangers' of ethnographic
research so that this professor could play the big man and
knock us down in front of his graduate students. We found
out later that the professor had been one of those most vocifer-
ous in preference for a large-scale survey when our project
had first been mooted.

(Scott 1984:175)

Outside academia there may be less knowledge but equal or
greater hostility. The comment of a constable in the Royal Ulster
Constabulary, cited by Brewer (1991:16), provides an example:
'If anything gets me down it's bloody sociology. I think it's the
biggest load of shite, simple as that.' Brewer notes that for
many police officers the word 'sociologist' sounds too much like
'socialist'. But this is not the only source of problems; he quotes
a senior police officer:

I think most policemen can't relate to sociology at all, because,
you see, the way we're taught everything is black and white:
those who do bad should be punished, those who do good
should be rewarded. Sociology just seems to turn all that on
its head. It would seem to say that all those who are right
and honest are wrong. Just to say a man doesn't earn as much
money as me and he has to steal to keep his family, well,
sociology says that's OK. Another thing, sociology would
seem to be saying that those who have wealth and do well
do so at the expense of the poor unfortunate.

Where such attitudes prevail, people may challenge the legitimacy of the research and the credentials of the researcher, as
Brewer's colleague Kathleen Magee found in their research on
the RUC:

PC 1. Look, just hold on a wee minute. What gives you the
right to come here and start asking us these personal questions about our families and that?... You're not going to

learn anything about the police while you're here. They're not going to tell you anything ... And you know why? Because you're always walking around with that bloody notebook writing everything down, and you're not getting anywhere near the truth ... Like, what use is this research you're doing anyway? Is it going to do me or my mates any good? What you doing it for? 'Cos let me tell you, the only people who are going to be interested in your bloody research are the authorities.

This verbal assault continued for some time, but it ended on a less hostile note:

PC 1. . . . Maybe the police has made me this way, but do you not see that if you're going to come in here asking me questions about my family, if you're going to want to know all these things, I've got to be able to trust you? Like, after this tonight, I'd let you come out in a vehicle with me.

(Brewer 1991:21–2)

As this example shows, whether or not people have knowledge of social research, and whatever attitude they take towards it, they will often be more concerned with what kind of person the researcher is than with the research itself. They will try to gauge how far the ethnographer can be trusted, what he or she might be able to offer as an acquaintance or friend, and perhaps also how easily he or she could be manipulated or exploited. (For a striking analysis of this process, see Edgerton 1965.) The management of 'personal front' (Goffman 1955) is important here. As in other situations where identities have to be created or established, much thought must be given by the ethnographer to 'impression management'. Impressions that pose an obstacle to access must be avoided or countered as far as possible, while those that facilitate it must be encouraged, within the limits set by ethical considerations.

IMPRESSION MANAGEMENT

Personal appearance can be a salient consideration. Sometimes it may be necessary for the researcher to dress in a way that is very similar to the people to be studied. This is most obviously true in the case of covert research, where the fieldworker will be much more sharply constrained to match his or her personal front to that of the other participants. Patrick's research on a Glasgow gang reveals what 'passing' in this way can involve:

Clothes were another major difficulty. I was already aware of the importance attached to them by gang members . . . and so, after discussion with Tim, I bought [a midnight-blue suit, with a twelve-inch middle vent, three-inch flaps over the side pockets and a light blue handkerchief with a white polka dot (to match my tie) in the top pocket]. Even here I made two mistakes. Firstly, I bought the suit outright with cash instead of paying it up, thus attracting both attention to myself in the shop and disbelief in the gang when I innocently mentioned the fact. Secondly, during my first night out with the gang, I fastened the middle button of my jacket as I was accustomed to. Tim was quick to spot the mistake. The boys in the gang fastened only the top button – 'ra gallous wae'.

(Patrick 1973:15)

Much the same sort of attention to dress is required in research that is destined to be overt, but where an initial period of gaining trust is necessary. However, in the case of Wolf's research on 'outlaw bikers', it was important not only that he looked like a biker – shoulder-length hair and a heavy beard, leather jacket and studded leather wrist bands, a cut-off denim jacket with appropriate patches, etc. – but also that he had a 'hog', a bike, that would stand scrutiny by experts (Wolf 1991:214).

Even where the research is overt, the researcher's appearance can be an important factor in shaping relationships with people in the field. Van Maanen reports that, having done participant observation as a student at the police academy, in studying the police on the street he

still carried a badge and a gun. These symbols of membership signified to others my public commitment to share the risks of the police life. Aside from a few special events, parades, and civic ceremonies where uniformed bodies were in short supply, I was, as the police said, out of the bag. I dressed for the street as I thought plainclothes officers might – heavy and hard-toed shoes, slit or clip-on ties, and loose-fitting jackets that would not make conspicuous the bulge of my revolver.

I carried with me chemical Mace, handcuffs, assorted keys, extra bullets, and sometimes a two-way portable radio and a concealed two-inch revolver loaned to me by co-workers who felt that I should be properly prepared.

(van Maanen 1991:37–8)

He reports that his 'plainclothes but altogether coplike appearance' caused some confusion for citizens, who tended to assume he was a high-ranking police officer!

Similar considerations, but a rather different outfit, were involved in Henslin's research on the homeless. He sought to dress in a way that would allow him to 'blend in' with the inhabitants of the skid rows he visited. This was necessary both to facilitate rapport and to avoid marking himself out as a target for muggers. At the same time, he needed to look sufficiently like a researcher to have his announcement of that identity believed by people working in shelters for the homeless whom he wished to interview. He solved this problem by carrying an old briefcase that was cheap-looking and whose stitching had unravelled at one corner 'making it look as though I had just snatched it up out of the trash'. He reports:

When I would announce to shelter personnel that I was a sociologist doing research on the homeless, they immediately would look me over – as the status I had announced set me apart from the faceless thousands who come trekking through the shelters – making this prop suddenly salient. To direct their attention and help them accept the announced identity, I noticed that at times I would raise the case somewhat, occasionally even obtrusively setting it on the check-in counter (while turning the side with the separating stitching more toward myself to conceal this otherwise desirable defect).

(Henslin 1990:56–8)

In her research on an elite girls' school in Edinburgh, Delamont recounts a similar concern with dressing in a way that enabled her to preserve relationships with multiple audiences:

I had a special grey dress and coat for days when I expected to see the head and some pupils. The coat was knee-length and very conservative-looking, while the dress was mini-length, to show the pupils I knew what the fashion was. I would keep the coat on in the head's office, and take it off before I first met pupils.

(Delamont 1984:25)

While those engaged in overt research do not have to copy closely the dress and demeanour of the people they are researching, they may need to alter their appearance and habits a little in order to reduce any sharp differences. In this way they can make people more at ease in their presence; but this is not the only reason for such adjustments, as Liebow notes:

> I came close in dress (in warm weather, tee or sport shirt and khakis or other slacks) with almost no effort at all. My vocabulary and diction changed, but not radically. . . . Thus, while remaining conspicuous in speech and perhaps in dress, I had dulled some of the characteristics of my background. I probably made myself more acceptable to others, and certainly more acceptable to myself. This last point was forcefully brought home to me one evening when, on my way to a professional meeting, I stopped off at the carry-out in a suit and tie. My loss of ease made me clearly aware that the change in dress, speech, and general carriage was as important for its effect on me as it was for its effect on others.

(Liebow 1967:255–6)

In some situations, however, it may be necessary to use dress to mark oneself off from particular categories to which one might otherwise be assigned. Thus, in her research in Nigeria, Niara Sudarkasa found that in order to be able to get answers to her questions in settings where the people did not already know her she had to avoid dressing like a Yoruba woman: 'People were suspicious of the woman with the notebook, the more so because she did not look like the American student she claimed to be.' They suspected she was a Yoruba collecting information for the government:

> I was so often 'accused' of being a Yoruba that when I went to a market in which I was not certain I would find a friend to identify me, I made a point of speaking only American-sounding English (for the benefit of the English speakers there) and of dressing 'like an American'. On my first trip to

such a market, I even abandoned my sandals in favour of moderately high heels and put on make-up, including lipstick.

(Sudarkasa 1986:175)

In overt participant observation, then, where an explicit research role must be constructed, forms of dress, can 'give off' the message that the ethnographer seeks to maintain the position of an acceptable marginal member, perhaps in relation to several audiences. They may declare affinity between researcher and hosts, and/or they may distance the ethnographer from constraining identities.

There can be no clear prescription for dress other than to commend a high degree of awareness about self-presentation. A mistake over such a simple matter can jeopardize the entire enterprise. Having gained access to the Edinburgh medical school, for instance, Atkinson (1976 and 1981a) went to see one of the influential gatekeepers for an 'informal' chat about the actual fieldwork. He was dressed extremely casually (as well as having very long hair). He had absolutely no intention of going on to the hospital wards looking like that. But the gatekeeper was taken aback by his informal appearance, and started to get cold feet about the research altogether. It took a subsequent meeting, after a hair-cut and the donning of a lounge suit, to convince him otherwise.

To some extent we have already touched on more general aspects of self-presentation. Speech and demeanour will require monitoring, though as we have seen it is not necessarily desirable for them to be matched to those of participants. The researcher must judge what sort of impression he or she wishes to create, and manage appearances accordingly. Such impression management is unlikely to be a unitary affair, however. There may be different categories of participants, and different social contexts, which demand the construction of different 'selves'. In this, the ethnographer is no different in principle from social actors in general, whose social competence requires such sensitivity to shifting situations.

The construction of a working identity may be facilitated in some circumstances if the ethnographer can exploit relevant skills or knowledge he or she already possesses. Parker illustrates the use of social skills in the course of his work with a Liverpool gang. He wrote that blending in was facilitated by certain basic skills. One of the most important involved being 'quick': although I was regarded as normally 'quiet' and socially marginal, this placidity is not always a good idea. Unless you are to be seen as something of a 'divvy' you must be able to look after yourself in the verbal quickfire of the Corner and the pub . . . Being able to kick and head a football reasonably accurately was also an important aspect of fitting into the scheme. Again, whilst I was 'no Kevin Keegan' and indeed occasionally induced abuse like 'back to Rugby Special', I was able to blend into a scene where kicking a ball around took up several hours of the week. I also followed The Boys' football team closely each week and went to 'the match' with them when I could. This helped greatly. Indeed when everyone realized I supported Preston (as well as Liverpool, of course) it was always a good joke since they were so often getting beaten. 'Why don't you play for them they couldn't do any worse?'; 'Is there a blind school in Preston?' (Danny).

(Parker 1974:217–19)

One sort of expertise, of a rather different sort, that anthropologists often find themselves trading on is that of superior technical knowledge and resources. Medical knowledge and treatment constitute one form of this. The treatment of common disorders, usually by simple and readily available methods, has long been one way in which anthropologists in the field have succeeded in ingratiating themselves. This can create problems, of course, as McCurdy (1976) found out, with surgery time capable of taking up the whole day. Nevertheless, this is one way in which the fieldworker can demonstrate that he or she is not an exploitative interloper, but has something to give. Legal advice, the writing of letters, and the provision of 'lifts', for example, can perform the same role. Moreover, sometimes providing such services can directly aid the research. In his study of 'survivalists' Mitchell (1991:100)

offered to compose a group newsletter on my word processor and, in doing so, became the recipient of a steady stream of members' written opinions and perceptions. Being editor of 'The Survival Times', as the newsletter came to be known, in turn, legitimated the use of tape recorders and cameras at group gatherings, [and] provided an entrée to survivalist groups elsewhere around the country.

Participants sometimes come to expect the provision of services, and it may be costly to disappoint them. While in his study of a political campaign organization Corsino often helped out stuffing envelopes, delivering materials, clipping newspapers, etc., on one occasion he refused to scrub floors and help prepare someone's home for a fund-raising reception, on the grounds that he could more usefully spend his time observing the organizational preparations for the event. He describes the result:

> The reactions of the campaign manager and volunteer director were more antagonistic than I expected. Over the next several days, I noticed a polite but unmistakable cooling in my relationship with these officials. . . . I began to feel more and more like an ingrate. . . . This, in turn, resulted in a rather barren period of fieldwork observations. . . . At best, I had to become a passive observer.
> (Corsino; quoted in Adler and Adler 1987:18)

This is not to say that all the expectations of those in the field are legitimate or should be honoured. Sometimes the ethnographer will have to refuse requests and live with the consequences. Indeed, one must take care not to offer too much, to the detriment of the research.

The value of pure sociability should not be underestimated as a means of building trust. Indeed, the researcher must often try to find ways in which 'normal' social intercourse can be established. This requires finding some neutral ground with participants where mundane small-talk can take place. It may be very threatening to hosts if one pumps them constantly about matters relating directly to research interests. Especially in the early days of field negotiations it may be advantageous to find more 'ordinary' topics of conversation, with a view to establishing one's identity as a 'normal', 'regular', 'decent' person.

Beynon (1983) comments on this aspect of his research in an urban secondary school for boys, outlining the strategies he used to establish rapport with the teaching staff:

> Although I did not consciously search these out, I stumbled upon topics in which they and I shared a certain degree of

interest to serve as a backcloth, a resource to be referred to for 'starters', or for 'gap fillers' to keep the conversational door ajar.

(Beynon 1983:40)

Needless to say, such 'neutral' topics are not actually divorced from the researcher's interests at hand, since they can throw additional and unforeseen light on informants, and yield fresh sources of data. Beynon also lists as a 'way in' his own local connections: 'being regarded as "a local" was an important step forward, especially when it became known that I lived within comfortable walking distance of Victoria Road. This considerably lessened the sense of threat which some felt I posed.' (Beynon 1983:41).

This would not lessen such 'threats' in all cases, however. In some settings the participants might feel less threatened by a stranger, and feel more uneasy about the possible significance of an observer's local knowledge. The same applies to another of Beynon's 'ways in':

More significant by far, however, was my own background in teaching and experience in secondary schools, which I unashamedly employed to show staff that I was no stranger to teaching, to classrooms, and to school life in general. I was too old to adopt the now-familiar ethnographic persona of 'naive student', and found it best to present myself as a former teacher turned lecturer/researcher.

(Beynon 1983:41)

Beynon goes on to quote the following exchange, which illustrates how such experience was a 'bonus' in his particular circumstances. At the same time, the extract illustrates a reaction to the attentions of a research worker typical of many settings:

MR. BUNSEN: Where did you teach in London?

J.B.:   South London and then Hertfordshire.

MR. PIANO: (who had been reading the staff notice board): Good Lord, I didn't realise you were one of us! I thought you were one of the 'experts' who never taught, but knew all about it.

J.B.:   I don't know all about it, but I have taught.

MR. PIANO: How long?

J.B.:   Ten years, in a Grammar and then a Comprehensive.

MR. PIANO: That's a fair stretch. Well, well, I can start thump-
ing them now!

(Beynon 1983:42)

We can note in passing the common resentment on the part
of some occupational practitioners, and especially teachers, of
detached, often invisible, 'experts' – though a fieldworker's willingness to stay and learn can often overcome such hostilities,
irrespective of prior membership or expertise.

Beynon himself goes on to note that the employment of such
strategies in establishing 'mutuality' was more than him pander-
ing for the teachers' approval. Not only did such exchanges
facilitate the collection of data, but they were data in their own
right. However, he also notes some feelings of personal disquiet,
wondering whether he was unduly exploitative in offering
'friendship' in return for data.

A problem that the ethnographer often faces in such circumstances is deciding how much self-disclosure is appropriate or
fruitful. It is hard to expect 'honesty' and 'frankness' on the part
of participants and informants, while never being frank and
honest about oneself. And feminists have stressed the importance of this from an ethical point of view also (see, for example,
Oakley 1981). At the same time, just as in many everyday situations, as a researcher one often has to suppress or play down
one's own personal beliefs, commitments, and political sympathies. This is not necessarily a matter of gross deception. The
normal requirements of tact, courtesy, and 'interaction ritual', in
general (Goffman 1972), mean that in some ways 'everyone has
to lie' (Sacks 1975). For the researcher this may be a matter of
self-conscious impression management, and may thus become
an ever-present aspect of social interaction in the field. One
cannot bias the fieldwork by talking only with the people one
finds most congenial or politically sympathetic: one cannot
choose one's informants on the same basis as one chooses
friends (for the most part).

Particular problems arise where the researcher's own religious
or political attitudes differ markedly from those of the people
being studied. This is illustrated by Klatch's research on women
involved in right-wing organizations. She comments:

I often faced an uneasy situation in which the women concluded that because I did not challenge their ideas, I must

agree with them. Nodding my head in understanding of their words, for example, was interpreted as acceptance of their basic beliefs. Thus, the women I interviewed often ended up thanking me for doing the study, telling me how important it was for a like-minded person to convey their perspective. As one pro-family activist told me, 'We need people like you, young people, to restore the faith.' Having successfully gained her trust, this woman then interpreted that trust, and my enthusiasm for learning, as concurrence with her own beliefs.

(Klatch 1988:79)

Sometimes, the fieldworker may find him- or herself being 'tested' and pushed towards disclosure, particularly when the group or culture in question is founded upon beliefs and commitments (such as religious convictions, political affiliations, and the like). Here the process of negotiating access and rapport may be a matter of progressive initiation. The fieldworker may find the management of disclosure a particularly crucial feature of this delicate procedure. The same can apply with particular force to the investigation of deviance, where members of stigmatized groups may require reassurance that the ethnographer does not harbour feelings of disapproval, nor intends to initiate action against them.

THE PERSONAL CHARACTERISTICS OF THE RESEARCHER

There are, of course, aspects of personal front that are not open to 'management' and that may limit the negotiation of identities in the field, and these include so-called 'ascribed' characteristics. Although it would be wrong to think of the effects of these as absolutely determinate or fixed, such characteristics as gender, age, 'race', and ethnic identification may shape relationships with gatekeepers, sponsors, and people under study in important ways.

The researcher cannot escape the implications of gender: no position of genderless neutrality can be achieved, though the implications of gender vary according to setting and are intertwined with sexual orientation (Roberts 1981, Golde 1986; Whitehead and Conaway 1986; Warren 1988). Revealingly, most concern with the effects of gender has focused on the role of women fieldworkers: in particular, the way in which their gender bars them from some situations and activities, while opening up others that are not accessible to men. This has long been a theme in the methodological writings of anthropologists, where it has been noted that women may find themselves restricted to the domestic world of fellow women, children, the elderly, and so on. In Golde's study of the Nahua the problem was exacerbated by other characteristics:

> What was problematic was that I was unmarried and older than was reasonable for an unmarried girl to be, I was without the protection of my family, and I traveled alone, as an unmarried, virginal girl would never do. They found it hard to understand how I, so obviously attractive in their eyes, could still be single. . . . Being an unmarried girl meant that I should not drink, smoke, go about alone at night, visit during the day without a real errand, speak of such topics as sex or pregnancy, entertain boys or men in my house except in the presence of older people, or ask too many questions of any kind.
>
> (Golde 1986:79–80)

In much the same way, male researchers may find it difficult to gain access to the world of women, especially in cultures where there is a strong division between the sexes.

However, the anthropologist's status as a foreigner can allow some distance to be created from such restrictions. Reflecting on her experience in studying purdah, Papanek (1964) points out that as a woman she had access to the world of women, which no man could ever attain, while her own foreignness helped to remove her from the most restricting demands of female modesty. Rainbird's experience was similar:

> Being female affected my relations in the field insofar as certain activities were exclusive to one sex or the other. Nevertheless, the fact that I towered over most peasants, wore trousers and was an outsider of high social status placed me in a rather ambiguous category that allowed me to attend meetings and visit people freely around the countryside as men did, but not to drink with the men unless other women were present. . . . On the other hand, I had good access to

women's activities and gossip networks, their warmth and affection.

(Rainbird 1990:78–9)

Similar problems and freedoms tied to gender can also arise in research within Western societies. Easterday *et al.* (1977) note that in male-dominated settings women may come up against the male 'fraternity', from which they are excluded; that women may find themselves the object of 'hustling' from male hosts; that they may be cast in the role of the 'go-fer' runner of errands, or may be adopted as a sort of mascot. These possibilities all imply a lack of participation, or non-serious participation, on the part of the woman. Not only may the female researcher sometimes find it difficult to be taken seriously by male hosts, but other females may also display suspicion and hostility in the face of her intrusions. At the same time, Easterday *et al.* also recognize that female researchers may find advantageous trade-offs. The 'hustling' informant who is trying to impress the researcher may prove particularly forthcoming to her, and males may be manipulated by femininity. Similarly, in so far as women are seen as unthreatening, they may gain access to settings and information with relative ease. Thus, common cultural stereo-types of females can work to their advantage in some respects.

Warren provides illustrations of both the restrictions and the leeway that can arise from being a woman researcher:

When I did my dissertation study of a male secretive gay community during the late 1960s and early 1970s, I was able to do fieldwork in those parts of the setting dedicated to sociability and leisure – bars, parties, family gatherings. I was not, however, able to observe in those parts of the setting dedicated to sexuality – even quasi-public settings such as homosexual bath houses . . . and 'tearooms'. . . . Thus, my por-trait of the gay community is only a partial one, bounded by the social roles assigned to females within the male homo-sexual world.

She contrasts this with research in a drug rehabilitation centre:

This institution was open to both male and female residents. But as a female researcher, and over several months of obser-vation, I found that men were generally much more ready to talk to me than women. Furthermore, I was generally per-

ceived as harmless by the males, and afforded access border-
ing on trespass. I vividly remember one day deciding to go
upstairs, an action expressly forbidden to anyone not resident
in the facility. Someone started to protest; the protest was
silenced by a male voice saying, 'aah, what harm can she do,
she's only a broad'. Upstairs I went.

(Warren 1988:18)

'Race', ethnicity, and religious affiliation, like gender, can also
set limits and pose problems. 'Race' is, of course, not merely a
matter of physical characteristics, but relates to culture, power,
and personal style. Keiser (1970), reflecting on his work with
the 'Vice Lords', a Chicago street gang, notes that it was difficult
for him, as a white man, to establish relationships with black
informants. While some were willing to accept him as a 'white
nigger', others displayed strong antagonisms. Similar problems
may arise, however, even where both researcher and researched
are black. Whitehead (1986) was seen by the Jamaicans he studied as a 'big', 'brown', 'pretty-talking man'. 'Big' referred not to
his size, but to his status as an educated foreigner, and 'pretty-
talking' indicated his use of standard rather than dialect English.
'Brown' was the term used by local Jamaicans to refer to a
combination of light skin colour and desirable economic and
social characteristics. He reports that one of the effects of his
being seen in this way was that

when I tried to hold casual conversations or formal interviews
with a number of low-income men, they avoided looking me
in the face and often suggested that I talk to someone else
who was considered a bigger man than they. Frequently they
answered me with meaningless 'yes sirs' and 'no sirs'.

(Whitehead 1986:215)

Similarly, Peshkin's experience researching a fundamentalist
Protestant school showed that the ethnicity and religious affiliation of the ethnographer can be an important factor in the
establishment of field relations:

At Bethany I wanted to be the non-Christian scholar interested
in learning about the fundamentalist educational phenomenon
that was sweeping the country. [But] I discovered . . . that
being Jewish would be the personal fact bearing most on
my research; it became the unavoidably salient aspect of my

subjectivity. Bethanyites let me define my research self, but could never rest easy with my unsaved self. I became forcibly aware that the threats to my identity as a Jew were not just a matter of history.

For in the course of inculcating their students with doctrine and the meaning of the Christian identity, Bethany's educators taught us both that I was part of Satan's rejected, humanist world; I epitomized the darkness and unrighteousness that contrasts with their godly light and righteousness. They taught their children never to be close friends, marry, or to go into business with someone like me. What they were expected to do with someone like me was to proselytize.

(Peshkin 1985:13–15)

While this did not force Peshkin out of the setting, it did shape the whole character of the fieldwork.

A similar problem was faced by Magee, a Catholic woman, studying the (predominantly Protestant) Royal Ulster Constabulary in Northern Ireland; but she too managed to establish good relations with many of those in the field:

Over a twelve-month period a field-worker's persistent inquisitiveness is bound to become something of an irritant. . . . But leaving aside instances of momentary irritation, of which there were many . . . most respondents became confident enough in the field-worker's presence to express what were undoubtedly widely held fears about the research. Sometimes these concerns were expressed through humour and ribaldry. The field-worker became known as 'Old Nosebag', and there were long-running jokes about spelling people's names correctly in Sinn Fein's *Republican News*.

(Brewer 1991:21)

Sometimes, belonging to a different ethnic or national group can even have distinct advantages. Hannerz (1969), discussing his research on a black ghetto area in the United States, points out that, while one of his informants jokingly suggested that he might be the real 'blue-eyed blond devil' that the Black Muslims talked about, his Swedish nationality distanced him from other whites.

Age is another important aspect of the fieldworker's persona. Although it is by no means universally true, there appears to be a tendency for ethnography to be the province of younger research workers. In part this may be because the younger person has more time to commit to the fieldwork (often studying full time for a higher degree); in part it may suggest that junior people find it easier to adopt the 'incompetent' position of the 'outsider' or 'marginal' person. This is not to imply that ethnography is properly restricted to younger investigators, but one must at least entertain the possibility that age will have a bearing on the kinds of relationships established and the data collected. The junior research student may well establish quite different working relationships from those available to, say, the middle-aged professor.

One reason for this is the effects of age on the researcher's *modus operandi*, as Henslin illustrates, comparing his research on cab drivers, at age 29, with that on the homeless, at age 47:

[In the participant observation study of cab drivers] I gave little thought to danger, as I was caught up in the excitement of the sociological pursuit. Although two or three cabbies were stabbed the first week that I drove a cab, certain that such a thing would not happen to me, I gave the matter little thought.

Now, however, I was once again face to face with street realities, and at this point in my life things no longer looked the same. Age had accomplished what it is rumored to accomplish: It had brought with it a more conservative . . . approach to street experiences. I found myself more frequently questioning what I was doing, and even whether I should do it.

He goes on to describe his hesitation in approaching a group of runaways:

Down the block I saw about half a dozen or so young males and two females clustered in front of a parking lot. Somehow they did not look like the midwestern suburban youth I had come to know. What was most striking about this group was the amount of 'metal' they were displaying, notably the studs protruding from various parts of their bodies.

A few years back those youths would have struck me as another variant group that likely had engrossing experiences to relate. No longer. They now impressed me as a group that discretion would indicate as being better off left alone.

(Henslin 1990:69–70)

He did in fact make contact with them. They told him that they slept in abandoned buildings, and he immediately began to wonder about how they found these, how they protected themselves from other intruders, etc. However, despite his curiosity he decided that to stay with them at night would be too dangerous.

Age and its associated features can also affect the way people react to the researcher, along with what he or she is and is not allowed to do. An extreme example is provided by Corsaro's (1981) research on nursery school children:

Two four-year-old girls (Betty and Jenny) and adult researcher (Bill) in a nursery school:

BETTY: You can't play with us!
BILL: Why?
BETTY: Cause you're too big.
BILL: I'll sit down. (sits down)
JENNY: You're still too big.
BETTY: Yeah, you're 'Big Bill'!
BILL: Can I just watch?
JENNY: OK, but don't touch nuthin!
BETTY: You just watch, OK?
BILL: OK.
JENNY: OK, Big Bill?
BILL: OK

(Later Big Bill got to play.)

(Corsaro 1981:117)

We have limited discussion here to some of the standard face-sheet characteristics of the ethnographer and their implications for research relationships. It is perhaps worth emphasizing that this discussion has not exhausted the personal characteristics that can make a difference. Oboler provides a striking example of this, discussing her husband's acceptance among the Nandi of Kenya:

His first trip to the river to bathe was a crucial test. In a spirit of camaraderie, as same-sex communal bathing is customary, he was accompanied by a number of young men. Tagging along was an enormous group of curiosity-seeking children and younger adolescents . . . everyone wanted to know the answer. . . . Was Leon circumcised? In Nandi, male initiation involving adolescent circumcision is the most crucial event in the male life-cycle, without which adult identity, entry into the age-set system, and marriage are impossible. It is also viewed as an important ethnic boundary marker. . . . Fortunately Leon, a Jew by ancestry and rearing, passed the test. I believe that an uncircumcised husband would have made fieldwork in Nandi extremely difficult for me.

(Oboler 1986:37)

In the course of fieldwork, then, people who meet, or hear about, the researcher will cast him or her into certain identities on the basis of 'ascribed characteristics', as well as aspects of appearance and manner. This 'identity work' (Goffman 1959) must be monitored for its effects on the kinds of data collected. At the same time, the ethnographer will generally try to shape the nature of his or her role, through adaptation of dress and demeanour, in order to facilitate gaining the necessary data.

FIELD ROLES

In the early days of fieldwork, the conduct of the ethnographer is often little different from that of any layperson faced with the practical need to make sense of a particular social setting. Consider the position of the novice or recruit – a student fresher, a military rookie, a person starting a new job – who finds him- or herself in relatively strange surroundings. How do such novices get to 'know the ropes' and become 'old hands'? Obviously, there is nothing magical about this process of learning. Novices watch what other people are doing, ask others to explain what is happening, try things out for themselves – occasionally making mistakes – and so on. The novice thus acts like a social scientist: making observations and inferences, asking informants, constructing hypotheses, and acting on them.

When studying an unfamiliar setting, the ethnographer is also a novice. Wherever possible he or she must put him- or herself into the position of being an 'acceptable incompetent', as

Lofland (1971) neatly describes it. It is only through watching, listening, asking questions, formulating hypotheses, and making blunders that the ethnographer can acquire some sense of the social structure of the setting and begin to understand the culture(s) of participants.

Styles provides an example of the early stages of learning to be a participant observer in his research on gay baths. He comments that before he started he assumed that as a gay man he was 'among the "natural clientele" of the baths. It never occurred to me that I might not understand what was going on' (Styles 1979:151). Before going to the bath house he consulted a gay friend who frequented it:

> From this conversation, I saw no major problems ahead and laid some tentative research plans. I would first scout out the various scenes of sexual activity in the bath and diagram the bath's physical and sexual layout. After observing the interaction in the various areas, I would start conversations with one or two of the customers, explaining that I was a first-time visitor, and ask them questions about their bath-going. To write fieldnotes, I could use the isolation of some of the downstairs toilets, described by my friend, which had doors that could be locked to ensure privacy.

As might have been expected, his plans did not work out as intended:

> The bath was extremely crowded, noisy, and smelly. My first project – scouting out the layout of the bath itself – consisted of twenty or thirty minutes of pushing my way between, around, and beside naked and almost-naked men jamming the hallways. . . . I gave up on field notes when I saw the line to the downstairs toilets had half a dozen men in it . . . more lining up all the time. I did identify the major sexual arenas . . . but these were, for the most part, so dimly lit that I could see few details of behavior and gave up on the orgy room when, after squeezing through a mass of bodies, I stumbled around in the dark, bumped into a clutch of men engaging in group sexual activity, and had my towel torn off while one of them grabbed for my genitals. I gave up on the steam room after the steam poured in and my glasses fogged over. The blaring rock Muzak, the dour looks of the cus-

tomers, and the splitting headache I developed (from what I later learned was the odor of amylnitrite, a drug inhaled to enhance the sexual experience) effectively killed any desire I had for conversation.

(Styles 1979:138)

He comments that it was 'only through a slow trial-and-error process [that] I gradually came to understand some of the patterns of behavior in the bath' (Styles 1979:139).

The crucial difference between the 'lay' novice and the ethnographer in the field is that the latter attempts to maintain a self-conscious awareness of what is learned, how it has been learned, and the social transactions that inform the production of such knowledge. As we saw in Chapter 1, it is an important requirement of ethnography that we suspend a wide range of common-sense and theoretical knowledge in order to minimize the danger of taking on trust misleading preconceptions about the setting and the people in it.

'Strange' or 'exotic' settings quickly demolish the ethnographer's faith in his or her preconceptions, just as Schutz's (1964) stranger finds that what he or she knows about the new country will not suffice for survival in it. Laura Bohannon (under the *nom de plume* Elenore Bowen) wrote a vivid, semi-fictionalized account of her own initial encounters with an African culture. She captures the sense of alienation and 'strangeness' experienced by the fieldworker, and a feeling of being an 'incompetent':

I felt much more like a backyard child than an independent young woman. My household supported me, right or wrong, against outsiders, but made their opinions known after the fact, and so obviously for my own good that I could not be justifiably angry. I felt even less like a trained and professional anthropologist pursuing his researches. I was hauled around from one homestead to another and scolded for my lack of manners or for getting my shoes wet. Far from having docile informants whom I could train, I found myself the spare-time amusement of people who taught me what they considered it good for me to know and what they were interested in at the moment, almost always plants or people.

(Bowen 1954:40–1)

She documents the personal and emotional difficulties of coming to terms with such estrangement, but it is apparent from her account that this is integral to the process of learning.

This experience of estrangement is what is often referred to as 'culture shock' and it is the stock-in-trade of social and cultural anthropology. Confrontation of the ethnographer with an 'alien' culture is the methodological and epistemological foundation of the anthropological enterprise, whether it be from the point of view of a romantically inspired search for exotic cultures, or the less glamorous sort of encounter described by Chagnon from his fieldwork among the Yanomamö. He reports, with engaging frankness, how he set off into the field with a mixture of assumptions. On the one hand, he confesses to a Rousseau-like expectation as to his future relations with the Yanomamö: that they would like him, even adopt him, and so on. At the same time, by virtue of his seven years of training as an anthropologist, he carried with him a considerable load of social-scientific assumptions: as he puts it, that he was about to encounter 'social facts' inhabiting the village, all eager to recount their genealogies to him. In contrast to his romantic fantasies, and his social-scientific assumptions, he did not encounter a collection of social facts, nor indeed were his chosen people the noble or welcoming savages of his imagination. Quite the reverse:

> I looked up and gasped when I saw a dozen burly, naked, filthy, hideous men staring at us down the shafts of their drawn arrows! Immense wads of green tobacco were stuck between their lower teeth and lips making them look even more hideous, and strands of dark green slime dripped or hung from their noses. . . . I was horrified. What sort of welcome was this for the person who came here to live with you and learn your way of life, to become friends with you?
>
> (Chagnon 1977:4)

It is worth noting in passing that Chagnon's self-revelation shows not only the 'culture clash' of the Westerner encountering an 'exotic' culture, but also the problem of the social scientist who expects to uncover social facts, rules, institutions, organizations, and so on by direct observation of the social world. This is perhaps one of the hardest lessons to learn at the outset. One does not 'see' everyday life laid out like a sociology or anthropology textbook, and one cannot read off analytic concepts directly from the phenomena one experiences in the field. Some researchers, setting out on fieldwork, may even feel a sense of betrayal when they discover this, or alternatively experience a panic of self-doubt, believing themselves to be inadequate research workers because their observations do not fall neatly into the sorts of categories suggested by the received wisdom of 'the literature'.

In researching settings that are more familiar, it can be much more difficult to suspend one's preconceptions, whether these derive from social science or from everyday knowledge. One reason for this is that what one finds is so obvious. Becker provides a classic example:

> We may have understated a little the difficulty of observing contemporary classrooms. It is not just the survey method of educational testing or any of those things that keeps people from seeing what is going on. I think, instead, that it is first and foremost a matter of it all being so familiar that it becomes impossible to single out events that occur in the classroom as things that have occurred, even when they happen right in front of you. I have not had the experience of observing in elementary and high school classrooms myself, but I have in college classrooms and it takes a tremendous effort of will and imagination to stop seeing only the things that are conventionally 'there' to be seen. I have talked to a couple of teams of researchers and it is like pulling teeth to get them to see or write anything beyond what 'everyone' knows.
>
> (Becker 1971:10)

Another problem with settings in one's own society is that one may not be allowed to take on a novice role. We noted in the previous chapter how researchers are sometimes cast into the role of expert or critic. Moreover, ascribed characteristics, notably age, and latent identities – as in the case of Beynon's (1983) research on teachers – may reinforce this. In studying such settings the ethnographer is faced with the difficult task of rapidly acquiring the ability to act competently, which is not always easy even within familiar settings, while simultaneously privately struggling to suspend for analytic purposes precisely those assumptions that must be taken for granted in relations with participants.

The 'acceptable incompetent' is not, then, the only role that

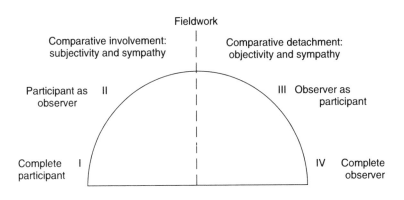

Figure 1 Theoretical social roles for fieldwork
Source: Junker 1960:36; reproduced by permission of University of Chicago Press

ethnographers may take on in the field, and, indeed, even where it is adopted it is often abandoned, to one degree or another, as the fieldwork progresses. There have been several attempts to map out the various roles that ethnographers may adopt in settings. Junker (1960) and Gold (1958), for example, distinguish between the 'complete participant', 'participant-as-observer', 'observer-as-participant', and 'complete observer' (see Figure 1).

In the 'complete participant' role, the ethnographer's activities are wholly concealed. Here the researcher may join an organization or group – Alcoholics Anonymous (Lofland and Lejeune 1960), Pentecostalists (Homan 1980), an army unit (Sullivan *et al*. 1958), a mental hospital (Rosenhahn 1973) – as though he or she were an ordinary member but with the purpose of carrying out research. Alternatively, complete participation may occur where the putative researcher is already a member of the group or organization that he or she decides to study. This was the case with Holdaway's (1982) research on the police, and Dalton's (1959) work on 'men who manage'. An extreme example is Bettelheim's (1970) account of life in German concentration camps.

'Complete participation' is, then, approximated in some circumstances. Some commentators have suggested that it is the ideal to which researchers should aim. Jules-Rosette (1978a and b), for instance, has argued for the necessity of 'total immersion' in a native culture: that is, not simply 'passing' as a member but actually becoming a member. In her case this was accompanied by conversion to the Apostolic Church of John Maranke, an indigenous African movement. This indeed is the criterion Jules-Rosette demands for what she calls 'reflexive ethnography': a usage of the term 'reflexive' that is somewhat different from our own.

'Complete participation' may seem very attractive. Such identification and immersion in the setting may appear to offer safety: one can travel incognito, obtain 'inside' knowledge, and avoid the trouble of access negotiations. There is some truth in this, and indeed in some settings complete participation may be the only strategy by which the data required can be obtained. However, 'passing' as a member over a protracted period usually places great strain on the fieldworker's dramaturgical capacities. And should the ethnographer's cover be 'blown', the consequences may be disastrous for the completion of the fieldwork project, and perhaps also for the researcher personally. Severe embarrassment is the least of the problems that can be expected:

> Athena appeared again, and excitedly told me some people wanted to talk to me. . . . and she led me into a room where five members of the Council were gathered – the Priests Armat and Wif, and the Masters Firth, Huf and Lare. The latter was the chairman of the Council.
>
> At first, as I walked in, I was delighted to finally have the chance to talk to some higher-ups, but in moments the elaborate plotting that had taken place behind my back became painfully obvious.
>
> As I sat down on the bed beside Huf, Lare looked at me icily. 'What are your motives?' she hissed.
>
> At once I became aware of the current of hostility in the room, and this sudden realization, so unexpected, left me almost speechless.
>
> 'To grow,' I answered lamely. 'Are you concerned about the tapes?'
>
> 'Well, what about them?' she snapped.
>
> 'It's so I can remember things,' I said.
>
> 'And the questions? Why have you been asking everyone

about their backgrounds? What does that have to do with growth?'

I tried to explain. 'But I always ask people about themselves when I meet them. What's wrong with that?'

However, Lare disregarded my explanation. 'We don't believe you,' she said.

Then Firth butted in. 'We have several people in intelligence in the group . . . We've read your diary . . . '.

At this point . . . I couldn't think of anything to say. It was apparent now they considered me some kind of undercover enemy or sensationalist journalist out to harm or expose the Church, and they had gathered their evidence to prove this. . . . Later Armat explained that they had fears about me or anyone else drawing attention to them because of the negative climate towards cults among 'humans'. So they were afraid that any outside attention might lead to the destruction of the Church before they could prepare for the coming annihilation. However, in the tense setting of a quickly convened trial, there was no way to explain my intentions or try to reconcile them with my expressed belief in learning magic. Once Firth said he read my diary, I realized there was nothing more to say.

'So now, get out,' Lare snapped. 'Take off your pentagram and get out.'

As I removed it from my chain, I explained that I had driven up with several other people and had no way back.

'That's your problem,' she said. 'Just be gone by the time we get back.' Then, threateningly, she added: 'You should be glad that we aren't going to do anything else.'

(Scott 1983:132–3)

Fortunately, Scott had already collected a substantial amount of data before her identity as a researcher was discovered; and the group she was involved with decided against violent reprisals.

Even if successfully maintained, the strategy of 'complete participation' will normally prove rather limiting. The range and character of the data that can be collected will often be quite restricted. The participant will, by definition, be implicated in existing social practices and expectations in a far more rigid manner than the known researcher. The research activity will therefore be hedged round by these pre-existing social routines and realities. It will prove hard for the fieldworker to arrange his or her actions in order to optimize data collection possibilities. Some potentially fruitful lines of inquiry may be rendered practically impossible, in so far as the complete participant has to act in accordance with existing role expectations.

These limitations of complete participation are indicated by Gregor (1977). During the early days of fieldwork in a Brazilian Indian village, Gregor and his wife attempted – in the interests of 'good public relations' – to live out their lives as villagers:

> Unfortunately we were not learning very much. Each day I would come back from treks through the forest numb with fatigue, ill with hunger, and covered with ticks and biting insects. My own work was difficult to pursue, for fishing and hunting are serious business and there is no time to pester men at work with irrelevant questions about their mother's brothers. Meanwhile, my wife was faring little better with the women.
>
> (Gregor 1977:28)

Hence the Gregors stopped 'pretending' that they were 'becoming' Brazilian villagers, and turned to systematic research activity.

In contrast to the 'complete participant', the 'complete observer' has no contact at all with those he or she is observing. Thus, Corsaro (1981) complemented his participant observation with nursery school children by observing them through a one-way mirror. Covert observation from a window of public behaviour in the street (Lofland 1973) also falls into this category, and perhaps also research like that by Karp (1980) on the 'public sexual scene' in Times Square.

Paradoxically, complete observation shares many of the advantages and disadvantages of complete participation. In their favour they can both minimize problems of reactivity: in neither case will the ethnographer interact as a researcher with members being studied. On the other hand, there may be severe limits on what can and cannot be observed, and the questioning of participants may be impossible. Adopting either of these roles alone would make it very difficult to generate and test accounts in a rigorous manner, though both may be useful strategies to adopt during particular phases of the fieldwork, and in some situations may be unavoidable.

Most field research involves roles somewhere between these two poles. Whether the distinction between participant-as-observer and observer-as-participant is of any value is a moot point. Indeed, in examining this distinction a serious problem with Junker's (1960) typology arises: it runs together several dimensions of variation that are by no means necessarily related. One of these, touched on earlier, is the question of secrecy and deception. Another is the issue of whether the ethnographer takes on a role already existing in the field or negotiates a new one – though no hard-and-fast distinction can be made here, and indeed we should beware of treating the roles already established in the setting as completely fixed in character (Turner 1962).

Of course, in secret research one has little option but to take on an existing role, though it may be possible to extend and modify it somewhat to facilitate the research (Dalton 1959). And sometimes even in open research there may be no choice but to adopt an established role, as Freilich (1970a and b) found out in his research on Mohawk steelworkers in New York. Having become friends with one of the Mohawks, he tried to revert to the role of anthropologist. As he remarks:

> It was soon clear that any anthropological symbol was taboo. . . . I could use no pencils, notebooks or questionnaires. I even failed in attempts to play the semi-anthropologist. For example I tried saying, 'Now that is really interesting; let me write that down so that I don't forget it.' Suddenly my audience became hostile, and the few words I jotted down cost me much in rapport for the next few days.
>
> (Freilich 1970a and b:193)

Currer (1992) reports much the same experience in negotiating access to Pathan women informants:

> Once permission to visit was given, the visits were on social terms: my agenda and public domain purpose were never referred to. When once I did so, the women concerned were very offended and our relationship was jeopardized. Yet the women, no less than the men, knew of my research purpose. Only in two cases did the relationship more closely combine the personal and the professional. In these cases I was able to take notes and to lead the exchange.

She concludes that she 'had to choose between insisting on my rules and being denied any real access or [visiting] on the women's terms' (Currer 1992:17–18).

Generally, though, in open research the ethnographer has some choice over whether or not to take on one of the existing roles in the field. Thus, for example, in research on schools, ethnographers have sometimes adopted the role of teacher (see, for example, Aggleton 1987; Mac an Ghaill 1991), but sometimes they have not (Brown 1987; Walker 1988; Stanley 1989; Riddell 1992). Perhaps not surprisingly, they have rarely taken on the role of school student (but see Llewellyn 1980), although in studies of higher education ethnographers do sometimes enrol as students (Moffat 1989; Tobias 1990).

Decisions about the sort of role to adopt in a setting will depend on the purposes of the research and the nature of the setting. In any case, anticipation of the likely consequences of adopting different roles can rarely be more than speculative. Fortunately, shifts in role can often be made over the course of fieldwork. Indeed, there are strong arguments in favour of moving among roles so as to allow one to discount their effects on the data. Thus, Sevigny (1981), studying art classes in a college, collected data by surreptitiously taking on the role of student, and by acting as tutor, as well as adopting a variety of researcher roles. Different roles within a setting can be exploited, then, in order to get access to different kinds of data, as well as to acquire some sense of the various kinds of bias characteristic of each.

MANAGING MARGINALITY

There is a third dimension of variation in research roles built into the typology developed by Junker and Gold: it ranges from the 'external' view of the observer to the 'internal' view of the participant. However, this dimension is surrounded by what Styles refers to as outsider and insider myths:

> In essence, outsider myths assert that only outsiders can con-
> duct valid research on a given group; only outsiders, it is
> held, possess the needed objectivity and emotional distance.
> According to outsider myths, insiders invariably present their
> group in an unrealistically favourable light. Analogously,
> insider myths assert that only insiders are capable of doing

valid research in a particular group and that all outsiders are inherently incapable of appreciating the true character of the group's life.

Insider and outsider myths are not empirical generalizations about the relationship between the researcher's social position and the character of the research findings. They are elements in a moral rhetoric that claims exclusive research legitimacy for a particular group.

(Styles 1979:148)

Of course, it is true that outsiders and insiders are likely to have immediate access to different sorts of information. And they are also exposed to different kinds of methodological dangers. The danger that attends the role of complete observer is that of failing to understand the perspectives of participants. Where this strategy is used alone, these perspectives have to be inferred from what can be observed plus the researcher's background knowledge, without any possibility of checking these interpretations against what participants say in response to questions. The risk here is not simply of missing out on an important aspect of the setting, but rather of seriously misunderstanding the behaviour observed.

A more common danger in ethnographic research, one that attends the other three roles in Junker's typology, is 'going native'. Not only may the task of analysis be abandoned in favour of the joys of participation, but even where it is retained bias may arise from 'over-rapport'. Miller outlines the problem in the context of a study of local union leadership:

Once I had developed a close relationship to the union leaders I was committed to continuing it, and some penetrating lines of inquiry had to be dropped. They had given me very significant and delicate information about the internal operation of the local [union branch]: to question closely their basic attitudes would open up severe conflict areas. To continue close rapport and to pursue avenues of investigation which appeared antagonistic to the union leaders was impossible. To shift to a lower level of rapport would be difficult because such a change would induce considerable distance and distrust.

(Miller 1952:98)

Having established friendly relations Miller found the possibilities of data collection limited. Indeed, he suggests that the leaders themselves might have fostered such close relationships as a strategy to limit his observations and criticisms. Miller also notes that over-rapport with one group leads to problems of rapport with others: in his study, his close rapport with union leaders limited his rapport with rank-and-file members.

The question of rapport applies in two senses, both of which may be glossed as issues of identification. In the sort of case outlined by Miller, one may be identified with particular groups or individuals so that one's social mobility in the field and relationships with others become impaired. More subtle, perhaps, is the danger of identifying with such members' perspectives, and hence of failing to treat these as problematic.

One well-known British ethnography that is flawed by such partial perspectives is Paul Willis's (1977) study of working-class adolescent boys. Willis's work is based primarily on conversations with twelve pupils who display 'anti-school' attitudes. These particular working-class boys describe themselves as 'lads' and distinguish themselves from those they call 'ear-'oles', who subscribe to the values of the school. The 'lads' not only see little chance of obtaining middle-class jobs but have no desire for them, enthusiastically seeking working-class employment. Willis argues that the counter-culture fits with the culture of the workplace for manual workers, even suggesting that the more conformist pupils are less well adapted to the culture of working-class jobs.

There are two senses in which over-rapport appears to be indicated in Willis's treatment of these youngsters. In the first place he seems to have devoted his attention almost entirely to the 'lads', and to have taken over their views in the analysis, where they did not conflict with his own. Hence, the book becomes as much a celebration of them as anything else: Willis appears unable or unwilling adequately to distance himself from their accounts. Second, the 'lads' are endorsed by Willis, since he treats them more or less as spokesmen for the working class. While he explicitly recognizes that working-class culture is variable, he nonetheless seems to identify the views held by the 'lads', or those of some of them, as representative in important respects of true working-class consciousness. Since the 'ear-'oles' or conformists are also from working-class backgrounds, this is problematic, to say the least. To a large extent, Willis is guilty of identifying with his chosen twelve, and his theoretical description of schooling is distorted by this.

In a striking parallel, Stein (1964) provides a reflexive account of his own identification with one set of workers, the miners in the gypsum plant he studied with Gouldner (1954):

> Looking back now I can see all kinds of influences that must have been involved. I was working out authority issues, and clearly I chose the open expression of hostile feelings that was characteristic in the mine rather than the repression that was characteristic on the surface. I came from a muddled class background which involved a mixture of lower-, upper-, and middle-class elements that I have not yet been able to disentangle fully. The main point is that I associate working-class settings with emotional spontaneity and middle-class settings with emotional restraint. I never quite confronted the fact that the surface men were as much members of the working class as were the miners.
>
> The descriptive writing became an act of fealty since I felt that writing about life in this setting was my way of being loyal to the people living in it. This writing came more easily than most of my other writing. But the efforts at interpreting the miners' behavior as a product of social forces, and especially seeing it as being in any way strategic rather than spontaneous, left me with profound misgivings.
>
> (Stein 1964:20-1)

While ethnographers may adopt a variety of roles, the usual aim throughout is to maintain a more or less marginal position, thereby providing access to participant perspectives but at the same time minimizing the dangers of over-rapport. As Lofland (1971:97) points out, the researcher can also generate creative insight out of this marginal position of simultaneous insider-outsider. The ethnographer needs to be intellectually poised between familiarity and strangeness; and, in overt participant observation, socially he or she will usually be poised between stranger and friend (Powdermaker 1966; Everhart 1977). As the title of the collection edited by Freilich (1970b) suggests, the ethnographer is typically a 'marginal native'.

THE STRAINS AND STRESSES OF FIELDWORK

Marginality is not an easy position to maintain, however, because it engenders a continual sense of insecurity. It involves living simultaneously in two worlds, that of participation and that of research. In covert research there is the constant effort to maintain one's cover and at the same time to make the most of whatever research opportunities arise. In overt participant observation there is the strain of living with the ambiguity and uncertainty of one's social position on the margin, and doing so in a way that serves the research but is also ethically acceptable. To one degree or another, as Thorne (1983:221) puts it, one is often 'running against the grain' of the settings in which one works.

Johnson (1975) has recorded in some detail his emotional and physical reactions to the stresses of fieldwork. Some of his fieldnotes document his response with notable frankness:

> Every morning around seven forty-five, as I'm driving to the office, I begin to get this pain in the left side of my back, and the damn thing stays there usually until around eleven, when I've made my daily plans for accompanying one of the workers. Since nearly all of the workers remain in the office until around eleven or twelve, and since there's only one extra chair in the two units, and no extra desks as yet, those first two or three hours are sheer agony for me every damn day. Trying to be busy without hassling any one worker too much is like playing Chinese checkers, hopping to and fro, from here to there, with no place to hide.
>
> (Johnson 1975:152–3)

The physical symptoms that Johnson describes are perhaps rather extreme examples of fieldwork stress. But the phenomenon in general is by no means unusual: many fieldworkers report that they experience some degree of discomfort by virtue of their 'odd', 'strange', or 'marginal' position. Some flavour of this can be gleaned from Wintrob's (1969) psychological appraisal of the anxieties suffered by anthropologists in the field: it is based on the experiences of a number of graduate students, and published autobiographical accounts.

Wintrob identifies various sources of stress, including what he glosses as the 'dysadaptation syndrome' which includes a wide range of feelings – incompetence, fear, anger, frustration. He cites one graduate student's account:

> I was afraid of everything at the beginning. It was just fear, of imposing on people, of trying to maintain a completely different role than anyone else around you. You hem and haw before making a leap into the situation. You want to retreat for another day. I'd keep thinking: am I going to be rejected? Am I really getting the data I need? I knew I had to set up my tent but I'd put it off. I'd put off getting started in telling people about wanting to give a questionnaire. I was neatly ensconced in —'s compound (an area of tents comprising one kin group). Everybody there knew what I was doing. I found it hard to move over to the other camp (a few miles away). I rationalised that a field worker shouldn't jump around too much.
>
> (Wintrob 1969:67)

Malinowski's diaries reveal many indications of similar kinds of stress and anxiety: indeed they are a remarkable document for what they reveal about his ambivalent feelings towards the Trobriand Islanders, his own intense self-absorption, and his preoccupation with his own well-being (Malinowski 1967). In a similar vein, Wax (1971) has provided an excellent account of her difficulties in working in a relocation centre for Japanese Americans after the Second World War. She describes her initial difficulties with collecting data, in the face of (understandable) suspicion and hostility: 'At the conclusion of the first month of work I had obtained very little data, and I was discouraged, bewildered and obsessed by a sense of failure' (1971:70).

We do not wish to convey the impression that the experience of fieldwork is one of unrelieved misery: for many it is often a matter of intense personal reward and satisfaction. At the same time, the stress experienced by the 'marginal native' is a very common aspect of ethnography, and it is an important one. In so far as he or she resists over-identification or surrender to hosts, then it is likely that there will be a corresponding sense of betrayal, or at least of divided loyalties. Lofland (1971:108–9) draws attention to the 'poignancy' of this experience. There is a sense of schizophrenia that the disengaged/engaged ethnographer may suffer. But this feeling, and equivalent feelings, should be managed for what they are. Such feelings are not necessarily something to be avoided, or to be replaced by more congenial sensations of comfort. The comfortable sense of being 'at home' is a danger signal. From the perspective of the 'marginal' reflexive ethnographer, there can thus be no question of total commitment, 'surrender', or 'becoming'. There must always remain some part held back, some social and intellectual 'distance'. For it is in the space created by this distance that the analytic work of the ethnographer gets done. Without that distance, without such analytic space, the ethnography can be little more than the autobiographical account of a personal conversion. This would be an interesting and valuable document, but not an ethnographic study.

Ethnographers, then, must strenuously avoid feeling 'at home'. If and when all sense of being a stranger is lost, one may have allowed the escape of one's critical, analytic perspective. The early days of fieldwork are proverbially problematic, and may well be fraught with difficulties: difficult decisions concerning fieldwork strategy have to be made; working relationships may have to be established quickly; and social embarrassment is a real possibility. On the other hand, it would be dangerous to assume that this is just a difficult phase that the researcher can simply outgrow, after which he or she can settle down to a totally comfortable, trouble-free existence. While social relations and working arrangements will get sorted out, and gross problems of strangeness will be resolved, it is important that this should not result in too cosy a mental attitude. Everhart (1977) illustrates the danger from his research on college students and teachers:

> saturation, fieldwork fatigue, and just plain fitting in too well culminated, toward the end of the second year, in a diminishing of my critical perspective. I began to notice that events were escaping me, the significance of which I did not realize until later. For example, previously I had recorded in minute detail the discussions teachers had on categorizing students and those conversations students had on labelling other students. While these discussions continued and were especially rich because of the factors that caused these perspectives to shift, I found myself, toward the end of the study, tuning out of such discussions because I felt I had heard them all before when, actually, many dealt with dimensions I had

never considered. On the one hand I was angry at myself for not recording and analyzing the category systems, on the other hand I was tired and found it more natural to sit with teachers and engage in small talk. The inquisitiveness had been drained from me.

(Everhart 1977:13)

This is not to deny that there will be occasions, many occasions, when one will need to engage in social interaction for primarily social and pragmatic reasons, rather than in accordance with research interests and strategies. Rather, the point is that one should never surrender oneself entirely to the setting or to the moment. In principle, one should be constantly on the alert, with more than half an eye on the research possibilities that can be seen or engineered from any and every social situation.

If one does start to feel at ease, and the research setting takes on the appearance of routine familiarity, then one needs to ask oneself some pertinent questions. Is this sense of ease a reflection of the fact that the research is actually finished? Have all the necessary data already been collected? (Obviously in principle there is always something new to discover, unforeseen events to investigate, unpredictable outcomes to follow up, and so on; but the line has to be drawn somewhere.) This is always a useful question to ask: there is no point in hanging on in the field to no good purpose, just for the sake of being there, just 'for interest', or from a lack of confidence that one has enough information.

Sometimes you will tell yourself that you are done: that you should either finish the fieldwork, or now move on to a new social setting. Alternatively, it may be the case that a sense of familiarity has been produced by sheer laziness. Further questions may be in order, if the research does not seem to be finished. Do I feel at ease because I am being too compliant? That is, am I being so 'nice' to my hosts that I never get them to confront any potentially troublesome or touchy topics? Likewise, does my social ease mean that I am avoiding some people, and cultivating others with whom I feel more comfortable? In many social contexts, we find ourselves in need of formal or informal sponsors, helpful informants, and so forth. But it is important not to cling to them. From time to time one should evaluate whether the research is being unduly limited by such a possibility. In general, it is well worth pausing to consider whether a sense of comfort and familiarity may be an artefact of laziness, and a limitation imposed on the research by a failure to go on asking new questions, by a reluctance ever to go against the grain, a fear of ever making mistakes, and an unwillingness to try to establish new or difficult social relationships. It is possible to carve out an inhabitable niche in the field during the early stages of a project: it is important not to stay there and never try one's wings in other contexts.

Marginality is not the only source of strain and stress in fieldwork, of course. Another is finding oneself in physical and social situations that one might not otherwise encounter and would normally avoid. Henslin provides an example from his participant observation research on the homeless:

> It was not the shelter's large size and greater impersonality ... that brought culture shock. It was, rather, its radically different approach to the homeless. For example, at check-in each man was assigned a number. At the exact designated time the man located a bed marked with that number, one that held at its foot a similarly-numbered basket. Each man then undressed at his bedside and waited in the nude until his number was called. Still nude, he then had to parade in front of the other hundred and nine men, carrying his clothing ... to a check-in center operated by clothed personnel. ... After showering, but still standing in the nude and surrounded by nude strangers, each man was required to shave, using the common razors laid out by the sinks. Finally, still nude, he took the long walk back to his assigned bed.
>
> This routine burst upon me as a startling experience. ... For me ... to parade nude in front of strangers, ... and to witness man after man parading nude was humiliating and degrading, a frontal assault on my sensibilities.
>
> Nor was that night spent peacefully. Gone now was my cuddly sleeping partner of the past dozen years. Gone were my familiar surroundings. And, especially, gone was the lock that protected me from the unknown. ...
>
> Then my mind insisted on playing back statements made by one of the directors of the shelter. Earlier that day, as I was interviewing him, ... he mentioned homosexual rapes

that had occurred in the dormitories. Then during the interview two men had to be removed from the dining hall after they drew a knife and a pistol on one another. When I told him that I was planning to spend the night and asked him if it was safe, instead of the reassurance I was hoping for, he told me about a man who had pulled a knife on him and added, 'Nothing is really safe. You really have to be ready to die in this life.'

That was certainly not the most restful night I have ever spent, but by morning I was sleeping fairly soundly. I knew that was so because in the early hours, at 5.35 to be exact, the numerous overhead lights suddenly beat onto my upturned face while simultaneously over the loudspeaker a shrieking voice trumpeted, 'Everybody up! Everybody up! Let's get moving!'

(Henslin 1990:60–1)

Women fieldworkers are sometimes thought to be especially vulnerable to attack, particularly sexual attack. As Warren (1988:30) notes, the question of sexuality in fieldwork first arose in the context of safety from rape of 'white women' alone in 'primitive' societies. She argues for a wider perspective, noting the reports of fieldworkers' sexual participation in the field (see also Fine 1993). Nevertheless, sexual harassment, at the very least, can be a problem. Warren reports the research of one of her students Liz Brunner among the homeless:

During her fieldwork, Liz slept, drank, talked, and shared meals with the homeless on Los Angeles streets – almost all of whom were male. After several episodes of unwanted physical touching, she learned to avoid being alone with particular men, or going into dark areas of the street with those she did not know well. . . . These homeless men – some of them de-institutionalised mental patients – often did not share, or perhaps know about, Liz's middle class, feminist values and beliefs concerning sexual expression and male-female relationships.

(Warren 1988:33–4)

Such problems are not, of course, restricted to contacts with the homeless on the streets, as Gurney reports from her research on lawyers:

One clear-cut example of a problem related to my gender was an instance of sexual hustling on the part of one of the prosecutors. He tried, on several different occasions, to get me to come over to his apartment on the pretense of having me use his computer.... When that failed, he asked me if I knew anyone who might be willing to come to his apartment to help him program his computer to analyze bank accounts in embezzlement cases. I said I did not know anyone, but offered to post an advertisement for him at the university. He rejected that idea and never raised the issue again.

(Gurney 1991:58–9)

Unpleasant fieldwork experiences do not arise solely from what may be done *to* the ethnographer, however. Even more distressing can be what the participant observer feels it necessary to do in order to maintain the participant role. This is a problem that is especially likely to occur where the complete participant observation role has been adopted, since here, as we noted earlier, there is usually less scope for manoeuvre. The situation is also exacerbated where the people with whom one is involved are prone to violence. In such circumstances, one may find oneself drawn deep into activities that are obnoxious and dangerous, as Mitchell found in his research on survivalists:

Alone, two thousand miles away from home, on the third day of the Christian Patriots Survival Conference, I volunteered for guard duty.... The Aryan nations were there, with the Posse Comitatus, and the Klan. In the names of Reason and Patriotism and God they urged repudiation of the national debt, race revolution, economic assistance to small farmers, and genocide.... Four of us were assigned the evening gate watch. Into the dusk we directed late-arriving traffic, checked passes, and got acquainted. The camp settled. Talk turned to traditional survivalist topics. First, guns: They slid theirs one by one from concealed holsters to be admired. 'Mine's in the car,' I lied. Then, because we were strangers with presumably a common cause, it was time for stories, to reconfirm our enemies and reiterate our principles. We stood around a small camp fire.... Our stories went clockwise. Twelve O'clock told of homosexuals who frequent a city park in his home community and asked what should be done with them in 'the future'. His proposal involved chains and trees and long-

fused dynamite taped to body parts. Understand these
remarks. They were meant neither as braggadocio nor exces-
sive cruelty, but as a reasoned proposal. We all faced the
'queer' problem didn't we? And the community will need
'cleansing' won't it? In solemn agreement we nodded our
heads. Three O'clock reflected for a moment, then proposed
a utilitarian solution regarding nighttime and rifle practice.
'Good idea,' we mumbled supportively.... One more car
passed the gate. It grew quiet. It was Nine O'clock. My turn.
I told a story, too. As I began a new man joined us. He
listened to my idea and approved, introduced himself, then
told me things not everyone knew, about plans being made,
and action soon to be taken. He said they could use men like
me and told me to be ready to join. I took him seriously.
Others did, too. He was on the FBI's 'Ten Most Wanted' list.
If there are researchers who can participate in such business
without feeling, I am not one of them nor do I ever hope to
be. What I do hope is someday to forget, forget those unmis-
takable sounds, my own voice, my own words, telling that
Nine O'clock story.

(Mitchell 1991:107)

Here we are reminded that field researchers do not always
leave the field physically and emotionally unscathed, and they
rarely leave unaffected by the experience of research. But even
where very distressing, the experience is rarely simply negative,
as Cannon indicates on the basis of her research on women with
breast cancer:

It would sound overdramatic to say that it 'changed my life'
(although it has a lasting effect) but it certainly 'took over'
my life in terms of emotional involvement in ways I was not
altogether prepared for, and taught me a number of 'extra
curricular' lessons about life and death, pain and endurance,
and human relationships.

(Cannon 1992:180)

LEAVING THE FIELD

With all research there comes a time when the fieldwork needs
to be terminated. Often this is determined by the non-avail-
ability of further resources, or by the approach of deadlines for

the production of written reports. With the exception of those who are doing research in a setting within which they normally live or work, ending the fieldwork generally means leaving the field – though sometimes the setting itself disintegrates, as Gallmeier (1991:226) found in his research on a professional hockey team:

> Compared to some other field researchers . . . I had a less difficult time disengaging from the setting and the participants. This was attributable largely to the fact that once the season is over the players rapidly disperse and return to summer jobs and families in the 'Great White North'. In late April the Rockets were eliminated in the third round of the playoffs and the season was suddenly over. In just a few days the majority of the Rockets left Summit City.

Virtually overnight, the people he had been studying dispersed geographically, though he was able to follow up individuals subsequently.

Most ethnographers, however, must organize leaving the field, and this is not always a straightforward matter. Like all other aspects of field relations it usually has to be negotiated. Indeed, sometimes participants are reluctant to let the researcher go, for a variety of reasons. David Snow's first attempts at disengagement from a group of Nichiren Shosnu Buddhists were met with a flurry of reconversion activity:

> No sooner had I finished (telling my group leader about my growing disillusionment) than he congratulated me, indicating that (such feelings) were good signs. He went on to suggest that . . . something is really happening in my life. . . . Rather than getting discouraged and giving up, I was told to chant and participate even more. He also suggested that I should go to the Community Center at 10:00 this evening and get further guidance from the senior leaders. . . . Later in the evening my group leader stopped by the apartment at 10:00 – unnannounced – to pick me up and rush me to the Community Center to make sure that I received 'guidance'.
>
> While I was thus trying to curtail my involvement and offer what seemed to be legitimate reasons for dropping out, I was yet being drawn back at the same time.
>
> (Snow 1980:110)

Leaving the field is not usually as difficult as this; it is generally more a matter of saying goodbye to those with whom one has established relationships, making arrangements for future contacts (for example in order to feed data or findings back to them), and generally smoothing one's departure. And leaving does not necessarily mean breaking off all relationships with those one has come to know while working there. Most ethnographers retain friends and acquaintances from their periods of fieldwork, sometimes for a long time. A sad exception is Cannon, whose friends from her research were progressively depleted as they died from cancer (Cannon 1992).

However smoothly managed, though, leaving can be an emotional experience. It can sometimes be strange and disorienting for people in the setting to find that the ethnographer is no longer going to be a part of their everyday world. Informants must adjust to the fact that someone they have come to see as a friend is going to turn back into a stranger, at least to some degree. For the ethnographer too the experience may sometimes be traumatic. An extreme case is that of Young, where the end of the fieldwork coincided with his retirement from the police:

> In the months since I retired and have been compiling the material for this book, I have become crucially aware that . . . I have been . . . involved in what I have decided can only be a deconstruction of an identity. Shedding the institutional framework and the heavy constraints of a disciplined organization after thirty-three years, like the snake sheds his skin, has been another culture shock. . . . During this time I have dreamed regularly (in full colour) of situations where I am in half or partial uniform, often, for example, in police tunic but civvy trousers, and without epaulettes on the jacket or buttons and badges of rank. In these dreams, in which I was often with ex-colleagues from the distant past, I somehow was aware that I was now standing outside my police identity, but had still to throw off the last vestiges of it.
>
> (Young 1991:391)

Frequently, the ethnographer leaves the field with mixed feelings, but sometimes with not a little relief.

CONCLUSION

In Chapter 1 we argued that the role of the researcher in generating the data collected must be recognized. Rather than seeking, by one means or another, to eliminate reactivity, its effects should be monitored and, as far as possible, brought under control. As we have seen, there is a variety of roles the ethnographer may adopt in the field, carrying with them a range of advantages and disadvantages, opportunities and dangers. In addition, by systematically modifying field roles, it may be possible to collect different kinds of data whose comparison can greatly enhance interpretation of the social processes under study. However, establishing and maintaining field relations can be a stressful as well as an exciting experience, and ethnographers must learn to cope with their own feelings if they are to sustain their position as a marginal native and complete the fieldwork.

The various roles which ethnographers establish within settings are, of course, the bases from which data can be collected. One form of data is researchers' descriptions of people's behaviour, of what they do and say in various circumstances. Equally important, though, is information that people in the setting can provide about their own beliefs and feelings, and about their own and others' behaviour now and in the past. In the next chapter we consider the role of such insider accounts in ethnographic research.

Chapter 5

Insider accounts: listening and asking questions

It is a distinctive feature of social research that the 'objects' studied are in fact 'subjects', and themselves produce accounts of their world. As we saw in Chapter 1, this fact is interpreted rather differently by positivism and naturalism. For the former these common-sense accounts are subjective and must be replaced by science; at most they are simply social products to be explained. For naturalism, by contrast, common-sense knowledge *constitutes* the social world: it must be appreciated and described, not subjected to critical scrutiny as to its validity, nor explained away. More recent ethnographic critics of naturalism retain an interest in insider accounts, though they adopt a variety of attitudes towards them. Some regard the role of the ethnographer as to amplify the voices of those on the social margins; and they therefore seek ways of representing insider accounts in rhetorically powerful ways. Here the ethnographer's role approaches advocacy. Others see the task as to deconstruct accounts in order to understand how they were produced and the presuppositions on which they are based. Here the ethnographer's role comes close to ideology critique. And associated with both these views, sometimes, is a tendency to reject that concept of the validity of accounts which implies a correspondence between them and the world.

Our position fits neatly into none of these categories. For us, there are two legitimate and equally important ways in which insider accounts can be used by ethnographers. On the one hand, they can be read for what they tell us about the phenomena to which they refer. We see no reason to deny (or for that matter to affirm) the validity of accounts on the grounds that they are subjective, nor do we regard them as simply constitutive of the phenomena they document. Everyone is a participant observer, acquiring knowledge about the social world in the course of participating in it. And, in our view, such participant knowledge on the part of people in a setting is an important resource for the ethnographer – though its validity should not be accepted at face value, any more than should that of information from other sources.

However skilful a researcher is in negotiating a role that allows observation of events, some information will not be available at first hand. For this reason, ethnographers have cultivated or even trained people as informants (Paul 1953). Indeed, at one time the use of informants seems to have been the staple research method in cultural anthropology. The central concern was the collection of specimens of 'primitive' life, whether material artefacts or myths and legends, as an extract from the field diary of Franz Boas illustrates:

> I had a miserable day today. The natives held a big potlatch again. I was unable to get hold of anyone and had to snatch at whatever I could get. Late at night I did get something (a tale) for which I had been searching – 'The Birth of the Raven'. . . . The big potlatches were continued today, but people found time to tell me stories.
> (Rohner 1969:38; quoted in Pelto and Pelto 1978:243)

As Pelto and Pelto remark: 'Most anthropologists today would be overjoyed at the prospect of observing a full-blown potlatch and would assume that crucially important structural and cultural data could be extracted from the details of the ceremony' (1978:243). While in more recent times ethnographers have shown rather different priorities and have come to place more reliance on their own observations, considerable use is still made of informants, both to get information about activities that for one reason or another cannot be directly observed, and to check inferences made from observations (Burgess 1985e).

Accounts are also important, though, for what they may be able to tell us about those who produced them. We can use what people say as evidence about their perspectives, and perhaps about the larger subcultures and cultures to which they belong. Knowledge of these perspectives and cultures will often form an important element of the analysis. Here the approach is along the lines of the sociology of knowledge (Berger and

Luckmann 1967; Curtis and Petras 1970), though, equally, we can frame it in post-structuralist terms: what is of interest here is the forms of discourse through which accounts are constituted. Also instructive is ethnomethodological work showing that accounts are not simply representations of the world; they are part of the world they describe and are thus shaped by the contexts in which they occur (Atkinson 1988).

Besides contributing to the analysis directly, this second approach to accounts can also aid our assessment of the validity of the information provided by particular informants. The more effectively we can understand an account and its context – the presuppositions on which it relies, who produced it, for whom, and why – the better able we are to anticipate the ways in which it may suffer from biases of one kind or another as a source of information. In this sense the two ways of reading accounts – what we might call 'information' and 'perspective' analyses, respectively – are complementary. The same account can be analysed from both angles, though in asking questions of informants we may have one or other concern predominantly in mind.

Separating the question of the truth or falsity of people's beliefs from the analysis of those beliefs as social phenomena allows us to treat participants' knowledge as both resource and topic, and to do so in a principled way.

UNSOLICITED AND SOLICITED ACCOUNTS

Not all insider accounts are produced by informants responding to an ethnographer's questions: they may be unsolicited. All human behaviour has an expressive dimension. Ecological arrangements, clothes, gesture, and manner all convey messages about people. They may be taken to indicate gender, social status, occupational role, group membership, attitudes, etc. However, the expressive power of language provides the most important resource for accounts. A crucial feature of language is its capacity to present descriptions, explanations, and evaluations of almost infinite variety about any aspect of the world, including itself. Thus, we find that in everyday life people continually provide linguistic accounts to one another: retailing news about 'what happened' on particular occasions, discussing each other's motives, moral character, and abilities, etc. Such talk occurs most notably when some kind of misalignment is perceived between values, rules, or normal expectations and the actual course of events (Hewitt and Stokes 1976). The resulting accounts may be concerned with remedying the discrepancy, or with finding some explanation for it, for example by categorizing someone as 'stupid', 'immoral', or whatever.

Ethnographers may find such accounts a useful source both of direct information about the setting and of evidence about the perspectives, concerns, and discursive practices of the people who produce them. Furthermore, there are some sites where the exchange of accounts among participants is particularly likely to take place; and these are often rewarding locations for the ethnographer to visit. For instance, Hammersley found the staff-room of the school he was studying an extraordinarily rich source of teacher accounts, notably about particular students, their actions, 'moods', characters, and likely prospects, but also about national political events. These accounts provided the basis for an analysis of the ideological framework on which teachers in the school drew in making sense of their world (Hammersley 1980, 1981, and 1991b).

Of course, accounts are not only provided by participants to one another, they are also sometimes given unsolicited to participant observers. Indeed, especially in the early stages of fieldwork, participants may be intent upon making sure that the researcher understands the situation 'correctly'. Very often the aim is to counteract what it is assumed others have been saying, or what are presumed to be the ethnographer's likely interpretations of what has been observed (Hammersley 1980; Hitchcock 1983).

Sometimes, ethnographers are unable to go much beyond observation and the collection of unsolicited accounts. Asking questions may be interpreted as threatening, and even where answers are provided they may be of little value; as Okely found in her research on Gypsies:

> The Gypsies' experience of direct questions is partly formed by outsiders who would harass, prosecute or convert. The Gypsies assess the needs of the questioner and give the appropriate answer, thus disposing of the intruder, his ignorance intact. Alternatively the Gypsies may be deliberately inconsistent.... I found the very act of questioning elicited

either an evasive and incorrect answer or a glazed look. It was more informative to merge into the surroundings than alter them as inquisitor. I participated in order to observe. Towards the end of fieldwork I pushed myself to ask questions, but invariably the response was unproductive, except among a few close associates. Even then, answers dried up, once it appeared that my questions no longer arose from spontaneous puzzlement and I was making other forms of discussion impossible.

(Okely 1983:45)

Agar's experience was similar in his research on drug addiction, though the threatening nature of questions was not the only reason they had to be avoided:

In the streets, though, I learned that you don't ask questions. There are at least two reasons for that rule. One is because a person is vulnerable to arrest by the police, or to being cheated or robbed by other street people. Questions about behaviour may be asked to find out when you are vulnerable to arrest. Or they may be asked to find out when or in what way you can be parted from some money or heroin. Even if one sees no direct connection between the question and those outcomes, it might just be because one has not figured out the questioner's 'game' yet.

The second reason for not asking questions is that you should not have to ask. To be accepted in the streets is to be hip; to be hip is to be knowledgeable; to be knowledgeable is to be capable of understanding what is going on on the basis of minimal cues. So to ask a question is to show that you are not acceptable and this creates problems in a relationship when you have just been introduced to somebody.

(Agar 1980:456)

While questioning may occasionally have to be avoided or abandoned, it is sometimes possible to overcome initial resistance through modification of the way in which questions are asked. Lerner (1957) reports the defensive reactions he met when he started interviewing members of French elites, and the strategy he developed to deal with them:

Our first approaches to interviewing were modest, tentative, apologetic. Trial-and-error, hit-and-miss (what the French love to call *'L'empiricisme anglo-saxon'*) finally produced a workable formula. To each prospective respondent, the interviewer explained that his Institute had undertaken a study of attitudes among the elite. As Frenchmen do not respond readily to questionnaire, he continued, we were seeking the counsel of specially qualified persons: 'Would you be so kind as to review with us the questionnaire we propose to use and give us the benefit of your criticisms? In responding yourself, you could explain which questions a Frenchman would be likely to resist and why; which questions would draw ambiguous or evasive responses that could not be properly interpreted; and which questions could be altered in such a way as to require reflective rather than merely stereotyped answers.'

By casting the interviewee in the role of expert consultant, we gave him the opportunity to indulge in a favourite indoor sport – generalizing about Frenchmen.

(Lerner 1957:27)

As a result of the influence of naturalism, it is not uncommon for ethnographers to regard solicited accounts as less valid than those produced spontaneously. Thus, for example, Becker and Geer (1960) argue that it is important to ensure that conclusions about the perspectives of participants are not entirely reliant on solicited answers, otherwise we may be misled by reactivity, by the effects of the researcher's questions on what is said. Similarly, there is a tendency among ethnographers to favour non-directive interviewing in which the interviewee is allowed to talk at length in his or her own terms, as opposed to more directive questioning. The aim here is to minimize, as far as possible, the influence of the researcher on what is said, and thus to facilitate the open expression of the informant's perspective on the world.

Now it is certainly true that the influence of the researcher on the production of data is an important issue, but it is misleading to regard it simply as a source of bias that must be, or can be entirely, removed. For one thing, neither non-directive interviewing nor even reliance on unsolicited accounts avoids the problem entirely. Hargreaves *et al.* (1975) report the difficulties they faced in developing a non-reactive way of eliciting teachers' accounts of classroom events:

Our principal method was to observe a lesson and from these

observations to extract those teacher statements and/or actions which consisted of a reaction to a deviant act. . . . We then reported the reaction back to the teacher at a later stage, asking for his commentary upon what he did. . . . We often merely quoted what the teacher had said, and the teacher was willing to make a commentary upon his action without any direct question from us. On other occasions we reported the teacher's statement back and then asked why the teacher had said or done something.

(Hargreaves *et al.* 1975:219)

They comment that even where no question was asked the teacher's account was still shaped by what he or she assumed would be seen as 'an appropriate, reasonable and meaningful answer to our unspoken question' (Hargreaves *et al.* 1975:220).

In fact, even where the researcher plays no role at all in generating the account, one can never be sure that his or her presence was not an important influence. For instance, where the researcher is not a party to the interaction but is simply within earshot, knowledge of his or her presence may still have an effect. Sometimes this influence is only too obvious, as the following fieldnote from Hammersley's study of staffroom talk among secondary school teachers makes clear:

(The researcher is sitting in an armchair reading a newspaper. Two teachers are engaged in conversation nearby, in the course of which the following exchange occurs.)

LARSON: You ought to be official NUT (National Union of Teachers) convenor.
WALKER: I'm only in the NUT for one reason.
LARSON: (looking significantly at the researcher): In case you get prosecuted for hitting someone.
WALKER: That's right.

Of course, the influence of the researcher can be eliminated through adoption of the 'complete observer' or 'complete participant' role, but not only does this place serious restrictions on the data collection process, as we saw in the previous chapter, it also in no sense guarantees valid data. The problem of reactivity is merely one aspect of a more general phenomenon that cannot be eradicated: the effects of audience, and indeed of context generally, on what people say and do. All accounts must be interpreted in terms of the context in which they were produced. Thus, Dean and Whyte (1958) argue that rather than asking, for example, 'How do I know if the informant is telling the truth?' we should consider what the informant's statements reveal about his or her feelings and perceptions, and what inferences can be made from these about the actual environment or events he or she has experienced. The aim is not to gather 'pure' data that are free from potential bias. There is no such thing. Rather, the goal must be to discover the correct manner of interpreting whatever data we have.

Of course, this is not to suggest that how we collect data, or what data we collect, is of no importance. The point is that minimizing the influence of the researcher is not the only, or always even a prime, consideration. Assuming we understand how the presence of the researcher may have shaped the data, we can interpret the latter accordingly and it can provide important insights, allowing us to develop or test elements of the emerging analysis.

There is no reason, then, for ethnographers to shy away from the use of interviews, where these are viable. Interviewing can be an extremely important source of data: it may allow one to generate information that it would be very difficult, if not impossible, to obtain otherwise – both about events described and about perspectives and discursive strategies. And, of course, some sorts of qualitative research rely very heavily if not entirely on interview data, notably life-history work (Bertaux 1981; Plummer 1983).

At the same time, it should be noted that there are distinct advantages in combining participant observation with interviews; in particular, the data from each can be used to illuminate the other. As Dexter notes from his research on the United States Congress, one's experience as a participant observer can have an important effect on how one interprets what people say in interviews:

[In my research] I sometimes appear to rely chiefly upon interviews, but in fact I was living in Washington at the time, spent much of my 'free' time in a congressional office, saw a good deal of several congressional assistants and secretaries socially, worked on other matters with several persons actively engaged in relationships with Congress (lobbying and

liaison), had participated in a number of congressional cam-
paigns, had read extensively about congressional history and
behaviour, and had some relevant acquaintance with local
politics in several congressional districts. All these factors
made my analysis of interviews somewhat credible. And, as
I look back, interviews sometimes acquired meaning from the
observations which I often made while waiting in congressional offices – observation of other visitors, secretarial
staffs, and so forth. And, finally, most important of all, it
happened that interviews with constituents, lobbyists, congressmen of different views and factions, could be and
were checked and re-checked, against each other. Yet in the
book we say little about all this; and in fact it is only now,
that I realize how much these other factors affected what I
'heard'.

(Dexter 1970:15)

The effect may also work the other way. What people say in
interviews can lead us to see things differently in observation,
as Woods (1981) illustrates, discussing his research on secondary
school students. The way in which the students talked about
boredom cued him into the experience of it:

One of my outstanding memories from the enormous mass
of experience at the school is that of pupils talking to me
about boredom. They managed to convey, largely in a very
few words, years of crushing *ennui* that had been ingrained
into their bones. Great wealth of expression was got into
'boring, 'boredom', 'it's so bo-or-ring here'. The word, I
realized now, is onomatopoeic. I could never view lessons in
company with that group again without experiencing that
boredom myself. They would occasionally glance my way in
the back corner of the room with the same pained expression
on their faces, and I knew exactly what they meant. This,
then, provided a platform for my understanding of the school
life of one group of pupils.

(Woods 1981:22)

Any decision about whether to use interviews, alone or in
combination with other sources of data, must be made in the
context of the purpose of one's research and the circumstances
in which it is to be carried out. And here, as elsewhere, there

are no right and wrong decisions, only better and worse ones; and sometimes these can only be recognized with hindsight. What is important to remember, though, is that different research strategies may produce different data, and thereby, perhaps, different conclusions.

ETHNOGRAPHIC INTERVIEWING: SELECTING INFORMANTS

A crucial issue that arises once the decision has been made to collect data via interviews is: who should be interviewed? Sometimes, particularly in the context of participant observation, people select themselves or others for interview, as Cannon found in her research on women with breast cancer:

> Liz told me that she thought Yvonne was ready for another interview, 'she's not stopped talking all weekend'. A number of times women rang me to ask me to see them because they 'needed someone to talk to' about a particular event.
>
> (Cannon 1992:171)

Here the driving force was the therapeutic value of the interviewing, but self-selection for interview can occur for other reasons. Most obviously, it may arise where ethnographers encourage informants to keep them updated, hoping that they will initiate contacts to report any news:

> One of my key informants, Sylvia Robinson, always came to tell me what was going on in the school. She told me what happened on days when I was outside school, she talked to me about aspects of school policy that had been discussed at school meetings that I did not or could not attend, attributing remarks to particular teaching staff. Furthermore, she always updated me and any other teacher within earshot of the latest gossip in the school.
>
> (Burgess 1985c:149–50)

Such informants are of considerable use to an ethnographer, and 'interviews' with them may be initiated by either side.

Gatekeepers or other powerful figures in the field sometimes attempt to select interviewees for the ethnographer. This may be done in good faith to facilitate the research, or it may be designed to control the findings, as happened in Evans's study of a school for the hearing-impaired:

> In the course of time I learned from another administrator that Mr Gregory [the head of the school] would definitely require handling with kid gloves. This fact came to light when I asked the former if he could direct me to some key people on the high school campus. The naivete of the question, and the political dimensions of my work, were noted quickly by his response:
>
> > No, I couldn't do that. Mr Gregory will send you to those he picks out. If you try to do any interviews without his approval and knowledge, then he will close it up tight.
>
> ... Days later Gregory met with me again and announced, 'We have selected for you the "cream of the crop".' That is, four teachers had been handpicked for interviews.
>
> (Evans 1991:170–1)

While welcoming self-selection, and perhaps even selection by others, the ethnographer must retain the leeway to choose candidates for interview. Otherwise there is a grave danger that the data collected will be misleading in important respects, and the researcher will be unable to engage in the strategic search for data that is essential to a reflexive approach. However, gaining access to informants can be quite complex, sometimes as difficult as negotiating access to a setting. Indeed, it may even be necessary to negotiate with gatekeepers before one can contact the people one wants to interview:

> If the sample of navy wives was to be broad, it was essential that the cooperation of the naval authorities was secured.... The Royal Navy was approached to elicit its cooperation and support and to gain access to their personnel listings.... This was not some polite formality prior to being given a free hand, but a delicate series of negotiations....
>
> Research on service personnel inevitably encounters security problems. Therefore, it was hardly surprising that the Royal Navy was apprehensive about any organization having access to personnel files. Access to such records was limited, even within the Royal Navy, and they were certainly not for

outside eyes. There was an additional problem. The Ethics Committee of the Royal Navy had in the past developed regulations, it was claimed, to protect the civilian status of naval wives; they were not to be contacted by civilian or naval authorities without the prior permission of their husbands. Although the Navy was clearly interested in the consultative value of . . . outside research, initially these problems seemed to be major stumbling blocks. Eventually, however, a compromise was reached and a listing of all the personnel in the administrative region of Western Area was sent to the Family Services section of a local naval establishment. No names or addresses were permitted to be removed from these premises, but all replies to a questionnaire survey and later invitations to an interview were returned to the Polytechnic. This means of contacting women was cumbersome, but it protected their anonymity and fitted in with the Navy's regulations on security.

(Chandler 1990:124)

Even where gatekeepers are not involved, identifying and contacting interviewees may not be straightforward, as Shaffir found in his research on people who had left ultra-Orthodox Jewish groups. His hope was that, having identified one or two *haredim*, they would be able to supply the names of others, so producing a 'snowball sample'; but this plan was initially frustrated:

I quickly learned that there was no institutional framework within which to locate such persons. Thus I arranged a meeting with a journalist who recently had written a sensitive piece on the topic and who claimed that she located respondents through an ad in her newspaper inviting former *haredim* to contact her. The similar ad I inserted yielded only one individual who claimed to know of no others like himself. Although he did not lead me to further contacts, my conversation with him sensitized me to the pain, anguish, and desperation that characterized his departure from the ultra-Orthodox world – a theme that proved central in the account of every former *haredi* I was to meet.

The snowball technique that proved so effective for meeting Chassidic and newly observant Jews was largely unhelpful in the *haredi* project. Ex-*haredim* with whom I met suspected that there were others like themselves, but they did not know where to find them. Although at first I was suspicious of this claim, I gradually appreciated the extent to which former *haredim* were cut off from their previous circle such that they knew little, if anything, about other individuals who had defected recently. The important exception was Chaim.... At the end of my conversation with him, I asked whether he knew of others like himself with whom I might meet. 'Yes, I do,' he replied, 'I have names and telephone numbers. How many people do you want to meet?'

(Shaffir 1991:76)

Sometimes the difficulty of getting access to informants determines who will and will not be interviewed. But usually there is a choice of potential interviewees, and then decisions have to be made about how many to interview and whom these should be. These are not decisions that have to be taken once and for all; usually in ethnographic work they will be made recurrently. But, of course, in making them the researcher has to take account of the time and resources available and of the opportunity costs of different decisions. In life-history work, there may be only a single informant, who is interviewed repeatedly. More usually, ethnographers interview a range of people, but some of these may need to be interviewed more than once, for example because the aim is to trace patterns of change over time, or because it is discovered that further information, or checking of previously supplied information, is required.

The criteria by which ethnographers choose people for interview can vary considerably, even over the course of the same research project. In survey research the aim, typically, is to seek a representative sample. And, sometimes, this is the goal in ethnographic research too, though what is usually involved is sampling *within* rather than *across* cases (see Chapter 2). When studying a large organization, one may not have the time and resources to interview *all* the occupants of a particular role, and may therefore try to select a sample of them that is representative.

Doing this may be approached in much the same way as in survey research, selecting a suitably sized sample at random, or a stratified sample that takes account of known heterogeneity among the members of the population. However, such system-

atic sampling requires the existence of relatively clear boundaries around the population, and the existence and availability
of a full listing of its members. Such conditions may be met in
organizational contexts, but they will not be in others. Equally,
often the time is simply not available to interview a large
sample. In such circumstances, the researcher will have to select
interviewees as best he or she can in order to try to achieve
representativeness – though it may be possible to check the
success of this by asking informants for their judgments about
what are and are not representative views, and/or by comparing
the characteristics of the sample with what is known about the
population as a whole.

However, a representative sample of informants is not always
what is required in ethnographic research. This is especially so
where the primary concern is with eliciting information rather
than with documenting perspectives or discursive practices.
Here the aim will often be to target those people who have the
knowledge desired and who may be willing to divulge it to
the ethnographer. Identifying such people requires that one
draw on assumptions about the social distribution of knowledge
and about the motives of those in different roles. Dean *et al.*
provide an elaborate illustration of the sort of thinking that may
lie behind such strategic selection of interviewees:

1 *Informants who are especially sensitive to the area of concern*
  The outsider who sees things from the vantage point of
  another culture, social class, community, etc.

  The rookie, who is surprised by what goes on and notes the
  taken-for-granted things that the acclimatized miss. And, as
  yet, he may have no stake in the system to protect.

  The nouveau statused, who is in transition from one position to another where the tensions of new experience are
  vivid.

  The naturally reflective and objective person in the field.
  He can sometimes be pointed out by others of his kind.

2 *The more-willing-to-reveal informants*
  Because of their background or status, some informants are
  just more willing to talk than others:

The naive informant, who knows not whereof he speaks. He may be either naive as to what the fieldworker represents or naive about his own group.

The frustrated person, who may be a rebel or malcontent, especially the one who is consciously aware of his blocked drives and impulses.

The 'outs', who have lost power but are 'in-the-know'. Some of the 'ins' may be eager to reveal negative facts about their colleagues.

The habitué or 'old hand' or 'fixture', who no longer has a stake in the venture or is so secure that he is not jeopardized by exposing what others say or do.

The needy person, who fastens onto the interviewer because he craves attention and support. As long as the interviewer satisfies this need, he will talk.

The subordinate, who must adapt to superiors. He generally develops insights to cushion the impact of authority, and he may be hostile and willing to 'blow his top'.

(Dean *et al.* 1967:285)

Along the same lines, in his research on educational research policy-makers, Ball (1994) reports how he discovered early on that there was limited value in interviewing government ministers currently in office, that a much more effective strategy was to concentrate on those who had left office, since they were much more likely to feel free to provide inside information. Informants may also be selected on the basis of what Glaser and Strauss (1967) call 'theoretical sampling', choosing those whose testimony seems most likely to develop and test emerging analytic ideas.

Who is interviewed, when, and how will usually be decided as the research progresses, according to the ethnographer's assessment of the current state of his or her knowledge, and according to judgments as to how it might best be developed further. Of course, not everyone whom one might wish to interview will be willing. And, even with those who are willing in principle, it may take a considerable time, and may involve some cost, to obtain an interview. Nor will the account obtained always be illuminating, as Thomas reports from his research on top business executives:

> Unless you have some sort of leverage with which to get their attention, chances are you will get it for only half the time you think you need. Journalists I know are pleased to get an hour with an executive; but journalists have a source of leverage most sociologists do not. A staff writer for the *Wall Street Journal* or *Fortune* magazine can at least imply that he won't say nice things – or he won't say anything at all (which can be worse) – if he does not get access to the executive he wishes to interview. Even then, if you do get the 30 minutes, you may find that an emergency or someone more important bumps you off the schedule. If you get in the door, you will find that the executive does not intend to answer your questions or has a script of her own that she'd like to repeat. All of this can happen (and has happened to me) after you've spent several months and hundreds of dollars to get to the executive's office in the first place.
>
> (Thomas 1993:82–3)

As with any other data collection technique, the quality and relevance of the data produced by interviews can vary considerably, and is not always predictable. Selection of informants must be based on the best judgments one can make in the circumstances. However, one may need to revise these judgments on the basis of experience.

INTERVIEWS AS PARTICIPANT OBSERVATION

Interviews in ethnographic research range from spontaneous, informal conversations in places that are being used for other purposes, to formally arranged meetings in bounded settings out of earshot of other people. In the case of the former the dividing line between participant observation and interviewing is hard to discern. In the case of formal interviews it is more obvious. Here the interview represents a distinct setting, and it follows from this that the participant understandings elicited there may not be those which underlie behaviour elsewhere (Silverman 1973). This problem has been highlighted in research on teachers' typifications of students. Hargreaves *et al.* (1975), using observation and formal interviews, presented a picture of teachers' typifications as elaborate and individualized. Woods (1979) challenged their account, arguing, in part, that their data were a product of the interview situation and of their own analytical orientation. He claims that teachers would not be able to operate on the basis of such elaborate typifications in the secondary school classroom, given the sheer number of students they deal with each day. Whatever the merits of the arguments on each side, the fact that there is a problem about relating perspectives elicited in interviews to actions in other settings comes through clearly (Hargreaves 1977).

However, as we suggested earlier, the distinctiveness of the interview setting must not be exaggerated, and it can be viewed as a resource rather than as a problem. Just as the impact of the participant observer on the people observed is not simply a source of bias, so too with that of the interviewer. Indeed, to the extent that the aim in ethnography goes beyond the provision of a description of what occurred in a particular setting over a certain period of time, there may be positive advantages to be gained from subjecting people to verbal stimuli different to those prevalent in the settings in which they normally operate. In other words, the 'artificiality' of the interview when compared with 'normal' events in the setting may allow us to understand how participants would behave in other circumstances, for example when they move out of a setting or when the setting changes. Labov's (1969) work on 'the logic of non-standard English' illustrates this when he compares interviews in which the interviewer takes different roles. We might expect that the monosyllabic responses of some children in his formal interviews, while not an accurate indicator of their linguistic resources, may have been a genuine reflection of their behaviour in other similar circumstances, such as interviews with counsellors and social workers, or lessons in school. It may be that by varying features of the interview situation in this way we can identify which aspects of the setting produce particular responses.

Thus, while it is true that the perspectives elicited in interviews do not provide direct access to some cognitive and attitudinal base from which a person's behaviour in 'natural' settings is derived, they may still be capable of illuminating that behaviour. Similarly, while we must not treat the validity of people's reports of their attitudes, feelings, behaviour, etc., as beyond all possible doubt, as a privileged source of information, there is no reason to dismiss them as of no value at all, or even to treat them as of value only as displays of perspectives or discourse strategies.

The differences between participant observation and interviewing are not as great as is sometimes suggested, then. In both cases we must take account of context and of the effects of the researcher. There are other parallels too. Thus, both the participant observer and the interviewer need to build rapport. When interviewing people with whom one has already established a relationship through participant observation, little further work may be required. But where the research does not have a participant observation component, or where the ethnographer has had little or no previous contact with the person being interviewed, the task of building rapport is important. Much of what we wrote in the previous chapter about building relationships in participant observation applies here too. The personal characteristics of the researcher, and how these relate to those of the interviewee, can be important, though their effects are never entirely determinate. And they can be controlled to some degree by the interviewer's presentation of self. Measor (1985), for example, indicates the care she took with dressing appropriately when doing life-history interviews with teachers. This meant wearing very different clothes according, for example, to the age of the teacher concerned. She also reports drawing on shared interests and biographical experiences, and indeed developing some new interests, to facilitate the interview process. As in participant observation, so also in interviewing, it may be possible by careful self-presentation to avoid the attribution of damaging identities and to encourage ones that might facilitate rapport.

Building rapport is not the only concern, however. Equally necessary may be establishing and maintaining the interview situation itself. This is especially likely to be a problem when one is interviewing relatively powerful people:

> Elites are used to being in charge, and they are used to having others defer to them. They are also used to being asked what they think and having what they think matter in other people's lives. These social facts can result in the researcher being too deferential and overly concerned about establishing

positive rapport. . . . I have found it important for the inter-viewer to establish some visible control of the situation at the very beginning, even if the elite subject is momentarily set off balance. This came to my attention especially on one occasion when an elite board member of one of the family and child welfare agencies I was studying suggested that I meet him for our interview at 7:30 in the morning at an elegant downtown restaurant where he had a table in his name and breakfasted daily. I agreed and wondered aloud to a friend how I would convey the message from the outset – to myself as well as to him – that I was going to structure the social situation in which we found ourselves, even though we were clearly in his space and not mine. My friend suggested that I begin by arriving early and be sitting at his table when he came in. That would give me some time to get accustomed to the space and claim some of it as my own before he arrived. It worked like a charm. He appeared briefly taken aback and began by deferring to me and my research interests. It was a very successful interview, frank and substantive.

(Ostrander 1993:19–20)

This problem of establishing the interview context may also arise outside of the study of elites, as Currer (1992) found in her attempts to interview Pathan women, who insisted on treat-ing the event as a social occasion. And, as that example illus-trates, it is a problem that is not always so easy to resolve.

The initial few minutes of an interview can be particularly significant in establishing its nature and tone. At that point there may be some implicit, and perhaps even explicit, negotiation about the form the interview will take. One element of this will usually be information offered by the researcher about the reason for the interview, along with reassurances about confi-dentiality and the right of the interviewee to refuse to answer any question to which they would prefer not to respond. Small-talk may also take place at this stage, perhaps while a decision is made about where to sit, where to put the audio-recorder (if one is being used), etc.

The interviewer's manner while the informant is talking can also be very important. The latter will often be looking for some indication of whether the answers being provided are appropriate, and also perhaps for any sign of judgmental reaction. Generally, then, the interviewer needs to give clear indications of acceptance. Equally important, though, are signs that the ethnographer is following what is being said, and here appropriate responses on her or his part are essential. As Measor notes, God forbid that one should fail to laugh at an informant's joke! This underlines an important feature of much ethnographic interviewing: that within the boundaries of the interview context the aim is to facilitate a conversation, giving the interviewee a good deal more leeway to talk on their own terms than is the case in standardized interviews.

Frequently, the researcher him- or herself is the only other person present at an interview, and the guarantee of confidentiality implies that no one else will ever hear what the informant has said in a way that is attributable to him or her. Under these circumstances informants may be willing to divulge information and express opinions that they would not in front of others. However, this does not mean that this information is necessarily true or that the opinions they present are more genuine, more truly reflect their perspectives, than what they say on other occasions. Whether or not this is the case, and in what senses it is true, will depend in part on how their orientations towards others, including the researcher, are structured. Furthermore, informants are often aware that they are in some sense 'speaking for posterity', and this too will have an effect on what they say and how they say it. They may even doubt the ethnographer's assurances of confidentiality and seek to use him or her to 'leak' information to others.

Sometimes, of course, ethnographers conduct interviews where more than one other person is present, and here the question of audience is even more complex. On occasions, the presence of others cannot be avoided, as Lee reports:

> Where possible, couples were interviewed separately, but joint interviews were necessary in a number of cases. This was particularly so with some of the more recently married couples who lived in quite small flats. I found it embarrassing to ask one partner to wait in another room – usually the bedroom – while I interviewed the other.
>
> (Lee 1992:136)

Chandler had the same problem in her study of navy wives, and it had a significant effect:

Although appointments were made to interview only the women, on two occasions husbands were present. His presence transformed the interview; he altered the questioning, the woman's answers and sometimes he joined in. Even when he did not speak he communicated what he felt by means of what has come to be known as body language and his reactions were monitored by the women in their replies.

(Chandler 1990:127)

Such interventions need not always be counterproductive, however, as Hunter notes. During an interview he was carrying out with a councillor at his home in a wealthy suburb of Chicago, the latter's wife came in:

After listening briefly as an observer, she began to add asides and commentary on her husband's responses. Slowly, what had been heretofore a very focused and somewhat formal interview about issues and politics soon became transformed into a three-way conversation about particular persons among the elite. The wife was adding more 'social commentary' about people, who got along with whom, who was respected or not, and the interview was transformed into a very informative and revealing 'gossip situation'.

(Hunter 1993:48)

Sometimes, of course, ethnographers intentionally arrange interviews with more than one person at a time. In addition to the fact that group interviews allow a greater number of people to be interviewed, they also have the advantage that they may make the interview situation less strange for interviewees and thus encourage them to be more forthcoming. In particular, this may overcome the problem of the shy and retiring person, as in the case of Carol, quoted by Helen Simons:

INTERVIEWER: Does the lesson help the shy ones or does it make them stand out more?

ANGELA: They're so quiet and then all of sudden one of them'll speak and you think 'What's come over them?' I suppose they've got their opinion in their head and they hear everyone else talking so they think they will.

PATRICIA: Carol's quiet.

INTERVIEWER: You didn't like speaking?

CAROL: I'd only talk when I was asked a question.

ANGELA: Sort of speak when you're spoken to. I noticed that when I first met her, I thought she was quiet.

INTERVIEWER: But now you speak when you want to put your point of view.

CAROL: Yes. When I think someone's wrong, I'll say what I think.

INTERVIEWER: And how long did it take you to get to this stage?

CAROL: Well, it was more friendly, we sat in a circle and we could speak to each other. That was better and it didn't take long, only a few lessons.

ANGELA: I noticed after three or four lessons Carol started speaking more.

PATRICIA: I spoke the first lesson.

ANGELA: So did I.

CAROL: It gets me mad when people say you're very quiet though. I enjoy other people's views as well.

ANGELA (to Patricia):   Probably the way you shout, you probably frighten them to death.

(Simons 1981:40)

Of course, whether or not group interviews are successful in relaxing those who would find a one-to-one interview intimidating very much depends on the composition of the group.

What is said, as well as who speaks, is also likely to be affected by whether a group or individual format is used. For example, in a group the interviewer will usually find it more difficult to maintain control over topic. On the other hand, this may be all to the good in that informants can prompt one another – 'Go on, tell him', 'What about when you . . .?' – using information not available to the researcher and in ways which turn out to be productive (Woods 1979). Douglas used an interesting variation on this strategy in his attempts to get an informant to 'spill the beans' about massage parlours:

we had long known that the ultimate insider in the massage parlors was a local lawyer who represented the massage parlor association and about 80 per cent of the cases. We wanted to open him up, so we tried to set him up for it. We wanted to make it manifest to the lawyer that we were on the inside and could thus be trusted. We knew it wouldn't do any good to give him verbal commitments – 'Hey, man, we're on your side, you can trust us.' He was used to every possible deception and double cross from all angles. It would have to be made manifest, physically real.... We got two young masseuses to go with [us] for the interview, showing by their presence and trust in [us] what angle [we were] coming from. As [we] were ushered into the lawyer's office, two employees at the parlor where one of the girls ... worked came out and they had a grand reunion right there. (Researchers need luck as much as anyone else.) As the interview progressed, the two girls talked of their work. One of them, as we knew well, was under indictment for her work in a parlor. They talked about that. She was impressed by the lawyer and shifted her case to him. At the end of the interview, the lawyer told [us we] could use all his files, make xerox copies of them, use his name in doing [our] research, accompany him on cases, etc. We felt sure there were some things he wasn't telling us (and one of the girls later started working with him to get at more and check it out), but that seemed okay for the first hour.

(Douglas 1976:174–5)

At the same time, of course, the effects of audience must be monitored. Woods provides an illustration of the need for this from his group interviews with secondary school students:

For added ribaldry, the facts will probably have suffered some distortion.... Consider this example:

TRACY: Dianne fell off a chair first and as she went to get up, she got 'old of me skirt, she was having a muck about, and there was I in me petticoat, me skirt came down round my ankles and Mr. Bridge came in (great screams of laughter from girls). He'd been standing outside the door.

KATE: 'E told her she'd get suspended.

TRACY: He 'ad me mum up the school, telling her what a horrible child I was.

KATE: 'Nobody will marry you,' said Miss Judge.

TRACY: Oh yeah, Miss Judge sits there, ''n, nobody will want to marry you, Jones,' she said. I said, 'Well you ain't married, anyway.'

(Shrieks of laughter from girls.)

(Woods 1981:20)

The possibility of distortion is always present in participant accounts, since (as in the above example) they are often worked up for purposes where truth is probably not the primary concern. On the other hand, group discussions may provide considerable insight into participant culture: in other words, what is lost in terms of information may be compensated for by the illumination that the accounts provide into the perspectives and discursive repertoires of those being interviewed.

Pollard employed a further, novel variation on the manipulation of audience in the interviewing strategy he used in his research on a middle school:

> children were invited to form a dinner-time interviewing team to help me, as I put it, 'find out what all the children think about school'. This group very quickly coined the name 'The Moorside Investigation Department' (MID) for themselves and generated a sense of self-importance. Over the next year the membership of MID changed gradually, but I always attempted to balance it by having members of a range of groups. Normally about six children were involved at any one time and the total number of children involved during the year was thirteen. . . . My intention in setting up a child interviewing team was to break through the anticipated reticence of children towards me as a teacher. I spent a lot of time with the MID members discussing the type of things I was interested in and establishing the idea of immunity to teacher-prosecution and of confidentiality. We then began a procedure of inviting groups of children – in twos, threes or fours to give confidence – to be interviewed by a MID member in a building which was unused at dinner-times. Sometimes the interviewers would interview their own friends, sometimes they would interview children whom they did not know well. Initially, I did not try to control this but left it very much to the children.
>
> (Pollard 1985:227–8)

Here again, of course, the effects of audience need to be taken into account. And the data produced will have been affected not only by the particular children involved, but also by Pollard's background role.

As important as who is present at an interview, and who carries it out, often, is where and when it takes place. Again, though, the location of interviews is something which the eth-nographer may not be able to control. Two of the couples Lee interviewed in his study of religious intermarriage in Northern Ireland only agreed to meet him

> on the condition that our initial contact was made in a public place, and that they would have a description of me but I would have no description of them. In this way they were able to 'look me over' and make a judgment about the possi-ble threat I might pose before deciding whether or not to make themselves known to me. Obviously I passed the test since both couples did make themselves known and both were interviewed. In neither case, though, was I invited to the couple's home and each interview took place on 'neutral' territory, presumably so that the couples could ensure that their address remained unknown.
>
> (Lee 1992:131)

Even where the ethnographer is able to decide where the interview will take place, finding a suitable locale is not always easy. Burgess notes that in his study of a secondary school he conducted interviews in classrooms and departmental work-rooms, both of which were far from ideal. Others researching schools have ended up in broom cupboards; and Hammersley's (1980) most successful interview with a student took place at the bottom of a stairwell!

Where there is some choice of locale, several considerations have to be borne in mind. Dexter notes the need to take account of likely distractions:

> One mistake which I have made on a number of occasions is to try to carry on an interview in an environment unsuited for it. A legislator who is standing outside the legislative chamber, while half his attention is focused on buttonholing colleagues, is not a good subject for an interview; though one might learn something from observing him. I do not know whether, if confronted with such a situation again, I would have the nerve to say in effect, 'I need your full attention . . .' but I hope I would ask whether I can arrange some time when he is less preoccupied. The most common difficulty is a man who really lacks a private office; for instance, state legislators or an executive assistant whose room is used as a

passageway to his chief's. In all such cases, I shall in the future ask if there is a conference room or if we can have a cup of coffee, or, if worst comes to worst, even meet for a lunch.

(Dexter 1970:54)

Whose 'territory' (Lyman and Scott 1970) it is can make a big difference to how the interview goes, as Skipper and McCaghy's (1972) research on striptease artistes illustrates. They recount how one of the respondents asked them to come to the theatre, view her performance, and carry out the interview backstage:

On stage her act was highly sexual. It consisted primarily of fondling herself in various stages of undress while carrying on risqué banter with the audience. The act ended with the stripper squatting on the floor at the front of the stage, sans G-string, fondling her pudendum and asking a customer in the first row: 'Aren't you glad you came tonight? Do you think you can come again?'

Backstage, it was difficult for us to feign indifference over her appearance when she ushered us into her dressing room. As she sat clad only in the G-string she had worn on stage and with her legs on the dressing table, we became slightly mesmerized. We had difficulty in even remembering the questions we wanted to ask let alone getting them out of our mouths in an intelligible manner. To compound our difficulties, we felt it was obvious to the stripper what effect she was having on us. She seemed to enjoy the role. For over a half an hour she responded to our inquiries in what we perceived as a seductive voice, and her answers were often suggestive. After about forty minutes, she said very quickly, as if she had decided she had had enough, 'Doesn't it seem to be getting chilly in here? I'm freezing.' She rose, put on a kimono, and walked out of her dressing room and started talking to another stripper. When she did not return, we knew the interview had been concluded. . . .

When we returned to our office to record our impressions, we discovered we had not collected as much of the data as we had intended. We either had forgotten to ask many questions or had obtained inappropriate answers to those asked. In short, we had not conducted an effective interview. Our sheltered backgrounds and numerous courses in sociological methodology simply had not prepared us for this kind of research environment. . . . It was very clear to us that the nudity and perceived seductiveness of the stripper, and the general permissiveness of the setting, had interfered with our role as researchers. The respondent, not we, had been in control of the interaction; we had been induced to play her game her way even to the point that she made the decision when to end the interview.

(Skipper and McCaghy 1972:239–40)

In response to this experience the researchers arranged for future interviews with the strippers to take place in a restaurant!

The physical features of a context and their arrangement can also have an effect on responses in interviews, as Burgess notes:

In the office of a head or a deputy head there are comfortable chairs as well as a desk and chair. Choosing to sit around a coffee table helps to break down the fact that the tape-recorded conversation did not occur spontaneously but was pre-set. In contrast, talking to a deputy head across a desk with a tape-recorder placed beside us may give the individual I am talking to some confidence, as he or she is surrounded by props: a filing cabinet that may be consulted, a file that can be opened. Yet it also adds to the formality and communicates something about the status of individuals and the way in which they perceived themselves.

(Burgess 1988:142)

With many people, interviewing them on their own territory, and allowing them to organize the context the way they wish, is the best strategy. It allows them to relax much more than they would in less familiar surroundings. However, as we noted earlier, sometimes one may need to establish the interview as a distinct setting in which the interviewer is in control, and choice of locale and/or manipulation of its topography by the researcher can be an effective strategy for doing this.

Equally important in thinking about the context of interviews is to look at how the interview fits into the interviewee's life. There is a great temptation for the researcher to see interviews purely in terms of his or her own schedule, regarding them as time-out from the everyday lives of participants. However, other people may not view them like this at all. This may well have been one source of the trouble that Skipper and McCaghy ran into. Equally, though, there are people of whom one might say that talk is their business and indeed being interviewed may be a routine part of life for them. Dexter's senators and congressmen provide the obvious example. Their attitude to and behaviour in an interview will be very different to those who are unfamiliar with, or inexperienced in, this form of social interaction. Also, how people respond on any particular occasion may be affected by what else is going on in their lives, and how they currently feel. This was an important factor in Cannon's research:

> one day I had what I experienced as a particularly bad interview with Katherine, with whom I felt I had built a good deal of rapport and understanding. . . . I felt that all my worst fears concerning interviewing sick people were being realized, that I was only serving further to upset her, that she was ill and tired and really only stayed in the hospital to talk to me out of politeness. She seemed remote and distant and the conversation was punctuated by long sighs and silences, yet when I asked her if she felt too tired to go on she said she wanted to continue. . . . I worried about this encounter until the next time I saw her. . . . At the next interview I was able . . . to tell her how I had felt and the matter was resolved to both our satisfaction. She said she had wanted to talk but had found herself to be too depressed and tired to be able to do so. We decided that in future if this happened we would simply have a cup of tea and make another appointment. In fact it did not happen again until she became very ill and bedridden when she would sometimes say she would prefer to talk about matters other than her illness. This we would do, although the illness often emerged as the main topic of conversation in any case.
>
> (Cannon 1992:164)

ASKING QUESTIONS

The main difference between the way in which ethnographers and survey interviewers ask questions is not, as is sometimes assumed, that one form of interviewing is 'structured' and the other is 'unstructured'. All interviews, like any other kind of

social interaction, are structured by both researcher and informant. The important distinction to be made is between standardized and reflexive interviewing. Ethnographers do not usually
decide beforehand the exact questions they want to ask, and do
not ask each interviewee exactly the same questions, though
they will usually enter the interviews with a list of issues to be
covered. Nor do they seek to establish a fixed sequence in which
relevant topics are covered; they adopt a more flexible approach,
allowing the discussion to flow in a way that seems natural.
Nor need ethnographers restrict themselves to a single mode of
questioning. On different occasions, or at different points in the
same interview, the approach may be non-directive or directive,
depending on the function that the questioning is intended to
serve; and this will usually be decided as the interview progresses. In these senses, as we noted earlier, ethnographic interviews are closer in character to conversations than are survey
interviews (Burgess 1984a and 1988b). However, they are never
simply conversations, because the ethnographer has a research
agenda and must retain some control over the proceedings.

This is true even in the case of non-directive questioning.
Here questions are designed as triggers that stimulate the interviewee into talking about a particular broad area:

> Ordinarily, the questions should be of this nature: 'What do
> you hear from business?' (to the congressmen), 'What are they
> worrying you about?' not 'Do you hear from them about the
> tariff?'. Even better may be, 'What people do you hear from
> most?', 'Does anybody pressure you?'. Similarly, not 'How
> about the grants your agency is supposed to get from such-
> and-such a federal department?' but 'In what ways are you
> most affected in your work by national matters...?' and if
> someone starts telling you, as an official of a racing com-
> mission told me, about ex-FBI agents who are employed by
> some national authority, well and good, you have learned to
> redefine the impact of the federal government! A question
> which sharply defines a particular area for discussion is far
> more likely to result in omission of some vital data which
> you, the interviewer, have not even thought of.
>
> (Dexter 1970:55)

Non-directive questions, then, are relatively open-ended,
rather than requiring the interviewee to provide a specific piece

of information or, at the extreme, simply to reply 'yes' or 'no'. However, even here the interview format must be maintained, and this can be a problem where latent identities intrude, as Platt (1981) found in her research on fellow sociologists. Many of the respondents knew of Platt and her work, even if they did not know her personally. As a result, 'personal and community knowledge [was] used as a part of the information available to construct a conception of what the interview [was] meant to be about and thus affected what [was] said' (Platt 1981:77). A particular problem was the tendency of respondents to invite her to draw on her background knowledge rather than spelling out what they were saying. As a result, she sometimes gained responses lacking the explicitness and/or detail necessary to bear her interpretations.

For this reason and others, in non-directive interviewing the interviewer must be an active listener; he or she must listen to what is being said in order to assess how it relates to the research focus and how it may reflect the circumstances of the interview. Moreover, this is done with a view to how the future course of the interview might be shaped. While the aim is often to minimize the influence of the researcher on what the interviewee says, some structuring is necessary in terms of what is and is not relevant. And even where what is said is highly relevant, it may be insufficiently detailed or concrete, or some clarification may be necessary if ambiguity is to be resolved. Whyte (1953) provides an illustration of the non-directive 'steering' of an interview in the questions he puts to Columbus Gary, a union official handling grievances in a steel plant:

WHYTE: I'm trying to catch up on things that have happened since I was last here to study this case. That was back in 1950. I think probably the best thing to start would be if you could give your own impressions as to how things are going now, compared to the past. Do you think things are getting better or worse, or staying about the same? . . .

WHYTE: That's interesting. You mean that it isn't that you don't have problems, but you take them up and talk them over before you write them up, is that it? . . .

WHYTE: That's very interesting. I wonder if you could give me an example of a problem that came up recently, or not so recently, that would illustrate how you handled it sort of informally without writing it down. . . .

WHYTE: That's a good example. I wonder if you could give me a little more detail about the beginning of it. Did Mr. Grosscup first tell you about it? How did you first find out?. . .

WHYTE: I see. He first explained it to you and you went to the people on the job to tell them about it, but then you saw that they didn't understand it?

(Whyte 1953:16–17)

As we indicated, interviewing in ethnography is by no means always non-directive. Often one may wish to test hypotheses arising from the developing analysis and here quite directive and specific questions can be required, though of course one must bear in mind that the answers may be deceptive. Such questions might also be necessary if one suspects that informants have been lying. Nadel, a social anthropologist, reports that

the expression of doubt or disbelief on the part of the interviewer, or the arrangement of interviews with several informants, some of whom, owing to their social position, were certain to produce inaccurate information, easily induced the key informant to disregard his usual reluctance and to speak openly, if only to confound his opponents and critics.

(Nadel 1939:323)

Confrontation of informants with what one already knows is another technique of this kind, as Perlman illustrates from his research in Uganda:

Christian [men] did not like to admit, for example, that they had at one time (or even still had) two or more wives. But in those cases where I had learned the truth from friends, neighbors, or relatives of the interviewee, I would confront him with the fact, although always in a joking manner, by mentioning, for instance, the first name of a former wife. At that point the interviewee – realizing that I knew too much already – usually told me everything for fear that his enemies would tell me even worse things about him. Although he might insist that he had lived with this woman for only six months and that he had hardly counted her as a real wife, he had at least confirmed my information. Later, I checked his story on the length of time, coming back to confront him again and again if necessary. Although I visited most people only once or twice – after first learning as much as possible about them from others – I had to go back to see some of them as many as five times until I was satisfied that all the data were accurate.

(Perlman 1970:307)

Of course, not all interviewees will tolerate such repeated and directive questioning, as Troustine and Christensen (1982:70) note in the course of a study of community elites:

Respondents may be reluctant at first to offer candid views of their peers. . . . Sometimes a respondent will balk at virtually every question, finding it increasingly uncomfortable to share the inside views we are asking him or her to reveal. This won't happen often, but when it does we should be persistent but not belligerent. After all, . . . the respondent could, if he or she is well-connected, make things difficult for us with just a phone call.

(quoted in Hunter 1993:45)

Researchers are often warned to avoid the use of leading questions. While their dangers must be borne in mind, they can be extremely useful in testing hypotheses and trying to penetrate fronts. What is important is to assess the likely direction of bias that the question will introduce. Indeed, a useful tactic is to make the question 'lead' in a direction opposite to that in which one expects the answer to lie, and thus avoid the danger of misleadingly confirming one's expectations – though one must take care that this does not undermine one's identity as a competent participant in the eyes of interviewees.

Directive questioning and non-directive questioning are likely to provide different kinds of data, and thus may be useful at different stages of inquiry. But whatever kinds of questioning are employed, ethnographers must remain aware of the likely effects of their questions on what is, and is not, said by informants. (For useful discussions of different question formats, and of other matters relating to ethnographic interviewing, see Spradley 1979; and Lofland and Lofland 1984:ch.5.)

CONCLUSION

An important source of data for ethnographers is the accounts insiders provide. These may be produced spontaneously or elicited by the researcher. Interviews must be viewed as social events in which the interviewer (and for that matter the interviewee) is a participant observer. In interviews the ethnographer may be able to play a more dominant role than usual, and this can be capitalized upon, both in terms of when and where the interview takes place and who is present, as well as through the kinds of question asked. In this way different types of data can be elicited, as required by the changing demands of the research. While this feature of interviews heightens the danger of reactivity, this is only one aspect of a more general problem that cannot be avoided: the effects of audience and context on what is said and done.

The accounts produced by the people under study must neither be treated as 'valid in their own terms' and thus as beyond assessment and explanation, nor dismissed as epiphenomena or ideological distortions. They can be used both as a source of information about events, and as revealing the perspectives and discursive practices of those who produced them. Moreover, while it may sometimes be important to distinguish between solicited and unsolicited accounts, too much must not be made of this distinction. Rather, all accounts must be examined as social phenomena occurring in, and shaped by, particular contexts. Not only will this add to sociological knowledge directly, it can also throw light on the kind of threats to validity that we may need to consider in assessing the information provided by an account.

In this chapter we have rather assumed that insider accounts take an exclusively oral form. While this may be true in non-literate societies, for many settings written documents are an important source of data, as we shall see in the next chapter.

Chapter 6

Documents

Ethnographic work in its various guises has frequently been employed in the investigation of essentially oral cultures. Be they the non-literate cultures of much social anthropology, or the street cultures and *demi-monde* beloved of many sociological fieldworkers, the social worlds studied by ethnographers have often been devoid of written documents other than those produced by the fieldworkers themselves.

Although it was not the only rationale originally proposed for ethnographic fieldwork as a method, the fact that the 'exotic' societies studied by ethnographers had no written history was given as a major anthropological justification of the method, as well as of the synchronic functionalist analyses that often went with it. Rather than attempt to reconstruct an essentially unknowable past, the anthropologist was inclined to concentrate on the construction of a working version of the present. The anthropologists thus turned their backs on conjectural history. There was, therefore, more than a coincidental relationship between ethnographic methods and the investigation of non-literate cultures. (This is much less true today; indeed, anthropologists have taken a specific interest in literacy: Goody 1968, 1986, and 1987; Street 1984.)

In a rather similar way, many of the settings documented by sociologists of the Chicago School were ephemeral. It is not that they were 'outside' history or part of some timeless 'tradition' (a fiction even in anthropological contexts); rather, they were cultures that lacked conscious attempts to make documentary records of their activities. Whether or not their members were literate, their collective actions rarely depended on the production, distribution, and preservation of written documents and records. The urban cultures of hobos, prostitutes, drug-users, and so on are mostly non-literate in that sense.

It has been emphasized repeatedly that ethnography is a method ideally suited to the study of such non-literate cultures. But it must not be forgotten that many of the settings in which contemporary sociologists and anthropologists work are literate. Not only are their members able to read and write, but that capacity is also an integral feature of their everyday life and work (Smith 1987 and 1993). In many instances, therefore, ethnographers need to take account of documents as part of the social setting under investigation.

In recommending attention to written sources and accounts, in appropriate social settings, we are aware of their historical place in the intellectual tradition of interpretative social science. Research that emanated from the Chicago School, for instance, was sometimes based very heavily on written documents. For example, Thomas and Znaniecki (1927) in *The Polish Peasant in Europe and America* – generally regarded as an early classic of American sociology – relied substantially on written documents, mainly letters but also a life history. Thomas (1967) employed the same approach in *The Unadjusted Girl*. He collected personal documentary accounts, in the belief that 'the unique value of the personal document is its revelation of the situations which have conditioned the behaviour' (1967:42). In both cases what we have is a dense accumulation of personal accounts, which were arranged thematically and juxtaposed in order to draw out the regularities and contrasts in 'definitions of the situation': 'Not only concrete acts are dependent on the definition of the situation, but gradually a whole life-policy and the personality of the individual himself follow from a series of such definitions' (Thomas 1967:42).

In a rather similar vein, the early use of the term 'participant observation' was to designate the generation of documents by participants who might in contemporary parlance be called 'informants'. For instance, in the research that produced *The Gold Coast and the Slum*, Zorbaugh (1929) persuaded people who inhabited the exclusive society of Chicago's 'gold coast' to generate such 'inside' accounts. They were the participant observers as much as Zorbaugh himself.

In a literate culture, then, it is possible to draw on all sorts of 'inside' written accounts – documents produced especially for the purposes of the research and those generated routinely for other purposes. For the most part we find ourselves dealing with the latter variety: there are many contexts in which members of organizations and groups produce written accounts. We shall begin with a discussion of documents as 'secondary' sources for the ethnographer, and then turn our attention to a more detailed examination of the ethnography of settings where the production and use of documents are an integral feature of everyday life.

TYPES OF DOCUMENTARY SOURCE AND THEIR USES

There is, of course, a quite bewildering variety of documentary materials that might be of some relevance to the researcher. They may be ranged along a dimension ranging from the 'informal' to the 'formal' or 'official'. At the informal end of the spectrum there are many 'lay' accounts of everyday life that the enterprising and imaginative researcher can draw on for certain purposes. These include fictional literature, diaries, autobiographies, letters, and mass media products.

There are, for example, numerous categories of persons in contemporary society who publish versions of their own life story:

> More than ever before in history, men of affairs, including politicians, military leaders, and business executives, are intent upon recording their experiences, personal as well as public, for posterity. In recent decades a number of American governmental leaders, including those in the military, have, after resigning from their official posts, published their memories or personal accounts in which they seek public support for causes that the bureaucracy may have rejected during their period of office.
>
> (Sjoberg and Nett 1968:163)

In the decades since that observation, nothing has changed. The output of memoirs continues unabated.

There are, too, a fair number of first-hand accounts published by less eminent folk, including those drawn from the criminal underworld, and the realms of sports and entertainment. Similar personal accounts can be found in newspapers and magazines, or can be culled from radio and television documentaries and chat-shows, for example. We have an increasing number of personal accounts by or about leading scientists, musicians, and artists to add to the list of contemporary social types represented in published accounts.

Of course, such biographical and autobiographical accounts will rarely, if ever, be those of the actual people we study at first hand. They can, nevertheless prove valuable resources for the ethnographer. They can be a source of 'sensitizing concepts' (Blumer 1954): they can suggest distinctive ways in which their authors, or the people reported in them, organize their experiences, the sorts of imagery and 'situated vocabularies' (Mills 1940) they employ, the routine events, and the troubles and reactions, they encounter. Read in this light, they can be used to suggest potential lines of inquiry and 'foreshadowed problems'.

Documents of this sort have rather particular characteristics. Authors will have interests in presenting themselves in a (usually) favourable light; they may have axes to grind, scores to settle, or excuses and justifications to make. They are often written with the benefit of hindsight, and are thus subject to the usual problems of long-term recall. Authors have a sense of audience that will lead them to put particular glosses on their accounts. For some purposes, such considerations must be treated as potential sources of 'bias' in accounts of this sort. But the sources of 'bias' are, looked at from another perspective, data in themselves. As we noted in the previous chapter, as important as the 'accuracy' or 'objectivity' of an account is what it reveals about the teller's interests, perspectives, and presuppositions.

Such accounts can be used, with appropriate caution, for comparative purposes. They can furnish information (albeit partial and personal) on groups and settings that are not available for first-hand observation. As a general category of data, biographical and autobiographical sources are subject to a further sort of 'bias' in that they tend to over-represent the powerful, the famous, the extraordinary, and the articulate. But even that can also be a strength since it is precisely such social categories that are often difficult to research directly.

In recent years there has been a considerable resurgence of interest in the sociological analysis of biographical or autobiographical accounts. While that interest goes well beyond the scope of ethnographic research, ethnographers can incorporate many of the insights from this research field. The growth in scholarly interest reflects a renewed emphasis on narrative forms, temporality, and memory. It reflects too a focus on the intersection of the 'personal' and the 'social' (Erben 1993). As Stanley summarizes some of these concerns:

> I see a concern with biography and autobiography as funda-
> mental to sociology, because I perceive the grounds of their
> sociological interest lying within the epistemological problem-
> atics concerning how we understand 'the self' and 'a life',
> how we 'describe' ourselves and other people and events, how
> we justify the knowledge-claims we make in the name of
> the discipline, in particular through the processes of textual
> production.
>
> (Stanley 1993:50)

These sociological perspectives on 'lives' and 'documents' also often reflect commitments to a feminist standpoint. Documen- tary sources may be drawn on to recuperate the otherwise muted voices of women and other dominated groups, and fem- inst scholarship affirms the intersection of the personal and the social (Stanley 1992; Evans 1993).

In the collection and investigation of 'informal' documentary materials, the fictional – even the most popular and ephemeral – can be used profitably. The most banal ('pulp' or 'pot-boiler') fiction is often replete with images, stereotypes, and myths bear- ing on a vast range of social domains. Indeed, the lack of literary merit characteristic of such genres reflects the fact that it unques- tioningly trades on stocks of common knowledge and conven- tional wisdom. Here too, then, we can become sensitized to cultural themes pertaining to sex, gender, family, work, success, failure, class, mobility, regional variations, religious beliefs, political commitments, health and illness, the law, crime, social control, etc. These are not necessarily to be read at face value, as accurate representations of social reality, but can suggest themes, images, or metaphors. This is no less true of more 'serious' fiction: novels can suggest different ways of organizing experience, and alternative thematic models. We need not shy away from the careful use of literary sources. As various authors have pointed out, there is a long and complex set of relation- ships between literature and the social sciences (for example, Lepenies 1988; Cappetti 1993). And, as F. Davis (1974) notes, ethnographers and novelists alike find themselves telling 'stories'. (See Chapter 9 for further discussion of parallels between ethnography and literary analysis.)

The goal of comparative analysis, referred to earlier, is also a major use for published sources of a more 'formal' nature, including other published ethnographies. The development of generic concepts demands a broad and eclectic reading of textual sources (formal and informal, factual and fictional) on differing substantive topics. It is, however, important not to start searching out documentary sources only when 'writing up'. Wide and comparative reading should inform the generation of concepts throughout the research process. By and large sociologists and anthropologists are not conspicuously good at this. The textual variety of an Erving Goffman is a rare accomplishment.

There is every reason for the sociologist interested in, say, hospitals or clinics to examine works on a variety of other institutional settings – schools, courts, welfare agencies, religious houses, police stations, university departments, or emergency services, for example. The precise selection of settings, and the lessons drawn from them, will depend on the analytic themes being pursued. Through such comparisons one might trace the variety of 'degradation ceremonies', the conditions of 'information control', or the moral evaluation of 'clients'. There is, in principle, no limit to such comparative work, and no prescriptions can be offered. The part played by serendipitous discoveries and unpredicted insights will be considerable here, as in all creative work. One must establish the right conditions for serendipity, however, and that includes attention to sources of many sorts. As Glaser and Strauss remark with characteristic enthusiasm:

> theorizing begs of comparative analysis. The library offers a fantastic range of comparison groups, if only the researchers have the ingenuity to discover them. Of course, if their interest lies mainly with specific groups, and they wish to explore them in great depth, they may not always find sufficient documentation bearing on them. But if they are interested in generating theory, the library can be immensely useful – especially . . . for generating formal theory. Regardless of which type of theory the theorist is especially interested in, if he browses intelligently through the library (even without

much initial direction), he cannot help but have his theorizing impulses aroused by the happily bewildering, crazy-quilt pattern of social groups who speak to him.

(Glaser and Strauss 1967:179)

As in Goffman's work on topics like 'total institutions' (Goffman 1961), the imaginative use of secondary documentary sources allows for the elaboration of 'perspective by incongruity' (Burke 1964; Lofland 1980; Manning 1980): that is, the juxtaposition of instances and categories that are normally thought of as mutually exclusive. Such sources and devices are ideal for heuristic purposes: they can rejuvenate jaded imaginations and spark off novel conceptualizations. In his or her imagination the researcher is free to wander at large among diverse social scenes, gathering ideas, insights, hypotheses, and metaphors.

In addition to the sorts of documentary source we have referred to, in a literate culture it is possible to emulate researchers like Zorbaugh and draw on the ability of informants to generate written accounts specifically for research purposes. By such means one can gather information that complements other data sources in the field. Some versions of research have indeed drawn extensively on such indigenous written accounts. The entire tradition of 'mass observation' in Britain rested on the ability of literate volunteers to produce 'native' accounts of everyday life around them. The revival of the Mass Observation archive has again depended on such written documents:

The writing has been generated in response to a call from the Mass-Observation Archive, repeated at intervals over the years, for people to take part in a form of collective autobiography. No special skills, knowledge or qualifications are required, only an enjoyment of writing and a willingness to put thoughts and experiences on paper in a discursive way.

(Sheridan 1993:27)

This emphasis on the collection of demotic accounts, characteristic of Mass Observation, is but one version of wide possibilities for the collection of documentary evidence. The collection of diaries of different types is often an important adjunct to fieldwork. This strategy is advocated by Zimmerman and Wieder (1977), who used a diary technique in their study of counter-cultural life-styles. They comment that while they were committed to participant observation, there were settings and activities that remained hard for them to observe directly. They therefore recruited insider informants, who kept detailed diaries over seven-day periods. Subsequently, the researchers subjected each informant to a lengthy and detailed interview, based on the diaries, 'in which he or she was asked not only to expand the reportage, but also was questioned on the less directly observable features of the events recorded, on their meanings, their propriety, typicality, connection with other events and so on' (1977:484).

Solicited accounts, such as diaries, are especially useful ways of eliciting information about the personal and the private. When carefully managed, and with suitable co-operation from informants, the diary can be used to record data that might not be forthcoming in face-to-face interviews or other data collection encounters. Sexual behaviour is one obvious example. For instance, one major study among gay males made extensive use of personal diaries in order to obtain information on the types and frequencies of sexual practices (Coxon 1988).

Similarly, Davies used personal diaries in her study of student midwives (Davies and Atkinson 1991). Her research shows some of the anxieties and coping strategies associated with status passage, as experienced nurses became novice midwives. It is noticeable from the responses Davies obtained that the students were able to use the research diaries as a kind of personal confessional, often addressing the researcher directly about private anxieties, sources of anger, and frustrations. These personal accounts were complemented by interviews and observations.

Diaries of this sort can also be used to pick up the minutiae of day-to-day social action. Robinson (1971), in the course of an investigation of the experience of illness, persuaded a series of married women in South Wales to keep a diary on the health status of the members of their household. The diaries were kept over a four-week period. They enabled Robinson to gain some insight into the daily symptomatic episodes and health-related decisions characteristic of everyday living. Many of the episodes reported were minor, though by no means insignificant, and could easily have been overlooked in retrospective accounts from, say, interviews or questionnaires.

This sort of procedure has been drawn on widely in work on

educational settings. Ball (1981), for instance, used diaries in combination with a range of other techniques, including sociometric questionnaires on friendship choices. He explicitly notes the value of combining such data sources:

> The sociometric questionnaires failed to pick up the casual friendships that existed between pupils outside school, and made it appear that they had no such contact. In addition, they failed to pick up the cross-sex friendships that were established at this time. Perhaps the notion of 'friendships' is too narrow and ill-defined to account for these other kinds of adolescent relationships. . . . The entries in the diaries that several of the pupils wrote for me did, however, refer to these contacts.
>
> (Ball 1981:100)

Research-generated personal documents of this sort embody the strengths and weaknesses of all such personal accounts. They are partial, and reflect the interests and perspectives of their authors. They are not to be privileged over other sources of information, nor are they to be discounted. Like other accounts, they should be read with regard to the context of their production, their intended or implied audiences, and the author's interests. Equally, one must note that a written account is not a debased version. Given the historical and intellectual roots of ethnographic work, one can often detect a romantic legacy that privileges the oral over the literate. It is easy (but wrong) to assume that the spoken account is more 'authentic' or more 'spontaneous' than the written.

We have discussed a range of documentary sources, but we have not yet paid attention to the investigation of social activities that directly involve the production of documents. Fieldwork in literate societies – especially in formal organizations – is likely to encompass the production and use of documents of various sorts. In the following section we turn to such activities and their documentary products.

DOCUMENTS IN CONTEXT

In some settings it would be hard to conceive of anything approaching an ethnographic account without some attention to documentary material in use. For instance, in his study of locomotive engineers, Gamst drew on a range of documentary sources:

> Some documents are published, for example: rule books, timetables, technical manuals for use of equipment, and instructional, regulating, and investigating publications of many kinds used by railroads, trade unions, government, and other firms. Unpublished documents include: official correspondence, reports in mimeographed and other forms, railroad operating bulletins and circulars, train orders, operating messages, and sundry other items.
>
> (Gamst 1980:viii)

Whether or not one would draw on all such sources, one would certainly expect an ethnography of work on the railway to make full reference to such features as operating schedules and timetables (whatever disgruntled passengers might feel). A similar instance is provided by Zerubavel (1979) in his formal analysis of time in hospitals; he necessarily draws on such sources as timetables, work rosters and clinical rotations, as embodied in organizational documents. In many organizational settings the use and production of such documents are an integral part of everyday life.

Similarly, the ethnographic study of scientific work – especially the genre of 'laboratory studies' – cannot proceed adequately without acknowledgement of the work of writing. For instance, Latour and Woolgar (1979), in their classic study of a biomedical laboratory, document the centrality of written outputs. The scientific laboratory is fundamentally preoccupied with what they call 'inscriptions': that is, representations of natural phenomena, and the texts that are the products of the laboratory. Scientific papers are the currency that circulates within and between scientific research groups. One cannot address the complex social realities of scientific work and the production of scientific knowledge without paying serious attention to how and why scientific papers are written. The sociology of scientific knowledge is now replete with studies of written texts and other forms of representation (for example, Lynch and Woolgar 1990). And the same approach may be extended to all organizational and professional settings.

Douglas, writing in 1967, commented on the importance of 'official' data and enumerations in contemporary society, while simultaneously regretting a relative neglect of such topics by sociological commentators:

> Throughout the Western world today there exists a general belief that one knows something only when it has been counted. . . . Considering the importance of such statistics for the formation and testing of all kinds of common-sense and scientific theories of human action, it is a remarkable fact that there is at present very little systematic knowledge of the functioning of official statistics-keeping organizations.
>
> (Douglas 1967:163)

Since Douglas made those observations, there has been an increasing amount of work along the lines suggested. However, in comparison with the sheer volume of 'literate' record-keeping and documentation in contemporary society, the coverage remains at best patchy. There is still, apparently, a tacit assumption that ethnographic research can appropriately represent contemporary social worlds as essentially oral cultures. Many studies of medical settings, for instance, focus exclusively on spoken interaction between medical practitioners and their patients, or between health professionals, with relatively little attention to activities of reading and writing. As Rees remarks: 'Both medicine and medical sociology have to a large extent neglected the record. Indeed, so rarely is it mentioned that one could be forgiven for thinking that medicine is a purely oral discipline' (Rees 1981:55).

Pettinari (1988) demonstrates the value of close attention to 'writing' in a medical setting. Here is provided a detailed account of how surgeons write their reports on operations, and in particular of how junior surgeons learn such occupational skills. There are ways in which the operation is represented competently in surgeons' reports, and the appropriate forms are acquired over time with professional experience. The written account is a fundamental element in the everyday organization of surgical work. Its production and use are an important focus for an ethnographic account of surgery in general.

In a similar vein is Coffey's ethnography of accountants in training (Coffey 1993). Based on fieldwork in an office of an international accounting firm, Coffey documents aspects of trainees' acquisition of accountancy expertise. She studied bookkeeping skills together with the trainees, and describes how they acquired skill and judgment in reading documentary sources such as balance sheets. It would clearly be absurd to represent the world of the corporate accountant as non-literate – and indeed, as non-numerate – and a comprehensive ethnographic account must include reference to how organizational documents are read, interpreted, and used.

Because of the critique of 'official statistics' stemming largely from the ethnomethodological movement, some contemporary ethnographers may feel reluctant to engage in the systematic investigation or use of documentary data. We believe that they are right to treat seriously objections against 'official' data in that context, but that they would be wrong to ignore such materials. The point of departure for critics of 'data from official sources' was the contention that, traditionally, the tendency had been for sociologists to treat such information at face value, and not to pay adequate attention to its character as a social product.

It is, of course, a long-standing concern of sociologists that data derived from official sources may be inadequate in some way: that they may be subject to bias or distortion, or that bureaucracies' practical concerns may mean that data are not formulated in accordance with sociologists' interests. The ethnomethodologists, on the other hand, proposed more radical problems. Cicourel remarks, for instance:

> For years sociologists have complained about 'bad statistics and distorted bureaucratic record-keeping' but have not made the procedures producing the 'bad' materials we label 'data' a subject of study. The basic assumption of conventional research on crime, delinquency and law is to view compliance and deviance as having their own ontological significance, and the measuring rod is some set of presumably 'clear' rules whose meaning is also 'ontological and epistemologically clear'.
>
> (Cicourel 1976:331)

The argument is that rather than being viewed as more or less biased sources of data, official documents and enumerations should be treated as social products: they must be examined, not relied on uncritically as a research resource.

In this way attention is diverted towards the investigation of the socially organized practices whereby 'rates', categories, and statistics are produced by those whose job it is to generate and interpret such artefacts. An early example of work in this vein was that of Sudnow (1965) on the production of 'normal crimes' in a Public Defender's office. Sudnow details the practical reasoning that informs how particular crimes or misdemeanours become categorized in the course of organized activities such as plea bargaining. Thus, Sudnow looks 'behind' the categories of official designations and crime rates – based on convictions – to the work of interpretation and negotiation that generates such statistics. In addition to Sudnow's ethnographic study of crime rates, other studies of the same period included those of Cicourel (1967) on juvenile justice, and of Cicourel and Kitsuse (1963) on the organization of educational decision-making, the categorization of students, and their official biographies. More recent research in a similar vein includes a welter of constructionist accounts of social problems (see, for example, Holstein and Miller 1989). Similar in focus is Prior's study of the organization of death, with particular emphasis on the classification of causes of death (Prior 1985). In that context one should also note the observations of Prior and Bloor (1993) on the life-table as a cultural and historical artefact.

The origins of the 'official statistics' debate in sociology were potentially misleading, important though the general perspective was. Issues became polarized quite unnecessarily. The problems associated with data from official sources were important, and they related directly to classic problems of sociological analysis, such as the explanation of suicide (Douglas 1967; Atkinson 1978); but they were by no means unique. The careful ethnographer will be aware that all classes of data have their problems, all are produced socially, and none can be treated as unproblematically neutral or transparent representations of 'reality'. The recognition of reflexivity in social research entails such an awareness (Holstein and Miller 1993). As a result, there is no logical reason to regard documents or similar information as especially problematic or totally vitiated. As Bulmer remarks in this context:

Firstly, there is no logical reason why awareness of possible serious sources of error in official data should lead to their rejection for research purposes. It could as well point to the need for methodological work to secure their improvement. Secondly, a great many of the more thorough-going critiques of offical statistics relate to statistics of suicide, crime, and delinquency, areas in which there are special problems of reliable and valid measurement, notoriously so. The specific problems encountered in these fields are not, *ipso facto*, generalizable to all official statistics whatever their content. Thirdly, cases of the extensive use of official data – for example, by demographers – do not suggest that those who use them are unaware of the possible pitfalls in doing so. The world is not made up just of knowledgeable sceptics and naive hard-line positivists.

(Bulmer 1980:508)

In other words, then, while drawing some inspiration from the ethnomethodological critique of 'official statistics' and similar documentary sources, we by no means endorse a radical view which suggests that such sources are of no value. Data of this sort raise problems, to be sure, but they provide information as well as opening up a range of analytic problems. The ethnographer, like any other social scientist, may well draw on such documents and representations. Furthermore, he or she may be particularly well placed to engage in principled and systematic research bearing on their validity and reliability as data, through first-hand investigation of the contexts of their production and use.

Woods (1979) provides a good example of such an approach in his analysis of school reports. In writing these reports, Woods suggests, teachers draw on 'professional', 'educationist' conceptions of their task, rather than on the negotiated 'survival' ethos of everyday classroom life. Here models of the ideal student are reproduced, and teachers express their 'expert' evaluations of students' activities, motivation, and behaviour. The writing of such apparently authoritative accounts helps to 'cultivate the impression of detachment and omniscience, such as is attributed to the professions' (1979:185). Woods cites a number of striking examples where ideals of behaviour are announced in reports. For instance, the following clearly illustrate the teachers' appeals to norms of appropriate conduct for girls:

Apart from French and music, Sara's report is below standard for a 3rd year, 2nd term, pupil. Her slovenly ways, moodiness and inelegant speech are reflected in her work.

She is a cheerful girl who is rather boisterous, at times too much so. We must in this final year try to turn her into a quieter young lady.

Tends to make her presence heard forcibly and often uses rather strong language. I feel that if she can be made to see that this is not the behaviour we expect from young ladies, it will be to her advantage.

(Woods 1979:188)

Woods abstracts a number of typical categories that were used by teachers in formulating such normative characterizations:

Desirable	*Undesirable*
Concentration	Easily distracted
Quiet	Chatterbox
Industrious	Lazy
Willing/co-operative	Uncooperative
Responsible, mature	Immature
Courteous	Bad-mannered
Cheerful	Sullen
Obedient	Disobedient

(Woods 1979:173)

In many ways, as Woods points out, such typifications resemble those used by teachers in other contexts (such as staff-room conversations). It is important, however, to resist any temptation to condense all these different usages into a single category of 'teacher stereotypes'. In their differing social contexts, they may be formulated in different ways, for different practical purposes. The audiences for such statements differ, and their rhetoric may do the same accordingly.

Woods also touches on the fact that record-making can provide for the concrete display of 'professional' competence; such documents vouch for the fact that the work that should have been done has indeed been done, and renders that work accountable to superiors. Rees, in his work on medical records, makes the same point:

What the House Officer writes, and the way in which he goes about constructing the history and examination, is one way his seniors can make inferences about the standard of his other activities. The supposition others make is that a House

Officer who writes an organized and clearly thought out account of his work will be well organized in the way he carries out those activities. By paying attention to the construction of the account, and by ensuring that it conforms to the accepted model, the House Officer is able to influence one of the ways in which he will be judged by his seniors.

(Rees 1981:58–9)

This reflects Garfinkel's remarks on records, where he suggests that they should be thought of as 'contractual' rather than as 'actuarial'. That is, they are not literal accounts of 'what happened' but are tokens of the fact that the relevant personnel went about their business competently and reasonably. This is something taken up by Dingwall (1977b) in his study of the education of health visitors. He writes about the students' production of records of their visits to clients, and notes that since the actual conduct of the work is invisible to the supervisor, the record is the main focus of administrative control. Likewise, the record constitutes a major means of self-defence for the 'face-workers'.

In various ways, then, records have considerable importance in certain social settings. In some, the production of 'paperwork' is a major preoccupation. Even in organizations that have people-processing functions, this usually involves the translation of events into records of those events which can be filed, stored, and manipulated. Such files are a primary resource for members of the organization in getting through their everyday work. Often, the exigencies of record-making can play an important part in organizing the work that gets done, and the routines used to accomplish it. Records of previous encounters with clients can be used to formulate appropriate objectives and activities for a current consultation. As Dingwall writes of his student health visitors:

The good health visitor can derive sufficient data from the face sheet to identify the relevant areas of her knowledge about clients and the tasks she should be accomplishing in a visit. Unusual events are flagged in various ways. Thus, a child who is at risk may be marked by a red star on the card. Particular social problems may be pencilled on the cover.

(Dingwall 1977b:112)

Heath (1981) has also commented on this sort of use of medical records in the context of doctor-patient encounters. He explains how general practitioners use their record cards to open the encounter with the patient: 'It is often through the elaboration of the appropriate record's contents, prior to the initiation of first topic, that the doctor is able to render the relevant characteristics of the patient, and thereby design a "successful" first topic initiator' (1981:85).

Records, then, are used to establish actors as 'cases' with situated identities, which conform to 'normal' categories or deviate from them in identifiable ways. Records are made and used in accordance with organizational routines, and depend for their intelligibility on shared cultural assumptions. Records construct a 'documentary reality' that, by virtue of its very documentation, is often granted a sort of privilege. Although their production is a socially organized activity, official records have a certain anonymity, which warrants their treatment by members as objective, factual statements rather than as mere personal belief, opinion, or guesswork. (It is, of course, the case that some records may contain specific entries, such as differential medical or psychiatric diagnoses, that are explicitly flagged as tentative.)

It should be apparent from what we have outlined already that there are many locales where literate social activity is of some social significance, and may indeed be of major importance. Modern industrial and administrative bureaucracies, and professional or educational settings, are obvious cases in point. It requires little reflection to remind oneself of how pervasive are the activities of writing and reading written documents. And even in the case of settings where documents are not a central feature there is often an enormous amount of written material available that can be an invaluable research resource.

The presence and significance of documentary products provide the ethnographer with a rich vein of analytic topics, as well as a valuable source of information. Such topics include: How are documents written? How are they read? Who writes them? Who reads them? For what purposes? On what occasions? With what outcomes? What is recorded? What is omitted? What does the writer seem to take for granted about the reader(s)? What do readers need to know in order to make sense of them? The list can be extended readily, and the exploration of such questions would lead the ethnographer inexorably towards a systematic examination of each and every aspect of everyday life in the setting in question.

The ethnographer who takes no account of such matters, on the other hand, ignores at his or her peril these features of a literate culture. There is nothing to be gained, and much to be lost, by representing such a culture as if it were an essentially oral tradition. In the scrutiny of documentary sources, the ethnographer thus recognizes and builds on his or her socialized competence as a member of a literate culture. Not only does the researcher read and write, but he or she also reflects on the very activities of reading and writing in social settings. Thus, such everyday activities are incorporated into the ethnographer's topics of inquiry as well as furnishing analytic and interpretative resources.

Chapter 7

Recording and organizing data

FIELDNOTES

Fieldnotes are the traditional means in ethnography for recording observational data. In accordance with the ethnographer's commitment to discovery, fieldnotes consist of relatively concrete descriptions of social processes and their contexts. The aim is to capture these in their integrity, noting their various features and properties, though what is recorded will clearly depend on some general sense of what is relevant to the foreshadowed research problems. While it is impossible to provide any description without some principle of selecting what is and is not important, there are advantages (as well as some disadvantages) in adopting a wide focus. At least prior to the closing stages of data collection, then, there is usually no attempt at the point of observation to code systematically what is observed in terms of existing analytical categories. Indeed, the main purpose is to *identify* and *develop* what seem to be the most appropriate categories.

The writing of fieldnotes is not something that is (or should be) shrouded in mystery. It is not an especially esoteric activity. On the other hand, it does constitute a central research activity, and it should be carried out with as much care and self-conscious awareness as possible. A research project can be as well organized and as theoretically sophisticated as you like, but with inadequate note-taking the exercise will be like using an expensive camera with poor-quality film. In both cases, the resolution will prove unsatisfactory, and the results will be poor. Only foggy pictures result.

The completion of fieldnotes is not an entirely straightforward matter, then. Like most aspects of intellectual craft, some care and attention to detail are prerequisites: satisfactory note-taking needs to be worked at. It is a skill demanding repeated assessment of purposes and priorities, and of the costs and benefits of different strategies. Thus, the standard injunction, 'write down what you see and hear', glosses over a number of important issues. Among other things, the fieldworker will want to ask *what* to write down, *how* to write it down, and *when* to write it down.

The problems facing the novice ethnographer on this score stem in part from the relative invisibility of fieldnotes themselves. As is pointed out by various contributors to an edited collection on the topic (Sanjek 1990), anthropological fieldnotes have often been regarded as highly personal and private documents. Although fieldnotes are the basis of public-domain scholarship, their authors have rarely shared them with other scholars. For anthropologists, in particular, fieldnotes seem to be treated as almost 'sacred' objects (Jackson 1990). They certainly appear to be granted special – almost magical – potency. They have the power to evoke the times and places of the 'field', and call to mind the sights, sounds, and smells of 'elsewhere', when read and reread 'at home'.

At a mundane and practical level, the privacy of fieldnotes means that the novice rarely has models to follow, and there is remarkably little explicit advice available. The making of fieldnotes has been part of the invisible oral tradition of craft knowledge, and many who embark on their first project have to find their own way of doing things. So let us try to deal with some of the practical questions raised above. First, when to write notes? In principle, one should aim to make notes as soon as possible after the observed action. Most fieldworkers report that while they can train themselves to improve recall, the quality of their notes diminishes rapidly with the passage of time; the detail is quickly lost, and whole episodes can be forgotten or become irreparably muddled. The ideal would be to make notes during actual participant observation. But that is not always possible, and even when it is possible the opportunities may be very limited. There may be restrictions arising from the social characteristics of the research setting, as well as from the ethnographer's own social position(s).

If the research is covert, then note-taking in the course of participation will often be practically impossible. In most settings, participants are not visibly engaged in a continual process of jotting down notes, seizing notebooks during conversations, and similar activities. In many circumstances, such activity would prove totally disruptive to any 'natural' participation. It is hard to think of Laud Humphreys (1970), for example, taking copious notes while acting as 'watchqueen' in public lavatories so as to observe casual homosexual encounters. In a few contexts, of course, writing may be such an unremarkable activity that covert note-taking is possible. In a covert study of students' time-wasting strategies in a university library, spasmodic writing on the part of the ethnographer would be possible, though care might have to be taken not to appear too diligent. Perhaps surprisingly, observers in a covert study of patient life in mental hospitals found that they could take notes, since staff simply took this as a further sign of their mental illness (Rosenhahn 1973)!

However, overt research does not solve the problem of note-taking. To some extent our comments concerning covert participation apply here as well. The conduct of note-taking must be broadly congruent with the social setting under scrutiny. In some contexts, however 'well socialized' the hosts, open and continuous note-taking will be perceived as inappropriate or threatening, and will prove disruptive. In other contexts fairly extensive notes can be recorded without undue disruption. Thus, for example, Whyte (1981) reports how he took on the role of secretary to the Italian Community Club because it enabled him to take notes unobtrusively in their meetings.

Even in situations where note-taking is a 'normal' kind of activity, such as in educational settings, however, care must be exercised if disruption is to be avoided. Olesen and Whittaker's research on student nurses is a case in point:

> I feel it much easier to write when the students write, and listen when they do; I have noticed that when I attempt to write when the students are not, I attract [the tutor's] attention and on a few occasions she seems to falter in what she is saying ... Similarly when all the students are writing and I am not, but rather looking at her, I again seem to 'put her off'. And so it is that I've become a student, sometimes slightly at the loss of my self-esteem when I find myself lazily inserting a pencil in my mouth. (Fieldnotes: February, third year.)
>
> (Olesen and Whittaker 1968:28)

Many of the initial fieldnotes that ethnographers take, then, are jottings, snatched in the course of observed action. A common joke about ethnographers relates to their frequent trips to the lavatory where such hasty notes can be scribbled in private. Even the briefest of notes can be valuable aids in the construction of a more detailed account. As Schatzman and Strauss suggest: 'A single word, even one merely descriptive of the dress of a person, or a particular word uttered by someone usually is enough to "trip off" a string of images that afford substantial reconstruction of the observed scene' (Schatzman and Strauss 1973:95). Moreover, it is important to record even things that one does not immediately understand, because these might turn out to be important later.

Even if it proves possible to make fairly extensive notes in the field, they – like brief jottings – will need to be worked up, expanded on, and developed. Many social activities have a timetable of their own, and it may prove possible to match phases of observation with periods of writing up fieldnotes in accordance with such timetables. For instance, recent fieldwork by Atkinson on haematologists in American and British hospitals was structured round regular schedules of clinical 'rounds', 'grand rounds', 'conferences', 'mortality and morbidity reviews', and similar occasions for medical talk. The pattern of data collection was fitted into the rhythm of the hospital (cf. Zerubavel 1979), which allowed for periods of time in the canteen or the library, or back at the university, or at home, when detailed notes could be constructed.

In other settings, the phasing of observation and writing will be much less straightforward to organize, but there are usually times when participants are engaged in activities that are not relevant to the research. At the very least they sleep at regular times and at the risk of fatigue notes can be written up then. Carey (1972) reports a rare exception, that of 'speed freaks' (amphetamine users) who, under heavy doses, stay awake for several days in a hyperactive state:

The peculiar round of life wherein people stay up for three, four or five days at a time and then sleep for several days posed enormous practical difficulties for the research. Our conventional commitments (family, friends, teaching responsibilities) had to be put aside for a time so that we could adapt ourselves more realistically to this youthful scene. As we became more familiar with this particular universe, we developed a crude sampling plan that called for observations at a number of different gathering spots, and this relieved us somewhat from a very exacting round of life. If we were interested, however, in what happened during the course of a run when a small group of people started shooting speed intravenously, it meant that one or two fieldworkers had to be present at the beginning and be relieved periodically by other members of the team until the run was over. Fatigue was a constant problem and suggests that more than one fieldworker is required in this type of research.

(Carey 1972:82)

Clearly, in such cases, finding time to write up fieldnotes poses particularly severe problems. The problem remains serious, however, even with less exhausting schedules. But some time for writing up fieldnotes must always be set aside. There is no advantage in observing social action over extended periods if inadequate time is allowed for the preparation of notes. The information will quickly trickle away, and the effort will be wasted. There is always the temptation to try to observe everything, and the consequent fear that in withdrawing from the field one will miss some vital incident. Understandable though such feelings are, they must, in most circumstances, be suppressed in the interests of producing good-quality notes. Nevertheless, the trade-off between data collection and data recording must be recognized and resolved, in accordance with the overall research strategy and purpose. Thus, for example, the organization of periods of observation, with alternating periods of writing and other work, must be done with a view to the systematic sampling of action and actors (see Chapter 2).

It is difficult to overemphasize the importance of meticulous note-taking. The memory should never be relied on entirely, and a good maxim is 'if in doubt, write it down'. It is absolutely essential that one keep up to date in processing notes. Without the discipline of daily writing, the observations will fade from memory, and the ethnography will all too easily become incoherent and muddled.

What of the form and content of fieldnotes? One can never

record everything; social scenes are truly inexhaustible in this sense. Some selection has to be made. However, the nature of this is likely to change over time. During the early days of a research project, the scope of the notes is likely to be fairly wide, and one will probably be reluctant to emphasize any particular aspects. Indeed, one will probably not be in a position to make such a selection of topics. As the research progresses, and emergent issues are identified, the notes will become more restricted in subject matter. Moreover, features that previously seemed insignificant may come to take on new meaning, a point that Johnson illustrates from his research on social workers:

> Gradually I began to 'hear different things said' in the setting. This happened through a shift in attention from *what* was said or done to how it was said or done. The following excerpts from the fieldnotes illustrate several instances of my changing awareness. From the notes near the end of the sixth month of the observations:
>
> > Another thing that happened today. I was standing by Bill's desk when Art passed by and asked Bill to cover the phone for a couple of minutes while he walked through a request for County Supp over to Bess Lanston, an EW supervisor. Now I don't know how many times I've heard a comment like that; so many times that it's not even problematic any more. In fact, it's so routine that I'm surprised that I even made a note to remember it. The striking feature about this is that in my first days at Metro [the social work agency] I would have wanted to know all about what kind of form he was taking over there, what County Supp was, why and how one used it, got it, didn't get it, or whatever, who and where Bess Lanston was, what she did and so on. But all the time I've missed what was crucial about such a comment, the fact that he was walking it through. Before I would have only heard what he was doing or why, but today, instead, I began to hear the how.
>
> (Johnson 1975:197)

As analytical ideas develop and change, what is 'significant' and what must be included in the fieldnotes also changes. Over time, notes may also change in character, in particular becoming more concrete and detailed. Indeed, the preservation of concreteness is an important consideration in fieldnote writing. For most analytic purposes, compressed summary accounts will prove inadequate for the detailed and systematic comparison or aggregation of information across contexts or across occasions. As far as possible, therefore, speech should be rendered in a manner that approximates to a verbatim report and represents non-verbal behaviour in relatively concrete terms; this minimizes the level of inference and thus facilitates the construction and reconstruction of the analysis.

Below we reproduce two extracts from notes that purport to recapture the same interaction, taken from a study of the staff-room talk of secondary school teachers (Hammersley 1980). They are recognizably 'about' the same people and the same events. Neither lays any claim to completeness. The first obviously compresses things to an extreme extent, and the second summarizes some things, and explicitly acknowledges that some parts of the conversation are missing altogether:

1 The teacher told his colleagues in the staffroom about the wonders of a progressive school he had been to visit the day before. He was attacked from all sides. As I walked up with him to his classroom he continued talking of how the behaviour of the pupils at X had been marvellous. We reached his room. I waited outside, having decided to watch what happened in the hall in the build-up to the morning assembly. He went into his classroom and immediately began shouting at his class. He was taking it out on them for not being like the pupils at X.

2 (Walker gives an enthusiastic account of X to his colleagues in the staffroom. There is an aggressive reaction.)

GREAVES: Projects are not education, just cutting out things.

WALKER: Oh no, they don't allow that, there's a strict check on progress.

HOLTON: The more I hear of this the more wishy washy it sounds.

. . .

WALKER: There's a craft resources area and pupils go and do some dress-making or woodwork when they want to, when it fits into their project.

HOLTON: You need six weeks' basic teaching in woodwork or metalwork.

. . .

HOLTON: How can an immature child of that age do a project?

WALKER: Those children were self-controlled and well-behaved.

. . .

HOLTON: Sounds like Utopia.

DIXON: Gimmicky.

. . .

WALKER: There's no vandalism. They've had the books four years and they've been used a lot and I could see the pupils were using them, but they looked new, the teacher told me that if they damaged the books she would have to replace them herself.

. . .

HOLTON: Sounds like those kids don't need teaching.

((Walker and I go up to his room: he continues his praise for X. When we reach his room I wait outside to watch the hall as the build up for the morning assembly begins. He enters his room and immediately begins shouting. The thought crosses my mind that the contrast between the pupils at X he has been describing and defending to his colleagues and the 'behaviour' of his own pupils may be a reason for his shouting at the class, but, of course, I don't know what was going on in the classroom.))

(( )) = observer descriptions

. . . = omission of parts of conversation in record.

The second version is much more concrete in its treatment of the events; indeed, much of the speech of the actors is preserved. We can inspect the notes with a fair assurance that we are gaining information on how the participants themselves described things, who said what to whom, and so on. When we compress and summarize we not only lose 'interesting' detail and 'local colour', we can lose vital information.

The actual words people use can be of considerable analytic importance. The 'situated vocabularies' employed provide us with valuable information about the ways in which members of a particular culture organize their perceptions of the world, and so engage in the 'social construction of reality'. Situated vocabularies and folk taxonomies incorporate the typifications and recipes for action that constitute the stock-of-knowledge and practical reasoning of the members. Arensberg and Kimball provide an example from their study of interpersonal relations among family members in rural Ireland:

> The relations of the members of the farm family are best described in terms of the patterns which uniformity of habit and association build up. They are built up within the life of the farm household and its daily and yearly work. The relations of the fathers to sons and mothers to sons fall repeatedly into regular and expectable patterns of this kind that differ very little from farm to farm.
>
> If we are to understand them, then, we must trace them out of this setting and see in what manner they offer us explanation of Irish rural behaviour. In terms of a formal sociology, such as Simmel might give us, the position of the parents is one of extreme superordination, that of the children of extreme subordination. The retention of the names 'boy' and 'girl' reflects the latter position. Sociological adulthood has little to do with physiological adulthood. Age brings little change of modes of address and ways of treating and regarding one another in the relationships within the farm family.
>
> (Arensberg and Kimball 1968:59)

The potential significance and detail of the connotations of such members' terms apply equally to the use of argot. American hospital speech includes the term 'gomer', which is part of the rich and colourful vocabulary characteristic of most medical settings. George and Dundes summarize its use:

> What precisely is a 'gomer'? He is typically an older man who is both dirty and debilitated. He has extremely poor personal hygiene and he is often a chronic alcoholic. A derelict or down-and-outer, the gomer is normally on welfare. He has an extensive listing of multiple admissions to the hospital. From the gomer's standpoint, life inside the hospital is so much better than the miserable existence he endures outside that he exerts every effort to gain admission, or rather readmission to the hospital. Moreover, once admitted, the

gomer attempts to remain there as long as possible. Because of the gomer's desire to stay in the hospital he frequently pretends to be ill or he lacks interest in getting well on those occasions when he is really sick.

(George and Dundes 1978:570)

Of course, this brief account glosses over a wide range of uses and connotations associated with this one folk term. In practice, the research worker will not be content to generate such a composite or summary definition. The important task is to be able to document and retrieve the actual contexts of use for such folk terms.

Kondo's ethnography of the production of identities in Japan provides an exemplary documentation of the terms and idioms of identity in various social contexts (Kondo 1990). She examines, for instance, the idiomatic use of *Shitamachi* and *Yamanote*: literally, different parts of Tokyo, used to convey different orientations, life-styles and identities. Likewise, she explores the subtle usages and connotations of *ie* and *uchi*. Both terms have flexible, context-dependent meanings. The former refers to the inter-generational continuity of the group, the latter to the 'in-group' as defined on any particular occasion: 'Depending on the context, it can be any in-group: i.e. company, school, club, or nation . . .' (Kondo 1990:141). The ability to trace the social contexts of such idioms is dependent on the delicacy of one's ethnographic data: usage and social context must be identified with precision.

Making fieldnotes as concrete and descriptive as possible is not without its cost, however. Generally, the more closely this ideal is approximated, the more restricted the scope of the notes. Unless the focus of the research is extremely narrow, some concreteness and detail will have to be sacrificed for increased scope. Whatever the level of concreteness of fieldnotes, however, it is essential that direct quotations are clearly distinguished from summaries in the researcher's words, and that gaps and uncertainties in the record are clearly indicated. If speakers' original words cannot be reconstructed adequately, then indirect speech may be used to indicate the style and content. When we refer back to the notes there should be no ambiguity concerning the 'voices' that are represented. One should not have to puzzle over 'Is that what they themselves said?' The observer's own descriptive glosses should be kept clearly distinct.

It is equally important that records of speech and action should be located in relation to *who* was present, *where*, at what *time*, and under what *circumstances*. When it comes to the analysis stage, when one will be gathering together, categorizing, comparing, and contrasting instances, it may be crucial that 'context' (participants, audience, setting, etc.) can be identified. Spradley suggests one elementary checklist that can be used to guide the making of field records, adherence to which would preserve the sense of context:

1 *Space*: the physical place or places.
2 *Actor*: the people involved.
3 *Activity*: a set of related acts people do.
4 *Object*: the physical things that are present.
5 *Act*: single actions that people do.
6 *Event*: a set of related activities that people carry out.
7 *Time*: the sequencing that takes place over time.
8 *Goal*: the things people are trying to accomplish.
9 *Feeling*: the emotions felt and expressed.

(Spradley 1980:78)

Such lists are very crude and rest on arbitrary classifications. Nevertheless, they indicate a range of relevant features of context that might be noted.

Fieldnotes cannot possibly provide a comprehensive record of the research setting. The ethnographer acquires a great deal more tacit knowledge than is ever contained in the written record. The writer of ethnography uses 'head notes' or memory to fill in and recontextualize recorded events and utterances. One should not become totally wedded to the fieldnotes, as if they were the sum total of available information. Despite the scepticism of some commentators (for example, Agar 1980), however, the collection and maintenence of fieldnotes remain a major method of ethnographic recording.

Up to now, we have discussed fieldnotes in relation to observation, but they may also be used to record data from interviews. Sometimes, interviewees will refuse to allow the discussion to be audio-recorded; sometimes the ethnographer may judge that such recording will dissuade frankness or increase nervousness to an unacceptable level. Where fieldnotes are relied on in interviews, much the same considerations apply as in observation: decisions must be made about what is to be noted, when, and how. Once again reliance will most likely have to be placed on jotted notes, and the dilemma of summarizing versus verbatim reporting is just as acute. Similarly, note-taking in interviews can prove disruptive, much as in the tutorial cited by Olesen and Whittaker (1968), with the interviewee becoming self-conscious about what is being written down. Furthermore, the need to take notes makes very difficult the kind of interviewing we advocated in Chapter 5. Much of the interviewer's attention will be taken up with *recording* what has been said rather than thinking about it, especially as one should be recording not just the informant's responses but also the interviewer's questions.

Given these problems, the advantages of audio-recording of interviews are considerable. While interviewees will sometimes not give permission (because, for example, 'you can't argue with a tape'), agreement is normally forthcoming once it is explained that the purpose is simply to aid note-taking and that confidentiality will be maintained. Moreover, using a portable cassette-recorder may actually reduce reactivity rather than increase it. When the recorder is not in the informant's immediate line of sight, he or she is more likely to forget that the recording is being made than when the interviewer is hastily scribbling throughout the conversation. However, while the tape-recording provides a more complete, concrete, and detailed record than fieldnotes, non-verbal aspects and features of the physical setting go unrecorded, of course. For this reason it is usually advisable to supplement the tape-recording with jotted notes covering these matters.

PERMANENT RECORDINGS

We have already acknowledged that the 'pen-and-notebook' approach to fieldwork inevitably means the loss of much detailed information. The fine grain of speech and non-verbal communication is not easily reconstructed. It is very easy to demonstrate the major differences – in volume and detail – between a permanent recording and an observer's reconstruction of a strip of spoken action, for example. Since the technology of permanent recording is now readily available, in small and reliable formats, there are many possibilities. The uses of video or film, still photography, and audio-recording offer various options for data collection and storage.

For the reasons we have suggested, if at all possible the ethnographer will wish to audio-record interviews. However, the availability of portable cassette-recorders allows us to collect data in an enormous variety of other social settings as well. And whether recordings are derived from interviews or from 'naturally occurring' social interaction, many of the same issues of data preparation and storage apply.

It must be noted, though, that audio-recording does not provide a perfect and comprehensive record. In some cases background noise may make the recording virtually unintelligible. Also, recording is highly selective. Not only is non-verbal behaviour not captured but even such matters as who is being addressed are not always preserved. The availability of tape-recording facilities in the field does not remove the necessity for observation and the construction of fieldnotes, then. Indeed, an overemphasis on audio-recordings can distort one's sense of 'the field', by focusing data collection on what can be recorded, and concentrating attention on the analysis of spoken action. Further, there are considerable costs involved in the preparation of recorded materials. They must be transcribed. There are no hard-and-fast rules here, but the ratio of transcribing time to recorded time is always high (often in the range of five to one, or more).

We do not intend to provide detailed instructions as to the preparation of transcripts, but a number of general precepts can be noted. In the first place, a decision needs to be made about whether full transcription is necessary. An alternative is to treat the audio-tape as a document, indexing (by means of the revolution counter) and summarizing much of it, transcribing only what seems essential. This may save considerable time, though it risks relevant material being overlooked – especially since what is relevant changes over time.

Where transcription is to be carried out, a decision must be made about how detailed this should be. There are well-established conventions for the preparation of transcripts. These have been developed for the purposes of conversation analysis or discourse analysis. They use the typographical characters of the standard keyboard/printer to represent some basic features of speech (such as pauses, overlaps, and interruptions). They can be used to show when the speaker speeds up or slows down, where emphasis is placed, and when utterances are louder than others. These will be essential for some research purposes, less important for others; and obviously the more detailed the transcription, the more time it will take. The planning and conduct of research using audio-recorded data must therefore involve strategic decisions about the kind of data to be collected, and the degree of detail to be preserved in the transcription. (For further discussion of considerations involved in transcription, see Atkinson 1992b.)

The collection and use of visual materials are a large and specialized area. There has been a well-established tradition in social anthropology of ethnographic film – often made by professional film-makers, with the anthropologist acting as consultant or co-director. The ethnography, in the form of a monograph, is thus parallelled by one or more documentary films (cf. Crawford and Turton 1992). These ethnographic films have their own narrative conventions, and their distinctive genres (Loizos 1993). Despite the immediacy of the visual medium, the ethnographic film is not a direct or neutral representation of social reality. It is as dependent as any other medium on conventions of representation and readership (MacDougall 1992; Martinez 1992).

Much the same is true of the use of video-recording. The availability of relatively cheap and small portable camcorders has made this an attractive means of data recording. At the same time, the selectivity of video-records must be remembered, especially when used indoors. Decisions have to be made about whether the camera should be fixed or mobile, whether a single focus is to be adopted or whether the focus should shift – and if so where and on what basis. Where the position and focus are not fixed, operation of the camera is likely to be full-time – it will be difficult if not impossible to observe and take notes at the same time. Yet complementary observation and note-taking will almost certainly be necessary. Here too contextual features will need to be documented, since by no means everything will be 'in shot'. A team approach is advisable in such circumstances. Also, like audio-recordings, video-records are difficult to handle as data, and it may well be necessary to produce a transcript and/or index. And, especially where the transcript includes non-verbal behaviour, this will be even more time-consuming than the transcription of audio-tapes.

The use of photography is well established in anthropology (Collier and Collier 1986; Ball and Smith 1992), and to a much lesser extent in sociological research (Becker 1981). The use of visual data for more than illustrative purposes (and they are never without analytic import) requires considerable investment in detailed and specialized analysis of images. In other words, the collection of visual data does not remove the problems of selection and representation. We are used to thinking of film and photography as producing faithful, realistic images of the world about us; such habits of our own culture should not blind us to the fact that they are partial, interested, and conventional.

We still tend to think of written language as the privileged medium of scholarly communication. There are, therefore, some tensions in the use of visual materials in 'a discipline of words' (Ball and Smith 1992:5ff). In the near future, the use of 'hypermedia' software for the authoring and presentation of ethnographic (and other) information may change our notions of storing, analysing, and distributing data. As Seaman and Williams (1992) propose:

> The increasing availability of interactive multimedia and hypermedia database systems on personal computers will transform ethnographic methodologies. Gathering data in many different media has already been made possible by cheap, efficient technologies of electronic recording. Textual and audiovisual information made interactive will be able to provide the scholarly apparatus of referencing and contextualization necessary to create new forms of academic publication and knowledge dissemination. Ethnographers must therefore learn not only how to collect information in the different media formats but how to process, analyze and integrate it into forms that convey meaningful understanding.
>
> (Seaman and Williams 1992:300)

Hypertext and hypermedia will probably start to have an impact in the very near future. In the meantime, most ethnographers will remain committed to textual data for most practical purposes. Nevertheless, the use of visual recordings is an important, and often under-exploited, aspect of ethnographic fieldwork.

DOCUMENTS

We often need to collect and use documentary evidence from the research setting (see Chapter 6). Some documents are freely available and can be retained for later use. This is often true, for example, of such items as promotional material, guides, and circulars. Other documents can be bought or otherwise acquired. Even when documentary sources are not produced in large numbers, the researcher may be able to produce copies for retention. Photocopiers are available in some settings, of course, and the ethnographer may be allowed access to them. Alternatively, it may be possible to transcribe sections of documentary sources. Copying documents *in toto* is not necessarily the most effective recording strategy. While it avoids the dangers of omitting something important or losing the context, those advantages have to be set against the costs in time and money.

Frequently, there is no alternative to note-taking. Here too, though, there are different strategies that are available. One can index a document so that the relevant sections can be consulted as appropriate at later stages of the research. This can be done relatively quickly, but it requires easy and repeated access to the documentary sources. One may also summarize relevant sections or copy them out by hand. The choice between summarizing and copying revolves around a dilemma that we have met already in recording observational and interview data. By summarizing one can cover much more material in the same time, thus releasing scarce time for work of other kinds. On the other hand, summarizing involves some loss of information and introduces interpretation.

These three modes of note-taking – indexing, copying by hand, and summarizing – are not mutually exclusive, of course, and each should be used according to the accessibility of the documents and the anticipated use to which the notes will be put. Both these considerations may vary across different documents or even sections of documents. Where access to the documents is difficult and the precise wording used is likely to be important, there is little alternative to painstaking copying. Where the need is for background information, summaries might be sufficient. It should also be remembered that notes need not necessarily be made on the spot: where access is restricted it may be more efficient to read the indexes, summaries, or relevant sections into a portable tape-recorder, the recording being transcribed later.

ANALYTIC NOTES AND MEMOS, AND FIELDWORK JOURNALS

While reading documents, making fieldnotes, or transcribing audiovisual materials, promising analytic ideas often arise. It is important to make notes of these, as they may prove useful in analysing the data. It is important, though, to distinguish analytic notes from accounts provided by participants and from observer descriptions.

Equally important are the regular review and development of analytic ideas in the form of analytic memos. These are not fully developed working papers but occasional written notes whereby progress is assessed, emergent ideas are identified, research strategy is sketched out, and so on. It is all too easy to let one's fieldnotes and other types of data pile up day by day and week by week. The very accumuluation of material usually imparts a satisfying sense of progress, which can be measured in physical terms as notebooks are filled, interviews completed, periods of observation ticked off, or different research settings investigated. But it is a grave error to let this work accumulate without regular reflection and review. Under such circumstances the sense of progress may prove illusory, and a good deal of the data collection could be unnecessarily aimless.

As we have emphasized, the formulation of precise problems, hypotheses, and an appropriate research strategy is an emergent feature of ethnography. This process of progressive focusing means that the collection of data must be guided by the unfolding but explicit identification of topics for inquiry. The regular production of research memoranda will force the ethnographer to go through such a process of explication. Ideally, every period of observation should result in processed notes and the reflexive monitoring of the research process. As such memoranda accumulate, they will constitute preliminary analyses, providing the researcher with guidance through the corpus of data. If this is done there is no danger of being confronted at the end of the fieldwork with an undifferentiated collection of material, with only one's memory to guide analysis.

The construction of analytic notes and memos therefore

constitutes precisely the sort of internal dialogue, or thinking aloud, that is the essence of reflexive ethnography. Such activity should help one avoid lapsing into the 'natural attitude' and 'thinking as usual' in the field. Rather than coming to take one's understanding on trust, one is forced to question *what* one knows, *how* such knowledge has been acquired, the *degree of certainty* of such knowledge, and what further lines of inquiry are implied.

These analytic notes may be appended to the daily fieldnotes, or they may be incorporated into yet another form of written account, the fieldwork journal. Such a journal or diary provides a running account of the conduct of the research. This includes a record not only of the fieldwork, but also of the ethnographer's own personal feelings and involvement. The latter are not simply the basis for gratuitous introspection or narcissistic self-absorption. As we point out elsewhere in this book, feelings of personal comfort, anxiety, surprise, shock, or revulsion are of analytic significance. In the first place, our feelings enter into and colour the social relationships we engage in during fieldwork. Second, such personal and subjective responses will inevitably influence one's choice of what is note-worthy, what is regarded as strange and problematic, and what appears to be mundane and obvious. One often relies implicitly on such feelings; their existence and possible influence must be acknowledged and, if possible, explicated in written form. Similarly, feelings of anxiety can pose limitations on data collection, leading to a restricting tunnel vision. One of us (Atkinson 1992a) has reflected on how his personal feelings about general medicine and surgery clearly influenced the nature and balance of his published research on medical education.

There is a constant interplay between the personal and emotional on the one hand, and the intellectual on the other. Private response should be transformed, by reflection and analysis, into potential public knowledge. The fieldwork journal is the vehicle for such transformation. At a more mundane level, perhaps, the carefully made fieldwork journal will enable the conscientious ethnographer painstakingly to retrace and explicate the development of the research design, the emergence of analytic themes, and the systematic collection of data. The provision of such a 'natural history' of the research is a crucial component of the complete ethnography.

DATA STORAGE AND RETRIEVAL

It has always been common for ethnographers to keep written data records chronologically, as a running record in which the data are stored at the time of collection. Likewise, interview transcripts and the like are normally kept as complete records of the individual interview. Once analysis begins, however, reconceptualization – sometimes the physical reorganization – of the data into themes and categories generally becomes necessary. This involves the categorization of the data – often breaking the texts up into discrete chunks or segments and identifying them in accordance with an indexing or 'coding' system. (This is less common in conversation and discourse analysis, where the focus is often on local patterns.)

For many years ethnographers and researchers like them have manipulated their data by means of the physical indexing and sorting of precious manuscript and typescript texts. Recently, as we shall see, the functions of the computer – mainframe and microcomputer – have been used to facilitate the storage and retrieval of textual data for ethnographic purposes. To a considerable extent the computer software for ethnographic data storage and retrieval recapitulates the procedures associated with earlier, manual approaches. We shall comment on manual techniques before going on to discuss computer-based applications. It is important not to assume that all ethnographic data must now be stored and searched on computer. For many researchers there will still be a place for simple manual procedures.

The reorganization of the data into categories provides an important infrastructure for later searching and retrieval. It can also play an active role in the process of discovery, as the Webbs noted:

> It enables the scientific worker to break up his subject-matter, so as to isolate and examine at his leisure its various component parts, and to recombine the facts when they have been thus released from all accustomed categories, in new and experimental groupings.
>
> (Webb and Webb 1932:83)

Moreover the selection of categories is of some significance:

> As I gathered my early research data, I had to decide how I

was to organize the written notes. In the very early stage of exploration, I simply put all the notes, in chronological order, in a single folder. As I was to go on to study a number of different groups and problems, it was obvious that this was no solution at all.

I had to subdivide the notes. There seemed to be two main possibilities. I could organize the notes topically, with folders for politics, rackets, the church, the family, and so on. Or I could organize the notes in terms of the groups on which they were based, which would mean having folders on the Nortons, the Italian Community Club, and so on. Without really thinking the problem through, I began filing material on the group basis, reasoning that I could later redivide it on a topical basis when I had a better knowledge of what the relevant topics should be.

As the material in the folders piled up, I came to realize that the organization of notes by social groups fitted in with the way in which my study was developing. For example, we have a college-boy member of the Italian Community Club saying: 'These racketeers give our district a bad name. They should really be cleaned out of here.' And we have a member of the Nortons saying: 'These racketeers are really all right. When you need help, they'll give it to you. The legitimate businessman – he won't even give you the time of day.' Should these notes be filed under 'Racketeers, attitudes toward'? If so, they would only show that there are conflicting attitudes toward racketeers in Cornerville. Only a question-naire (which is hardly feasible for such a topic) would show the distribution of attitudes in the district. Furthermore, how important would it be to know how many people felt one way or another on this topic? It seemed to me of much greater scientific interest to be able to relate the attitude to the group in which the individual participated. This shows why two individuals could be expected to have quite different attitudes on a given topic.

(Whyte 1981:309)

Whyte's comments here emphasize the importance of context. No system of filing or coding and retrieval can ever remove the necessity to remain sensitive to the social context of speech and action.

The allocation of data to categories in ethnography has usually differed from the kind of coding typical in quantitative research, including content analysis (Krippendorff 1980). Here there is no requirement that items of data be assigned to one and only one category, or that there be explicit rules for assigning them:

> We code [the fieldnotes] inclusively, that is to say if we have any reason to think that anything might go under the heading, we will put it in. We do not lose anything. We also code them in multiple categories, under anything that might be felt to be cogent. As a general rule, we want to get back anything that could conceivably bear on a given interest. ... It is a search procedure for getting all of the material that is pertinent.
>
> (Becker 1968:245)

Indeed, Lofland (1971) argues that in the case of analytic categories it pays to be 'wild', to include anything, however long a shot.

The identification of categories is central to the process of analysis (although it should not be confused with analysis *per se*). As a result, the list of categories in terms of which the data are organized generally undergoes considerable change over the course of the research. In particular, there is typically a shift towards more analytic categories as the work develops (see Chapter 8).

Organizing and reorganizing the data in terms of categories can be done in a number of ways. The simplest is 'coding the record'. Here data are coded, that is, assigned to categories, on the running record itself (or a copy of it). Comments relating the data to descriptive or analytic categories are written in the margin, on the reverse, or on interleaved pages, depending on the format of the data themselves. This is quick, and preserves the sense of 'reading' the data. It is not, however, well adapted to subsequent procedures of searching and retrieving data segments. In a more sophisticated version of this strategy, an analytic index is produced. Here each data segment is indexed under a developing set of headings, stored on index cards or in a simple 'cardbox' microcomputer database. Identically or similarly coded segments can thus be found in the original hard copy of the data relatively easily.

An alternative method of data organization, used by many

ethnographers, is physical sorting. Multiple copies of the data are made, and each segment of the data is stored under all the categories to which it is deemed relevant. With this approach, ethnographers can find all the data collected together when they come to analyse and write up a particular theme. At the same time, the physical storage of multiple copies has limitations: not least the time taken to produce copies and the sheer space requirements of a large and complex data set. These methods, and others that have been used, such as punch cards with data extracts attached, reflect the same underlying approach. That is, they depend on the ethnographer segmenting and disaggregating the original data. The terminology of 'indexing' and 'coding' captures the essence of the tasks. They have been carried forward into the use of computer software for the storage, searching, and retrieval of ethnographic data. Only very recently have there been sustained attempts to use the intrinsic capacities of microcomputing to go beyond the manual techniques.

It is now perfectly commonplace for ethnographers and others to store textual data in microcomputer files. It is probably taken for granted in most academic settings that any textual data – such as fieldnotes, interview transcripts, diaries, and the like – can, and perhaps should, be prepared and stored via wordprocessing software on a microcomputer. The diskette and the hard disk are now the preferred storage media for many types of data. Where once the ethnographer relied on the scribbled note and the typescript, he or she is now likely to regard the microcomputer as a natural tool. There are, of course, constraints that may mean the ethnographer will in practice continue to rely on handwritten materials and other hard copy. Where fieldwork is conducted in remote settings, then the original data collection may remain in notebooks, and the time and cost of transferring them to wordprocessor may be too great once the data collection period is over. On the other hand, the existence of tiny pocket computers and the widespread use of laptops and other portable devices also mean that it becomes possible to envisage an environment in which data collection, storage, and retrieval are all conducted through microcomputing. Furthermore, the networking of workstations in most academic settings will permit the sharing of ethnographic data among members of research teams, graduate seminars, and the like.

Given our contemporary reliance on microcomputing environments, then, it often makes sense to go beyond the use of a wordprocessor and to employ available software to facilitate basic tasks of storage and retrieval. We do not equate such tasks with 'analysis', although the software and procedures are often referred to a 'Computer Assisted Qualitative Data Analysis'. They must be conducted in conjunction with the kinds of analytic processes we outline in the following chapter. There is a direct continuity between the systematic searching of data and the development of the analysis. The microcomputer may be used to store qualitative, textual data, to search them, and to retrieve specified items. Such basic procedures are common to most of the 'CAQDAS' software.

It is important to recognize at the outset, however, that many useful functions can be performed by generic wordprocessing software. The ethnographer who is familiar with an advanced, powerful wordprocessing package, and whose data retrieval needs are straightforward, may well find little or no need to look beyond the wordprocessor. The basic tasks of finding, marking, and relocating stretches of text (fieldnotes or interview transcript extracts, for example) may be performed by the functions of the wordprocessor (such as the insertion of 'bookmarks' and the capacity to 'copy' or 'cut and paste'). It is possible that such wordprocessing functions will actually serve all the needs of a particular user for a simple project. There is certainly no need to seek out more complex and more expensive solutions if the need does not arise. There is never any merit in using specialized software if its more sophisticated features are not in fact used and if generic applications will do the trick.

The majority of ethnographers who wish to use microcomputing software, however, will now turn to one or more applications that have been developed either for handling ethnographic data, or for more general textual work that is readily adapted to the ethnographer's needs Those software packages can be used for a variety of data handling tasks. In outlining them here we do not intend to review all the available software, nor to make systematic comparisons between their respective strengths and weaknesses. There are other sources to which the reader may be referred for such treatment, most notably the systematic review by Tesch (1990), which is an excellent account of the field. (See also Lee and Fielding 1991; and Dey 1993.) Tesch outlines a number of strategies for qualitative research and summarizes a wide range of software packages. Hers is as comprehensive a review as one could reasonably hope to achieve. Inevitably there are developments in such a field as this that quickly render all contributions obsolescent. Yet Tesch's book will remain a major source, and the reader is recommended to consult it for detailed guidance.

The most commonly advocated strategy is based on the *coding* of segments of text. There are several packages that reproduce this strategy which may be referred to as a 'code-and-retrieve' approach. There are some differences between them, but most of their basic functions are similar or identical. Currently available software includes *Ethnograph*, *Text Analysis Package*, *Textbase Alpha*, and *Qualpro*: some important variants that do other things as well will be commented on below. These computing strategies draw on and develop those of a previous era. They recapitulate the elementary approach whereby the text is classified and sorted according to thematic dimensions.

The element common to this family of software packages is the capacity – indeed the requirement – to attach 'codes' to specified segments of the notes or transcripts. There is nothing mechanical about this process. The software provides no automatic coding process. It always remains the task of the ethnographer to exercise his or her intellectual imagination to decide upon the analytically relevant codes to be used. Conceptually speaking, therefore, the task of coding for microcomputing applications is no different from 'manual' techniques for identifying and retrieving chunks of data. The data were once physically disaggregated or marked and indexed as part of a continuous record. The logic of code-and-retrieve remains the same. It is what Tesch (1990) calls 'decontextualizing' data segments, and 'recontextualizing' them into thematic files.

The microcomputing versions of this process have a number of practical advantages. While the coding process itself is no advance on previous approaches, the use of the software permits greater flexibility and sensitivity. The software allows the researcher to retrieve identically coded segments of text with considerable speed. All segments so coded are found. Any search is therefore comprehensive (provided only that the coding is equally so). There is, therefore, reduced danger of the ethnographer selecting only the most easily remembered instance, or the one that first comes to hand from the notebooks.

Furthermore the delicacy of the searching and retrieval process is enhanced, given the opportunity to combine codes in multiple searches. A package such as *Ethnograph* facilitates the multiple coding of segments; codes may overlap and be nested within one another. Segments may be retrieved using single or multiple code searches. Codes can be specified to be virtual synonyms, and others can be excluded. The procedures thus allow codes to be combined in an approximation of Boolean algebra – exploiting the opportunities of searching, for example, for 'X' and 'Y' or 'X' and not 'Y'.

Coding in these contexts is not a straightforward process. The ethnographer needs, of course, to decide on what codings are relevant to the emergent themes of the work and to the preliminary analyses that accompany data collection. They may index people, places, or things, and they may refer to relevant types of social encounter or event. The resulting coding system may need to become very complex and dense.

Ethnographers using software of this sort need to spend a considerable amount of time and effort devising and experimenting with codes relevant to their own data. The coding approach calls for some investment of time in preliminary analyses if codes are not to be devised and attached to data in an *ad hoc* fashion. Useful searches of the data can only be facilitated if the coding scheme itself is adequate in the first place. Software like *Ethnograph*, of course, permits the constant refinement and revision of coding schemes. In principle, the processes of coding and recoding may follow the emergence of ideas grounded in the data. They are never fixed. In practice, however, the tasks of entering and deleting codes are tedious. One strongly suspects that in many projects the codes themselves will rapidly become 'frozen' once data have been coded for the first time. There may readily develop an inertia that militates against progressive refinement and revision.

Furthermore, in themselves, the pure coding software applications are poor at the representation of analytic issues. *Ethnograph*, for instance, is poor at representing relationships between codes. In essence the coding strategy is a 'flat' one. Thus, the software cannot recognize some codes as being general categories that include more specific ones. Such software emulates manual searching quite efficiently and comprehensively. But its version of coding recapitulates what has been called 'the culture of fragmentation' (Atkinson 1992a) as a general approach to qualitative data. That is, it reflects a general assumption that data reduction and aggregation lie at the heart of data management. This is not necessarily faithful to all versions of ethnographic and other qualitative inquiry, particularly those concerned with detailed sequential analysis of social interaction.

The code-and-retrieve strategy may be complemented by an alternative strategy used to search text by means of 'indigenous' terms – that is, the identification of words and phrases actually used in the fieldnotes or interviews. This strategy of data retrieval may be especially useful when verbatim transcripts permit the identification of actors' own language. There are many microcomputing applications that can facilitate such data searching. They do not need to have been designed especially for ethnographic research purposes; there are many programs that have been developed for more general purposes, such as content analysis, indexing, and similar functions. All software of this sort allows the ethnographer to search for the occurrence of particular terms and to identify their location in the data texts. Among the many programs that have been described and used for this kind of data analysis are *FYI3000Plus*, *Golden Retriever*, and *IZE*. The systematic searching of the lexicon of transcripts and fieldnotes can aid important analytic tasks. Actors' and informants' own vocabularies may be inspected and chunks of data retrieved that contain specified terms. Some of this software allows for highly flexible and sensitive searching. Any word in the text may be used as a keyword without further marking. And a full Boolean logic allows words to be treated as synonyms (X or Y) as well as multiple searches (X and Y). The ethnographer may thus build up quite complex search strategies.

There are a number of microcomputer software packages that attempt to go beyond the simple code-and-retrieve function of the *Ethnograph* and cognate applications. They attempt to represent key features of analysis itself. The program *KWALITAN*, developed originally in The Netherlands, is an attempt to include aspects of 'grounded theory' building that go beyond coding the data. Hence the software supports not just keywords, but also analytic and methodological memoranda that may be attached to specific segments of data ('scenes' as they are called in this strategy). The intention is to provide a more faithful representation of the analytic process (not just storage and retrieval) in the microcomputing environment.

In a similar vein, *NUDIST*, originally developed in Australia for mainframe computers and now transferred to micro-computers, goes beyond the 'flat' coding of *Ethnograph* and similar basic code-and-retrieve applications. In the *NUDIST* system relations are established between codes themselves. As the coding scheme develops, semantic relationships are established, so that large numbers of codings may be arranged in a series of hierarchically ordered trees. More specific codings may thus be related to superordinate themes and categories. The specification of logical or sociological relationships between categories is an advance on other methods that simply map the occurrence or co-occurrence of coded segments. Approaches such as that supported by *NUDIST* may provide a genuine link between coding, retrieving, and *analysing* data. It is difficult to tell the actual benefits of the *NUDIST* approach over 'flat' coding methods. By no means all ethnographic projects in practice employ so many codewords, so delicately specified, that their taxonomic arrangement is a necessary advance in methodology: the analytic 'value-added' of such an approach may not be relevant for all researchers.

Even so, software like *KWALITAN* or *NUDIST* remains grounded in the basic approach of 'coding' or otherwise segmenting data. A more radically alternative approach to micromputing relies on the strategy known as 'hypertext'. This approach to the searching of qualitative data is entirely dependent on the capacities of the computer, and may be thought of as a genuine alternative strategy for the exploration of data. Here, indeed, the distinction between data retrieval and analysis becomes totally blurred. Rather than fragmenting the text into discrete segments, hypertext software allows the analyst to construct complex pathways and relationships within the database. Rather than thinking of 'finding' and 'retrieving' chunks of data, one should think rather of 'navigating' through the database. Elements of data can also be linked to annotations and commentary. The most widely implemented hypertext application is *Hyperqual*, based on the hypercard facility of the Macintosh computer. A similar application, based on the same computing environment, is *Hypersoft* (Dey 1993). A generic hypertext system that may be used for qualitative data in a PC environment is *Guide* (Weaver and Atkinson 1994). The possibilities of hypertext – and, more generally, hypermedia applications that link information of different sorts – are being explored by scholars in many disciplines.

With a fully realized hypertext application there is no real distinction between 'data' and other materials such as analytic memoranda, annotations, and the like. Equally 'data' such as interview transcripts or fieldnotes can be linked directly to other information, such as graphics, extracts of relevant literature, maps, even sounds. This high degree of integration and consequent flexibility may facilitate an analytic approach that is ultimately more faithful to the cognitive tasks and intellectual presuppositions of 'classic' ethnographic inquiry. They may also accommodate individual differences between researchers or research groups more readily than more conventional prestructured applications. The opportunity to create multiple links and trails may encourage the analyst to pursue dense networks of association and meaning. As Thomas (1993) suggests of future ethnographers:

> Using hypertext, a researcher could include not only a conventional description of the method of a study, but also graphics (photos or video segments) and sound to illustrate or clarify procedures. Qualitative researchers may find hypertext especially helpful, since they would be able to include, on a palm-sized disk, the anecdotes illustrating concepts, as well as the actual interview segments from which data were drawn.

And he goes on to comment:

> Imagine the richness of data if Becker's study of marijuana users, Manning's accounts of narcotics agents, or Irwin's analysis of prison culture included 3-D visuals and sound. This kind of communication would not only infuse ethnographic texts with richer detail, it would add a new level of accountability by giving the reader a view of the context from which the data and analysis is derived.
>
> (J. Thomas 1993:1)

Weaver and Atkinson did not go so far as to include sound and video in their use of *Guide*. They do, however, indicate how the ethnographer can create complex relationships within his or her data, and can also establish links 'out' to other sources and types of information. Moreover, as Thomas indicates, it is possible for 'the ethnography' itself to be presented in a hypertext format, so that the 'reader' is not confined to a linear hard-copy text. Rather, he or she may also choose alternative trails through the available data and other information. The 'reading' of the ethnography thus becomes more clearly interactive, and also recapitulates the kinds of 'analyses' traced out by the ethnographer.

Whatever merits are to be found in computer applications, however, we must recognize that they only provide adjuncts to the sociological or anthropological imagination. They certainly do not provide 'automatic' solutions to problems of representation and analysis. Understanding and interpretation are the outcome of interactions between the ethnographer and the data, which are themselves constructs. There is no mechanistic substitute for those complex processes of reading and interpretation.

CONCLUSION

While it is probably impossible to render explicit all the data acquired in fieldwork, every effort must be made to record it. Memory is an inadequate basis for subsequent analysis. Of course, data recording is necessarily selective and always involves some interpretation, however minimal. There is no set of basic, indubitable data available from which all else may be deduced. What is recorded, and how, will depend in large part on the purposes and priorities of the research, and the conditions in which it is carried out. Moreover, in using various recording techniques we must remain aware of the effects their use may be having on participants and be prepared to modify the strategy accordingly. Similarly, there is no finally correct way to store information or to retrieve it for analysis. The various systems – including currently available computing strategies – differ in appropriateness according to one's purposes, the nature of the data collected, the facilities and finance available, the size and scope of the research project, as well as personal convenience.

As with other aspects of ethnographic research, then, recording, storing, and retrieving data must be viewed as part of the reflexive process. Decisions are to be made, monitored, and – if necessary – remade in the light of methodological, practical, and ethical considerations. At the same time, however, these techniques play an important role in promoting the quality of ethnographic research. They provide a crucial resource in assessing typicality of examples, checking construct-indicator linkages, searching for negative cases, triangulating across different data sources and stages of the fieldwork, and assessing the role of the researcher in shaping the nature of the data and the findings. In short, they facilitate – but should not determine – the process of analysis, a topic to which we turn in the next chapter.

Chapter 8

The process of analysis

In ethnography the analysis of data is not a distinct stage of the research. In many ways, it begins in the pre-fieldwork phase, in the formulation and clarification of research problems, and continues through to the process of writing reports, articles, and books. Formally, it starts to take shape in analytic notes and memoranda; informally, it is embodied in the ethnographer's ideas and hunches. And in these ways, to one degree or another, the analysis of data feeds into research design and data collection. This iterative process is central to the 'grounded theorizing' promoted by Glaser and Strauss, in which theory is developed out of data analysis, and subsequent data collection is guided strategically by the emergent theory (Glaser and Strauss 1967; Glaser 1978; Strauss 1987; Strauss and Corbin 1990). However, much the same interactive process is also involved in other kinds of ethnographic research, including those which are directed not towards the generation of theory but to other research products, such as descriptions and explanations.

This commitment to a dialectical interaction between data collection and data analysis is not easy to sustain in practice, however; and much ethnographic research suffers from a lack of reflexivity in this respect. The data required to check a particular interpretation are often missing; the typicality of crucial items of data cannot be checked; or some of the comparative cases necessary for developing and testing an emerging set of analytic ideas have not been investigated. One reason for this is the influence of naturalism, with its emphasis on 'capturing' the social world in description (Hammersley 1992:ch.1). Naturalism reinforces what Lacey (1976:71) calls 'the it's all happening elsewhere syndrome', a common ailment in fieldwork where the researcher feels it necessary to try to be everywhere at once and to stay in the setting for as long as possible. As a result of this, a great deal of data is collected but little time is left for reflection on the significance of the data and the implications for further data collection. Likewise, the naturalistic commitment to 'tell it like it is' tends to force the process of analysis to remain implicit and underdeveloped.

However, there are also practical constraints on achieving the sort of close interaction between analysis, research design, and data collection that is desirable. Fieldwork is a very demanding activity, and the processing of data is equally time-consuming. As a result, engaging in sustained data analysis alongside data collection is often very difficult. However, some level of reflexivity can and should be maintained, even if it is not possible to carry out much formal data analysis before the main fieldwork has been completed. Some reflection on the data collection process and what it is producing is essential if the research is not to drift along the line of least resistance and to face an analytical impasse in its final stages.

Ethnographic research should have a characteristic 'funnel' structure, being progressively focused over its course. Over time the research problem needs to be developed or transformed, and eventually its scope is clarified and delimited, and its internal structure explored. In this sense, it is frequently well into the process of inquiry that one discovers what the research is *really* about; and not uncommonly it turns out to be about something rather different from the initial foreshadowed problems. An extreme example is some research by Shakespeare (1994), which started from a concern with how members of a housing co-operative accounted for its history, but eventually came to focus on the discursive structure of the 'confused talk' displayed by people suffering from various kinds of dementia. Here we have a dramatic change in substantive focus, though there is a continuing concern with the structure of interview discourse. Usually, shifts in research focus are less dramatic than this, more along the lines illustrated by Bohannon (1981). He identifies the various stages of a research project on poor residents of inner-city hotels, illustrating the importance of preliminary analysis; and he reports how the research problem was progressively redefined:

We did indeed begin this project with the 'notion' (it was

actually more formal than that – it was a hypothesis that proved wrong) that elderly individuals living in run-down hotels in the center city have established support networks. By and large they have not. Their networks are shallow and transient. It is [generally] part of the life adjustment of these people to run from the commitment that a support network implies.

(Bohannon 1981:45)

Starting from a view based on 'disorganization' or 'dislocation', Bohannon and his research team came to reformulate their research in terms of 'adaptation'. In the course of this they were able to argue that welfare policies predicated on the former were not soundly based.

Progressive focusing may also involve a gradual shift from a concern with describing social events and processes towards developing and testing explanations or theories. However, different studies vary considerably in the distance they travel along this road. Some remain heavily descriptive, ranging from narrative life histories of an individual, group, or organization to accounts of the way of life to be found in particular settings. Of course, these are in no sense pure descriptions: they are constructions involving selection and interpretation. But they may involve little attempt to derive any general theoretical lessons, the theory they employ remaining implicit, being used as a tool rather than forming the focus of the research. Such accounts can be of great value. They may provide us with knowledge of cultures hitherto unknown, and thereby shake our assumptions about the parameters of human life or challenge our stereotypes. Herein lies the interest of much anthropological work and of sociological accounts revealing the ways of life of low-status and deviant groups.

A variation on this theme is to show the familiar in the apparently strange (Goffman 1961; Turnbull 1973) or the strange in the familiar (Garfinkel 1967). An interesting recent application of this latter idea is Rawlings' explication of her knowledge as a participant in a therapeutic community. She takes an apparently ordinary first few minutes of a community meeting and shows that in many respects they were far from ordinary, that their appearance as ordinary was an interactional accomplishment, albeit a routine one (Rawlings 1988). Alternatively, descriptive accounts may contrast present conditions with an ideal, pointing up the discrepancy. Decision-making procedures within a political institution may be compared with an ideal type of democracy, for example; or personnel selection practices in a business organization may be compared with its official policy. Such comparisons are the stock-in-trade of ethnographic work.

By no means all ethnography remains at this descriptive level, however. Often, there is an attempt to draw out explanations or theoretical models of one kind or another. Here, features of the nature or history of the phenomenon under study start to be collected under more general categories. They are presented as examples of, for example, particular kinds of social orientation, discursive practice, interactional strategy, institutional form, etc. Going further, typologies may be developed identifying orientations, strategies, etc., of various related kinds which can be found in very different sorts of setting (Lofland 1971 and 1976). Finally, a whole range of analytic categories may be integrated into a model of some aspect of the social process (Glaser and Strauss 1967; Glaser 1978; Lofland and Lofland 1984). And this may then be subjected to test and further revision.

This is a long road to travel and there are many way-stations along its course. Moreover, as with all journeys, something is left behind. Concrete descriptions usually cover many different facets of the phenomena they describe: they give a rounded picture and open up all manner of theoretical possibilities. The development of explanations and theories involves a narrowing of focus and a process of abstraction. Theorized accounts provide a much more selective representation of the phenomena with which they deal. On the other hand, assuming that the theoretical ideas are well founded, they begin to give us much more knowledge about why events occur in the patterned ways they do.

In general, ethnographers deal with what is often referred to as 'unstructured' data. What this means is that the data are not already structured in terms of a finite set of analytic categories determined by the researcher, in the way that most survey research data are. Rather, they take the form of open-ended verbal descriptions in fieldnotes, of transcriptions of audio- or video-recordings, extracts of text from documents, etc. And the process of analysis involves, simultaneously, the development of a set of analytic categories that capture relevant aspects of these data, and the assignment of particular items of data to those categories.

There is a wide variety of approaches to analysis of this sort. This arises partly from the diverse purposes of social research. Someone concerned with how the sequencing of contributions to everyday conversation is organized is likely to adopt a very different approach compared with someone interested in, say, the strength of the ties among an elite group and how this affects their exercise of power. Closely related to such differences in topic or purpose, of course, are differences in theoretical approach. There are those who would dismiss the first topic as trivial, just as there are those who would regard the second as beyond the realm of rigorous investigation, at least given the current state of social-scientific knowledge. Our approach here will be a catholic one, ruling out neither of these forms of research. However, we cannot cover the full range of varieties of qualitative analysis in detail. Instead, we will focus on what we take to be central to much of it.

GENERATING CONCEPTS

The initial task in analysing qualitative data is to find some concepts that help us to make sense of what is going on in the scenes documented by the data. Often we will not be sure *why* what is happening is happening, and sometimes we may not even understand *what* is going on. The aim, though, is not just to make the data intelligible but to do so in an *analytical* way that provides a novel perspective on the phenomena we are concerned with or which promises to tell us much about other phenomena of similar types.

The development of analytical categories and models has often been treated as a mysterious process about which little can be said and no guidance given. One must simply wait on the theoretical muse, it is sometimes implied. While we would certainly not wish to deny or downplay the role of creative imagination in research, we should point out that it is not restricted to the *emergence* of analytical ideas, but is equally important in devising ways of *developing and testing* these. Moreover, in neither case does recognition of the role of imagination negate the fact that there are general strategies available.

Besides obscuring the importance of strategies for generating concepts and models, overemphasis on the role of creative imagination in the development of analytical ideas also leads us to forget the function that our existing knowledge of the social world performs in this process. It is only when we begin to understand that the imagination works via analogies and metaphors that this becomes plain. While it is rare for ethnographic analysis to begin from a well-defined theory, and indeed there are dangers associated with such a starting point, the process of analysis cannot but rely on the existing ideas of the ethnographer and those that he or she can get access to in the literature. What is important is that these do not take the form of prejudgments, forcing interpretation of the data into their mould, but are instead used as resources to make sense of the data. This requires the exercise of some analytic nerve, tolerating uncertainty and ambiguity in one's interpretations, and resisting the temptation to rush to determinate conclusions.

The first step in the process of analysis is, of course, a careful reading (indeed probably several readings) of the corpus of data, in order to become thoroughly familiar with it. At this stage the aim is to use the data to think with. One looks to see whether any interesting patterns can be identified; whether anything stands out as surprising or puzzling; how the data relate to what one might have expected on the basis of common-sense knowledge, official accounts, or previous theory; and whether there are any apparent inconsistencies or contradictions among the views of different groups or individuals, or between people's expressed beliefs or attitudes and what they do. Some such features and patterns may already have been noted in previous fieldnotes and analytic memos, perhaps even along with some ideas about how they might be explained. What sorts of pattern one is looking for depends, of course, on one's research focus and theoretical orientation. These will also affect how much data one collects and how one approaches the analysis. Some ethnographers, notably those employing conversation or discourse analysis, employ relatively small amounts of data and are concerned with local patterns visible within particular data sets. More usually, though, ethnographers collect quite large amounts of data of various kinds from different sources (observational fieldnotes and/or transcripts from various sites, interview notes and/or transcripts from different people, published and unpublished, official and personal documents, etc.);

and they seek relationships across the whole corpus. Here the aim is to compare and relate what happens at different places and times in order to identify stable features (of people, groups, organizations, etc.) that transcend local contexts.

Useful analytical concepts sometimes arise 'spontaneously', being used by participants themselves. And, indeed, unusual participant terms are always worth following up, since they may mark theoretically important or interesting phenomena (Becker and Geer 1957; Wieder 1974a and b; Becker 1993). Some forms of ethnography, especially those based on or influenced by 'ethnoscience', are devoted almost exclusively to the listing, sorting, and interpretation of such 'folk' terms. They are concerned with the more or less formal semantics of such inventories (see, for example, Tyler 1969). However, many ethnographies, while using folk types, attempt to do more than simply document their meaning. They are taken as evidence of knowledge, belief, and actions that can be located within more general analytic frameworks.

Alternatively, concepts may be 'observer-identified' (Lofland 1971); these are categories applied by the ethnographer rather than by members themselves. In the development of such classifications, the analyst may draw together under the aegis of a single type what for members is a diverse and unrelated range of phenomena. The formulation of such types can draw on general, common-sense knowledge and on personal experience. Equally, though, they can be generated by borrowing or adapting existing concepts from the literature. For instance, in their research on the transition of students from middle to high schools, Measor and Woods (1983) found that a variety of stories about life at the high school circulated among middle-school students, the most common one being that new entrants 'get their heads flushed in the loo' by older students. These stories had a standard form and seemed to reappear each year. Measor and Woods came to regard such stories as myths, and drew upon anthropological literature to understand the role they played in students' lives.

Sometimes, ethnographers find it necessary to formulate new terms to capture and characterize observer-identified types. Hargreaves provides an example with his development of the notion of 'contrastive rhetoric'. This refers to that interactional strategy whereby the boundaries of normal and acceptable practice are defined by institutionally and/or interactionally dominant individuals or groups through the introduction into discussion of alternative practices and social forms in stylized, trivialized and generally pejorative terms which connote their unacceptability.

(Hargreaves 1981:309)

Hargreaves uses the notion to analyse talk in a school staff meeting (Hargreaves 1981:314), but he notes that many parallel applications are to be found in the sociology of the mass media and of deviance. He also draws attention to the similarities with the 'atrocity stories' sometimes produced by those in subordinate positions in medical settings (Stimson and Webb 1975; Dingwall 1977a).

At this stage in their development, the concepts will not usually be well-defined elements of an explicit analytical model. Rather, they will probably take the form of a loose collection of 'sensitizing concepts' (Blumer 1954). These contrast with what Blumer calls 'definitive concepts', which 'refer precisely to what is common to a class of objects, by the aid of the clear definition of attributes or fixed bench-marks'. A sensitizing concept, on the other hand, lacks such specificity, and 'it gives the user a general sense of reference and guidelines in approaching empirical instances. Where definitive concepts provide prescriptions of what to see, sensitizing concepts merely suggest directions along which to look' (Blumer 1954:7). Sensitizing concepts are an important starting point; they are the germ of the analysis, and they can provide a focus for further data collection.

Reading through the corpus of data and generating concepts which make sense of it are the initial stages of ethnographic analysis. Very often, the concepts used to start with will be relatively mundane ones. Later, more analytically significant ones may be added. For instance, in his analysis of teachers' talk in a school staffroom Hammersley developed categories that ranged from the very concrete (teacher talk about students, about teaching, about national political events, etc.) to rather more abstract and analytic ones (trading news about students, exchanging mutual reassurances, accounting for decline and crisis, defending teacher competence, etc.). Needless to say, the process of coding the data is a recurrent one; as new categories emerge, previously coded data must be recoded to see if they contain any examples of the new codes. The ultimate aim, of course, is to reach a position where one has a stable set of categories and has carried out a systematic coding of all the data in terms of those categories. As we saw in the previous chapter, while there is no computer software which will do the coding automatically, there are various programs that facilitate the process and allow rapid retrieval or relating of data relevant to particular categories (see Dey 1993).

Having acquired some concrete and analytic categories for organizing the data, the next task is to begin to work on those which seem likely to be central to one's analysis, with a view to clarifying their meaning and exploring their relations with other categories. One strategy here is what Glaser and Strauss (1967) call the 'constant comparative method'. In this procedure, the analyst examines each item of data coded in terms of a particular category, and notes its similarities with and differences to other data that have been similarly categorized. This may lead to vaguely understood categories being differentiated into several more clearly defined ones, as well as to the specification of sub-categories. In this way, new categories or sub-categories emerge and there may be a considerable amount of reassignment of data among the categories

As this process of systematic sifting and comparison develops, so the mutual relationships and internal structures of categories will be more clearly displayed. However, the development of analytical ideas rarely takes the purely inductive form implied by Glaser and Strauss (heuristically useful though their approach is). Theoretical ideas, common-sense expectations, and stereotypes often play a key role. Indeed, it is these that allow the analyst to pick out surprising, interesting, and important features in the first place. Blanche Geer's (1964) famous account of her 'first days in the field' is a classic exemplification of the place of assumptions and stereotypes in the development of analytic themes.

Where a category forms part of a typology or model developed by others, however loosely constructed, relations with other categories may be implied that can be tentatively explored in the data. Where the fit is good and the model is well developed, it may even be possible to set about rigorously testing it. However, only rarely are sociological models sufficiently well developed for hypotheses to be derived and tested in this way. Generally, the process of testing requires considerable further development of the theory or explanation as a precondition, and in particular specification of what would be appropriate indicators for its concepts. (For discussions of the nature of theory development in ethnography, indicating some areas of disagreement, see Woods 1985 and 1987; Hammersley 1987a and b. And for questions about what constitutes theory in ethnography, see Hammersley 1992:ch.1.)

Of course, the ethnographer need not limit him- or herself to a single theory as a framework within which to analyse the data. Indeed, there are advantages to be gained from what Denzin (1978) terms 'theoretical triangulation', approaching data with multiple perspectives and hypotheses in mind. Bensman and Vidich (1960) provide an interesting example of this from their community study of Springdale. They report that they subjected their data to theoretical perspectives derived from Redfield, Weber, Tonnies, Veblen, Merton, Lynd, Warner, Mills, Sapir, and Tumin. In each case they asked themselves: 'What in [these] theories would permit us to comprehend our data?' Theories were not simply taken as off-the-peg solutions to research problems, but were used to provide focus for the analysis and for further fieldwork. They go on to note that

> When one set of theories does not exhaust the potentialities of the data, other sets can be employed to point to and explain the facts which remain unexplained. Thus, for any initial statement of the field problem a whole series of theories may be successively applied, each yielding different orders of data and each perhaps being limited by the special perspectives and dimensions on which it is predicated.
>
> (Bensman and Vidich 1960:165–6)

Not all ethnographers accept the validity of this approach; some see different theories as mutually incompatible, or rule out some theoretical approaches as incompatible with ethnography (Fielding and Fielding 1986; Silverman 1993:157). However, our view is that one should use whatever resources are available which help to make sense of the data.

DEVELOPING TYPOLOGIES

Very often the categories that have emerged in the analysis will be used simply to produce a description and/or explanation of the case or cases investigated. But sometimes ethnographers attempt to develop more systematic typologies that hold out the prospect of application to data from other situations. Here, a more or less exhaustive set of sub-types of some general category is identified. A very common pattern is the specification of various strategies which some category or group of actors adopt, or could adopt, to deal with a problem that they face routinely. However, typologies can have other sorts of foci too. For instance, Karp (1993) develops a typology of responses by patients to the prescription of anti-depressant drugs. These are: resistance, trial commitment, conversion, disenchantment, and deconversion. Rather than seeing these as alternative strategies he treats them as phases through which most patients go in their 'depressive careers', though of course there is the possibility of patients taking somewhat different routes through this set of responses. Karp explicitly draws a parallel with Robbins's (1988) work which identifies stages of recruitment, conversion, and deconversion of people to a variety of religious groups.

These are the sorts of relationships among categories that ethnographers look out for. And once having produced typologies like these they may become interested in why particular strategies are adopted by particular sorts of people in particular circumstances, or why particular kinds of people follow particular career patterns.

Typologies in ethnographic accounts vary considerably in the degree to which they have been systematically developed. Lofland has complained that in this respect much ethnographic research suffers from 'analytic interruptus'. In their development of categories, Lofland suggests, many analysts fail 'to follow through to the implied logical conclusion ... to reach [the] initially implied climax' (1970:42). Taking the example of typologies of strategies, Lofland argues that the investigator must take the time and trouble

1 to assemble self-consciously all his materials on how a [problem] is dealt with by the persons under study;
2 to tease out the variations among his assembled range of instances of strategies;

3 to classify them into an articulate set of . . . types of strategies; and

4 to present them to the reader in some orderly and preferably named and numbered manner.

(Lofland 1970:42–3)

Elsewhere, Lofland has provided an extended discussion of the varieties of typology and how they might be developed (Lofland 1971).

Lazarsfeld and Barton (1951) go even further in their recommendations for the systematic development of typologies. An initial set of categories differentiating a particular range of phenomena can be developed into a systematic typology, they argue, by specifying the dimensions underlying the discriminations it makes. Not only does this force clarification and perhaps modification of the categories already identified, it throws up other categories that may also be of importance.

We can illustrate this by reference to Glaser and Strauss's typology of 'awareness contexts'. They developed this concept to characterize the different kinds of social situation found among terminally ill hospital patients, their families, and medical personnel. The idea refers to the differential distribution of knowledge and understanding of the dying person's condition, from situations of 'closed awareness', when the patient is not informed of the diagnosis and prognosis, to 'open awareness', where the knowledge is shared openly by all parties. The idea of an awareness context is thus closely linked to the dynamics of information control characteristic of many medical encounters. However, in the following extract the notion is treated as a more general formal category. In such a formulation it is clearly applicable to a much wider range of social settings approximating to the general type of 'information games' (cf. Scott 1968). It is, for instance, directly applicable to the substantive issue of 'coming out' among homosexuals, and the management of the revelation or concealment of such an identity (Plummer 1975:177–96). Glaser and Strauss write:

We have singled out four types of awareness context for special consideration since they have proved useful in accounting for different types of interaction. An open awareness context obtains when each interactant is aware of the other's true identity and his own identity in the eyes of the other. A closed awareness context obtains when one inter-actant does not know either the other's identity or the other's view of his identity. A suspicion awareness context is a modi-fication of the closed one: one interactant suspects the true identity of the other or the other's view of his own identity, or both. A pretense awareness context is a modification of the open one: both interactants are fully aware but pretend not to be.

(Glaser and Strauss 1964:669)

PARTY A

PARTY B	Knows	Pretends not to know	Suspects	Doesn't know
Knows	*Open*		*Suspicion*	*Closed*
Pretends not to know		*Pretence*	*X*	*Y*
Suspects	*Suspicion*			*Z*
Doesn't know	*Closed*			

Figure 2 Typology of awareness contexts

By identifying the dimensions underlying this typology, along the lines suggested by Lazarsfeld and Barton, we find that there are rather more possibilities than Glaser and Strauss's initial typology allows (see Figure 2). Furthermore, some of these new possibilities look fruitful, such as cell X, where one party pre-tends while the other suspects, and cells Y and Z, where one pretends while the other does not know. Glaser (1978) warns us against what he calls the 'logical elaboration' of categories, and he is right to do so. Typologies should not be extended beyond their analytic value. Nonetheless, specification of the dimensions underlying a typology encourages us to think seriously and systematically about the nature of each category and its relation-ships with others. It may help us to spot previously uncon-sidered possibilities, or unsuspected relationships among categories. (For a useful discussion of the exploration of relation-ships among categories, in the context of using microcomputers for handling qualitative data, see Dey 1993.)

CONCEPTS AND INDICATORS

There is little point in developing highly systematized typologies and models if they provide little purchase on one's data.
The development of an effective typology is not a purely logical
or conceptual exercise: there must be constant recourse to the
material one is analysing. As the categories of the analysis are
being clarified and developed in relation to one another, so also
must the links between concepts and indicators be specified and
refined. Sensitizing concepts must be turned into something
more like definitive concepts. (This is a controversial proposal:
there are those who argue that sensitising concepts render
definitive concepts unnecessary in ethnographic research; see
Williams 1976. However, it is unclear to us how sensitising
concepts can be adequate for the later stages of analysis; see
Hammersley 1989a and b.)

In moving between data and concepts we must take great
care to note plausible alternative links to those made in the
emerging analysis, and these need to be tested. While in no
sense is it necessary, or even possible, to lay bare all the assumptions involved in concept-indicator linkages, it is important to
make explicit and to examine those assumptions to which strong
challenges can be made.

We can illustrate this by reference to Willis's (1977) classic
research on the adaptations of working-class boys to school.
Willis argues that the 'lads' he studied displayed a counter-
culture, an 'entrenched, general and personalized opposition to
"authority"'. In supporting this claim he uses descriptions of
the behaviour of the 'lads' as well as quotations from group
interviews such as the following comments about teachers:

JOEY: ... they're able to punish us. They're bigger than us,
    they stand for a bigger establishment than we do, like,
    we're just little and they stand for bigger things, and you
    try to get your own back. It's, uh, resenting authority I
    suppose.
EDDIE: The teachers think they're high and mighty 'cos
    they're teachers, but they're nobody really, they're just
    ordinary people ain't they?
BILL: Teachers think they're everybody. They are more,
    they're higher than us, but they think they're a lot higher
    and they're not.

SPANKSY: Wish we could call them first names and that . . . think they're God.

PETE: That would be a lot better.

PW: I mean you say they're higher. Do you accept at all that they know better about things?

JOEY: Yes, but that doesn't rank them above us, just because they are slightly more intelligent.

BILL: They ought to treat us how they'd like us to treat them. . . .

JOEY: . . . the way we're subject to their every whim like. They want something doing and we have to sort of do it, 'cos, er, er, we're just, we're under them like. We were with a woman teacher in here, and 'cos we all wear rings and one or two of them bangles, like he's got one on, and out of the blue, like, for no special reason, she says, 'take all that off'.

PW: Really?

JOEY: Yeah, we says, 'One won't come off', she says, 'Take yours off as well.' I said, 'You'll have to chop my finger off first.'

PW: Why did she want you to take your rings off?

JOEY: Just a sort of show like. Teachers do this, like, all of a sudden they'll make you do your ties up and things like this. You're subject to their every whim like. If they want something done, if you don't think it's right, and you object against it, you're down to Simmondsy (the head), or you get the cane, you get some extra work tonight.

PW: You think of most staff as kind of enemies . . .?

— Yeah.

— Yeah.

— Most of them.

JOEY: It adds a bit of spice to yer life, if you're trying to get him for something he's done to you.

(Willis 1977:11–12)

In assessing the way in which Willis links the concept of counter-culture with the various indicators he uses, we need to consider whether, for example, students' expressions of opposition to teachers reflect a general opposition to 'authority' as such, or only to particular types of authority. And, indeed, in the course of doing this, we may need to clarify the concept of authority itself. Would it make any sense, for example, to argue that Joey, who seems to be the leader of the 'lads', has authority among them? Whether or not we use the concept of authority in a broad or narrow sense, we need to be clear about exactly what it is that the analysis claims the 'lads' are rejecting.

Another question we might ask is whether the 'lads' are opposed to all aspects of teachers' authority or only to those teacher demands that they regard as overstepping its legitimate boundaries. For example, the 'lads' complain about rules relating to their personal appearance, a complaint also reported in a similar study by Werthman (1963), dealing with members of urban gangs in the United States. However, whereas Willis takes such complaints as an indicator of a general antipathy to authority, Werthman interprets them as signifying the boundaries of what the boys he studied regarded as a teacher's legitimate area of control. Clearly, such alternative interpretations have serious implications for the character and validity of the analysis produced.

While the nature of the alternative interpretations that must be considered will vary between studies, we can point to a number of issues that must be borne in mind when examining concept–indicator links. These correspond to the dimensions we discussed in Chapter 2 in relation to sampling within cases.

Social context

The issue of context is at the heart of the conflicting interpretations of student behaviour to be found in the work of Willis and Werthman. For Willis, opposition characterized the 'lads'' contacts with all forms of authority. For Werthman, on the other hand, the behaviour of gang members towards teachers varied across contexts according to the actions of the teacher and how these were interpreted.

We shall focus our discussion here on one of the most important elements of context: the audience to which the actions or accounts being used as data were directed. One important possible audience is, of course, the ethnographer. This is most obvious in the case of interviewing, an interactional format in which the researcher plays a key role through the questions he or she asks, however non-directive the interview is. In interviews the very structure of the interaction forces participants to be aware of the ethnographer as audience. Interviewees' conceptions of the nature and purposes of social research, of the particular research project, and of the personal characteristics of the interviewer may, therefore, act as a strong influence on what they say.

This can be both a help and a hindrance in the production of relevant data and valid interpretations of them. 'Well-trained' informants and respondents can act as highly effective research assistants in reporting relevant data, data of which the ethnographer might not otherwise become aware. They will also make the data collection process much more efficient, since they can select out what is relevant from the mass of irrelevant data that is available to them.

There are some dangers here, though. The more 'sophisticated' the interviewee the greater the tendency for him or her to move away from description into analysis. While there is no such thing as pure description, it is essential to minimize the inference involved in descriptions used as data in order to provide for the possibility of checking and rechecking, constructing and reconstructing, interpretations of them. If the interviewee gives heavily theorized accounts of the events or experiences he or she is describing, however interesting or fruitful the theoretical ideas are, the database has been eroded.

Spradley (1979) provides a particularly good example of this problem, that of Bob, an informant he worked with in the course of his study of tramps. Bob had spent four years on skid row; he was also a Harvard graduate, and had gone on to do postgraduate work in anthropology. Spradley recounts:

> On my next visit to the treatment center I invited Bob into my office. We chatted casually for a few minutes, then I started asking him some ethnographic questions. 'What kind of men go through Seattle City Jail and end up at this alcoholism treatment center?' I asked. 'I've been thinking about the men who are here,' Bob said thoughtfully. 'I would divide them up first in terms of race. There are Negroes, Indians, Caucasians, and a few Eskimo. Next I think I would divide them on the basis of their education. Some have almost none, a few have some college. Then some of the men are married and some are single.' For the next fifteen minutes he pro-

ceeded to give me the standard analytic categories that many social scientists use.

(Spradley 1979:53)

Where the researcher is particularly interested in the categories in terms of which participants view the world, this sort of account is of limited value. We must be careful, then, in analysing our material to be alert for the effects of audience in terms of people's views of the researcher's interests.

Even when the ethnographer is acting as observer, he or she may be an important audience for the participants, or at least for some of them. Informal questioning often forms part of participant observation, and Becker and Geer (1960) have pointed to the importance of distinguishing between solicited and unsolicited statements when assessing evidence. However, as we noted in Chapter 5, such a distinction is too crude. We cannot assume that unsolicited statements are uninfluenced by the researcher's presence. The same applies to other actions. It is now a central tenet of the sociological literature that people seek to manage impressions of themselves and of settings and groups with which they are associated (Goffman 1959). In a study of an Indian village community, Berreman (1962) only discovered the extent to which his data were the product of impression management by the villagers when he was forced to change his interpreter. This change modified his relationship with them, and produced different kinds of data.

Sometimes participants will actually tell an ethnographer that they have been presenting a front. Bogdan and Taylor quote the comment of an attendant in a state institution for the 'mentally retarded' made to an ethnographer at the end of the first day of fieldwork: 'Yeah, we didn't do a lot of things today that we usually do. Like if you wasn't here we woulda snitched some food at dinner and maybe hit a couple of 'em around. See before we didn't know you was an ok guy' (Bogdan and Taylor 1975:89). Of course, such admissions do not necessarily indicate that full access has finally been granted. While over the course of an extended stay in a setting participants generally acquire increasing trust in the ethnographer and find it more and more difficult to control the information available to him or her, members' creation and management of their personal fronts can prove a persistent problem. Thus, Punch (1979) reports how, at a party he attended some months after completing intensive and long-term fieldwork on police work in Amsterdam, one of his informants revealed to him, under the influence of alcohol, that he had been kept well away from evidence of police corruption. In the case of observational data too, then, one must be aware of the possible effects of the ethnographer as audience.

However, this concern with reactivity, with the effects of the researcher on the nature of the data he or she collects, can be somewhat misleading. Much as quantitative researchers seek to minimize reactivity through standardization, under the influence of naturalism ethnographers sometimes regard any effects of their presence or actions on the data simply as a source of bias. It is true that it can be a threat to the validity of inferences. However, participants' responses to ethnographers may also be an important source of information. Data in themselves cannot be valid or invalid; what is at issue are the inferences drawn from them. The point is that the ethnographer must try continually to be aware of *how* his or her presence may have shaped the data.

Similar considerations even apply in interpreting documents and data produced through secret research. Here too we must bear in mind the ways in which audience considerations may have shaped the actions and accounts produced. In secret participant observation, assuming cover has not been 'blown', the ethnographer cannot be an audience, as such. However, he or she may be an important audience in one or another participant identity. And we must remember that documents are always written for *some* audience, perhaps for several different ones simultaneously. This will shape the nature of the document, through what is taken as relevant, what can be assumed as background knowledge, what cannot or should not be said, and what must be said even if it is untrue. In the same way, in open participant observation and interviewing, consideration of the effects of audience must be extended beyond the role of the ethnographer. (One of the strengths of even open participant observation, of course, is that in 'natural' settings other audiences are generally much more powerful and significant for participants than the ethnographer, and their effects are likely to swamp those of the research.)

The significance of audience is heightened by the fact that the participants in a setting rarely perceive themselves as a homogeneous grouping. Different categories, groups, or factions are often involved, in relation to whom different fronts need to be maintained. And even within these divisions there will be more informal networks of communication that include some participants and exclude others, as Hitchcock shows in the case of a primary school's staff:

> On many occasions throughout the fieldwork, staff's comments would be prefaced by such statements as 'I know it's unprofessional of me talking like this . . .', 'I don't suppose I should really be telling you this', '. . . don't tell him I said this for goodness sake'. On other occasions when staff told me things these prefaces were not present; it was rather assumed that I wouldn't 'blow the scene' by telling someone else what had been said about them. That is, I was 'trusted' to keep things quiet or to keep what was said to myself.
>
> (Hitchcock 1983:30)

Different things will be said and done in different company. In particular we must interpret differently what is done 'in public' and what is done 'in private', since the category to which an action belongs may have important consequences for how it relates to actions and attitudes in other contexts. Of course, whether something is 'private' or 'public' is not always obvious, and there is a subtle shading between the two. One may have to know a setting very well in order to be able to recognize the public or private status of actions and even then it is easy to be mistaken. Indeed, what was public and private may get redefined retrospectively.

Even in the case of interviews, the ethnographer may not be the most significant audience, as we noted in Chapter 5. To one degree or another, and whatever assurances of confidentiality the ethnographer gives, interviewees may regard what they say as 'public' rather than 'private'; they may expect it to be communicated to others, or recorded for posterity. Krieger (1979a) provides an example from her research on a radio station. Reflecting on interviewees' confidence or trust, she remarks:

> I came to think it reflected an expectation that this telling in the interview situation was more than to one person, it was a telling to the world at large, and not only a bid for recognition by that world, but also perhaps for forgiveness.
>
> (Krieger 1979a:170–1)

Analysing data for the effects of audience is not, then, simply a matter of assessing the impact of the researcher, but also one of assessing the impact of any other audience the actor might be addressing, consciously or subconsciously. This applies to all forms of data and it is a crucial consideration if invalid inferences are to be avoided.

Time

What people say and do is produced in the context of a developing sequence of social interaction. If we ignore what has already occurred or what follows we are in danger of drawing the wrong conclusions. However, the temporal context of actions includes not only the host of events that occur before and after them but also the temporal framework in terms of which the people involved locate them. Glaser and Strauss (1968) provide a striking example in their study of how dying patients are dealt with by hospital staff. They note how staff construct and reconstruct conceptions of the dying trajectories of patients and how these play a key role in shaping their attitudes to the treatment of patients. Moreover, deviations from expected patterns can cause problems. How hospital staff react to signs of improvement in a patient, then, is dependent on the temporal context in terms of which they read those signs. Relevant here are not only what has happened in the past, but also estimates of what is likely to happen in the future. Nor is this restricted to the staff; patients' families may not always welcome signs of improvement in their condition, because these are seen as part of a painful and lingering death (Wright 1981).

Time is also an important consideration in the interpretation of interview data. Not only may what is said at one point in an interview be influenced by the interviewee's interpretation of what has been said earlier and what might be asked later, but it is also affected by what has happened to the person prior to the interview and what is anticipated in the near future. Ball (1983) has pointed out that many organizations are characterized by short- and long-term temporal cycles. Most universities and schools, for example, have terms whose beginnings and endings are important benchmarks for staff and students. Moreover, the different terms are not equivalent; they form part of a longer cycle based on the year – the autumn term is very different in many ways from the spring term, for example. For students, the years form part of an even larger cycle, their first year as freshers being very different in status from their final year as seniors. Data, of whatever kind, recorded at different times need to be examined in light of their place within the temporal patterns, short or long term, that structure the lives of those being studied. (For more on such patterns, see Roth 1963 and Zerubavel 1979).

From this point of view there are considerable advantages to be gained from combining interviews with participant observation. Each may provide information about temporal contexts whose implications for interpreting data can be assessed. The dangers of neglecting the effects of time are particularly great where reliance is placed upon a single data source, especially interviews or documents. Where interviews are used alone it is wise to give over some interview space to casual conversation about current events in the interviewee's life. Indeed, this may be a useful way of opening the interview to build rapport.

Once again, it is not a matter of accepting or rejecting data, but rather of knowing how to interpret them; there is a great temptation to assume that actions, statements, or interview responses represent stable features of the person or of settings. This may be correct, but it cannot be assumed. Actions are embedded in temporal contexts and these may shape them in ways that are important for the analysis.

Personnel

Who is doing or saying things is an equally important consideration when it comes to assessing the relationship between concept and evidence. People's identities or social locations (that is, the patterns of social relationships in which they are enmeshed) can have two kinds of effect on the nature of the accounts or actions they produce. First, social locations determine the kind of information available to people. They clearly affect what it is possible for people to see and hear 'at first hand'; they also determine what people will get to know about, and how they will get to know things 'second hand'. The other way in which identities affect actions and accounts is through the particular perspectives that people in various social locations tend to generate and that will filter their understanding and knowledge of the world, and shape their actions in it. In particular, the interpretation of information available to a person is likely to be selected and slanted in line with his or her prevailing interests and concerns. There may even be a strong element of wish-fulfilment involved. One must be aware of the possible effects of social location on all kinds of data, including ethnographers' own observational reports: we too occupy particular locations and what we observe, what we record, and how we interpret it will be influenced by these.

The implications of identity vary somewhat between information and perspective analysis. In the first, one is concerned with what information an account can provide about the cases being investigated. Here social location may be an important source of knowledge, but it is also a potential source of bias: it is a threat to validity that must be monitored. This kind of consideration must underlie the selection of informants and the interpretation of the data they provide, as well as the treatment of data from other sources. In perspective analysis, on the other hand, social location is no longer a source of bias, it is a key element in the analysis. Here the aim is precisely to document the perspectives of those in different social locations.

Of course, as we saw in Chapter 5, these two forms of analysis are complementary. And in the case of observational data produced by the ethnographer, their interaction is the essence of reflexivity.

The relationships between concepts and indicators must be assessed, then, by considering alternative interpretations of the data, and by following through the implications of particular interpretations to see if these are confirmed. And it is important here to take account of the dimensions of social context, time, and the people involved. However, some ethnographers have proposed more direct ways of testing these relationships. We will discuss two commonly mentioned strategies here: respondent validation and triangulation.

Respondent validation

A recognition of the importance of actors' social locations leads directly to the issue of 'respondent validation', a notion that has an uncertain and sometimes contested place in ethnographic analysis. Some ethnographers have argued that a crucial test for their accounts is whether the actors whose beliefs and behaviour they are describing recognize the validity of those accounts (Lincoln and Guba 1985). The aim is therefore to 'establish a correspondence between the sociologist's and the member's view of the member's social world by exploring the extent to which members recognize, give assent to, the judgments of the sociologist' (Bloor 1978:548–9).

In his own research on the decision rules employed by ENT (ear, nose, and throat) specialists, Bloor sent each specialist he studied a report describing their assessment practices. This was accompanied by a letter that asked each specialist to 'read through the report to see how far it corresponded with his own impressions of his clinic practice'. Bloor then discussed the reports in interviews with the doctors. He argues that for the most part the exercise was successful: 'some respondents endorsed my description of their practices, and where they did not the nature of the exercise was such as to enable me to correct the analysis so that this assent was no longer withheld' (1978:549). Using a different strategy, Ball (1981 and 1984), in his study of Beachside Comprehensive School, held two seminars for the school's staff at which he presented some of his findings. Ball's experience was rather less happy and fruitful, and suggests that while there is merit in the strategy, it is far from being problem-free.

The value of respondent validation lies in the fact that the participants involved in the events documented in the data may have access to additional knowledge of the context – of other relevant events, of temporal framework, of others' ulterior motives, for example – that is not available to the ethnographer. They may be part of information networks that are more powerful than those accessible to the ethnographer. In addition, they have access to their own experience of events, which may be of considerable importance. Such additional evidence may materially alter the plausibility of different possible interpretations of the data. Thus, Moffat (1989:329) reports how the conclusions of his research on students at Rutgers University were modified by their responses when he taught preliminary versions in his anthropology classes there.

At the same time, it is important to recognize the limitations of respondent validation. The information people receive through their networks may be false. Equally, we cannot assume that anyone is a privileged commentator on his or her own actions, in the sense that the truth of their account is guaranteed. As Schutz (1964) and others have noted, we can only grasp the meanings of our actions retrospectively. Moreover, these meanings must be reconstructed on the basis of memory; they are not given in any immediate sense. Nor will the evidence for them necessarily be preserved in memory. Much social action operates at a subconscious level, leaving no memory traces. Thus, in the case of Bloor's specialists, we cannot assume that they are consciously aware of the decision rules they use, or even that, infallibly, they can recognize them when someone documents them. In short, while people are well-placed informants on their own actions, they are no more than that; and their accounts must be analysed in the same way as any other data, with close consideration being given to possible threats to validity.

This is reinforced once we recognize that it may be in a person's interests to misinterpret or misdescribe his or her own actions, or to counter the interpretations of the ethnographer. Both Bloor and Ball point out that participants generally interpret data in the light of different concerns to, and sometimes by criteria at odds with, those of the ethnographer. Bloor acknowledges, for instance, that

I had expected the specialists to respond to the reports in a manner similar to that of an academic colleague when one asks him to criticize a draft paper one has written. I became aware of having made this assumption when it was violated – I suspected that some of the specialists had not read the report in the expected critical spirit. They had read the report, I felt, in the way that we today might read a nineteenth century religious tract – with a modicum of detached, superficial interest, with a feeling that it displayed a certain peculiar charm perhaps, but without being so moved by its content as to feel the necessity to define one's own beliefs and practices in accordance with it or in contrast to it. They were unversed in the conventions of academic sociological criticism and they were perhaps only marginally interested in the content of the reports.

(Bloor 1978:550)

As with all data collection and analysis, then, people's reactions to the ethnographer's account will be coloured by their social position and their perceptions of the research act. In the case of Bloor's doctors, they only had a marginal interest; Ball's school teachers, on the other hand, displayed a keener commitment. But this, too, was directly related to their social locations, and was at odds with that of the researcher:

> many of the staff had apparently read my chapter solely in terms of what it had to say about them or their subject. There was little or no discussion of the general issues I was trying to raise or the overall arguments of the chapter.... I had taken as my task as ethnographer the description and analysis of large scale trends which extended as I saw them across the whole school, an overview. The staff responded from their particular view of the school, from the vantage point of the position they held.
>
> (Ball 1984:18–19)

Ball's teachers interpreted his work as critical, and queried the validity of his findings. (Scarth reports a similar experience: Scarth 1986:202–3.)

Such feedback, then, can be highly problematic. Whether respondents are enthusiastic, indifferent, or hostile, their reactions cannot be taken as direct validation or refutation of the observer's inferences. Rather, such processes of so-called 'validation' should be treated as yet another valuable source of data and insight.

Triangulation

Respondent validation represents one kind of triangulation: the checking of inferences drawn from one set of data sources by collecting data from others. More specifically, data-source triangulation involves the comparison of data relating to the same phenomenon but deriving from different phases of the fieldwork, different points in the temporal cycles occurring in the setting, or, as in respondent validation, the accounts of different participants (including the ethnographer) differentially located in the setting. This last form of data-source triangulation can be extended indefinitely by showing each participant the others' accounts and recording his or her comments on them (Adelman

1977). This is very time-consuming but, besides providing a validity check, it also gives added depth to the description of the social meanings involved in a setting.

The term 'triangulation' derives from a loose analogy with navigation and surveying. For someone wanting to locate their position on a map, a single landmark can only provide the information that they are situated somewhere along a line in a particular direction from that landmark. With two landmarks, however, one's exact position can be pinpointed by taking bearings on both; one is at the point on the map where the two lines cross. In social research, if we rely on a single piece of data there is the danger that undetected error in our inferences may render our analysis incorrect. If, on the other hand, diverse kinds of data lead to the same conclusion, we can be a little more confident in that conclusion. This confidence is well founded to the degree that the different kinds of data have different likely directions of error built into them.

There are a number of other kinds of triangulation besides that relating to participants' accounts. First, there is the possibility of triangulating between different researchers. While team research has sometimes been used by ethnographers, often the data generated by different observers have been designed to be complementary, relating to different aspects of a setting or different settings, rather than intended to facilitate triangulation. Nevertheless, team research offers the opportunity for researcher triangulation. Of course, to maximize its potentialities the observers should be as different as possible, for example adopting very different roles in the field. Second, there is technique triangulation. Here, data produced by different data collection techniques are compared. To the extent that these techniques involve different kinds of validity threat, they provide a basis for checking interpretations. Ethnography often involves a combination of techniques and thus it may be possible to assess the validity of inferences between indicators and concepts by examining data relating to the same concept from participant observation, interviewing, and documents.

In triangulation, then, links between concepts and indicators are checked by recourse to other indicators. However, triangulation is not a simple test. Even if the results tally, this provides no guarantee that the inferences involved are correct. It may be that all the inferences are invalid, that as a result of systematic

or even random error they lead to the same, incorrect, conclusion. What is involved in triangulation is not the combination
of different kinds of data *per se*, but rather an attempt to relate
different sorts of data in such a way as to counteract various
possible threats to the validity of our analysis.

One should not, therefore, adopt a naively 'optimistic' view
that the aggregation of data from different sources will unproblematically add up to produce a more complete picture.
Although few writers have commented on it, differences
between sets or types of data may be just as important and
illuminating. Lever (1981) provides a valuable insight into this.
Researching sex differences in children's play, she collected data
by means of questionnaires and diaries. The former suggested
greater sex differences than the latter. Lever argues that this
reflects varying effects of stereotyping according to 'the nature
of the method or the posing of the question'. She claims that
this is why the children's statements of what they 'usually do'
collected in her questionnaire show stronger sex differences than
the information about what they 'actually do' collected in
diaries. In short, Lever suggests that 'abstract or unconditional
inquiries yield responses that more closely correspond to a person's perceptions of social norms than inquiries of a concrete or
detailed nature' (1981:205).

The lesson to be learned here, once again, is that data must
never be taken at face value. It is misleading to regard some as
true and some as false. Rather, as Lever's research indicates,
what is involved in triangulation is a matter not of checking
whether data are valid, but of discovering which inferences from
those data are valid. Incidentally, it is worth noting that the sort
of remarks offered by Zelditch (1962) on the suitability of different methods for field research, and by Becker and Geer (1957)
on participant observation and interviewing, can be read in this
light. These papers and others like them are normally cited
either to advocate one method against another, or to commend
the combination of different methods, but even more they lend
weight to the idea of reflexive triangulation.

THEORIES AND THE COMPARATIVE METHOD

Ethnographers have sometimes been reluctant to admit that one
of their concerns is the production of causal models. This stems

in part, no doubt, from the positivist connotations of the term 'causality', and perhaps also from a recognition of the extreme difficulty of assessing the validity of theoretical claims about causal relations. Nevertheless, theories implying causal relationships, not always clearly marked or expressed, are common in ethnographic work. It is important that the presence and significance of such theories are recognized and that they are explicated as fully as necessary, and, at some point, systematically developed and tested. (For a useful guide to the explication of causal models, see Hage and Meeker 1988.)

There is only one general method for testing causal relations – the comparative method – though there are different ways of using it. By assessing the patterning of social events under different circumstances, we can test the scope and the strength of the relationships posited by a theory. One version of the comparative method is the experiment. Here, at its simplest, a particular factor is varied across situations that are identical in all respects considered relevant. By holding constant factors involved in plausible rival theories, and by varying the cause specified in the theory being tested, the existence and strength of the presumed causal relation can be checked. Experiments are the most powerful means of assessing the validity of claims about causal relations. However, one can never be certain that all relevant variables have been controlled; and there are some serious disadvantages to the experimental method, notably its tendency to low ecological validity (its artificial character), as well as the political and ethical limits on its use. Given this, it is important to emphasize that experiments are not the only way in which the comparative method can be used to test causal hypotheses, even though they are taken as the ideal by positivism.

The positivist emphasis on the experiment as the model of scientific inquiry goes hand in hand with what Becker (1970) has called the 'single study model', which prescribes that all research be devoted to the rigorous testing of theoretical hypotheses. While ethnography can certainly be used to test theories, by no means all ethnographies are, or need to be, directed to this goal. As we saw earlier, instead they often provide relatively concrete descriptions or rather more developed typologies and models. And there is no obligation on the part of an ethnographer to engage in systematic theory testing in any particular study. At the same time, it should be said that theories do require rigorous testing, and that many theoretical models developed in ethnographic research are still waiting in vain for such treatment. In this respect, ethnography as a whole suffers from an even more serious form of 'analytic interruptus' than that which Lofland (1970) diagnosed (Hammersley 1985, 1987a and b).

There has been some ethnographic work that has grappled explicitly with the problems of testing theories. The procedural model usually adopted here is that of analytic induction. This involves the following steps:

1 An initial definition of the phenomenon to be explained is formulated (for example, addiction to opiate drugs, embezzlement, etc.).
2 Some cases of this phenomenon are investigated, documenting potential explanatory features.
3 A hypothetical explanation is framed on the basis of analysis of the data, designed to identify common factors across the cases.
4 Further cases are investigated to test the hypothesis.
5 If the hypothesis does not fit the facts from these new cases, either the hypothesis is reformulated or the phenomenon to be explained is redefined (so that the negative cases are excluded).
6 This procedure of examining cases, reformulating the hypothesis, and/or redefining the phenomenon is continued until new cases continually confirm the validity of the hypothesis, at which point it may be concluded that the hypothesis is correct (though this can never be known with absolute certainty).

This procedure is represented in Figure 3.

There are relatively few accounts of this method in use. Cressey's (1950) work on 'trust violation' provides a good example, as does that of Lindesmith (1947) on drug addiction. Analytic induction was originally developed by Znaniecki (1934) in explicit opposition to the statistical method. He claimed that it was the true method of the physical and biological sciences, and asserted its superiority on the grounds that it produces universal not probabilistic statements. However, Znaniecki's argument is not convincing. As Robinson (1969) has pointed

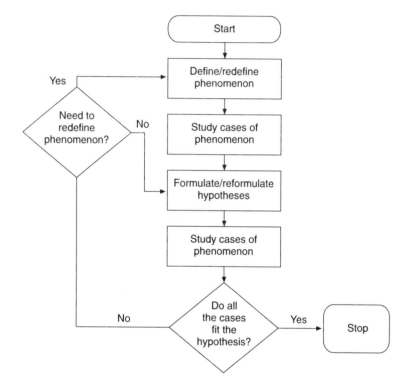

Figure 3 The process of analytic induction
Source: Hammersley 1989b:170

out, he drew too sharp a distinction between analytic induction and statistical method; and in fact the capacity of analytic induction to produce universal statements derives from being concerned only with necessary, and not with sufficient, conditions.

Besides the inclusion of sufficient as well as necessary conditions, there is another element we might add to analytic induction. The geneticist William Bateson is reported to have advised his students: 'Treasure your exceptions!' He argues that they are 'like the rough brickwork of a growing building which tells that there is more to come and shows where the next construction is to be' (quoted in Lipset 1980:54). Both Cressey and Lindesmith do this, but they do not seem actively to have searched for exceptions, a strategy rightly recommended by Popper (1972). While no number of confirming instances can ever guarantee the validity of a theory, we can increase the chances of our acceptance of it being well founded if we adopt this strategy.

Analytic induction, developed to cover both necessary and sufficient conditions, and to include the search for negative evidence, seems a plausible reconstruction of the logic of theoretical science, not just of ethnography concerned with the production of theory. In this sense Znaniecki was almost certainly correct in the claims he made for it. In many respects it corresponds to the hypothetico-deductive method. Where it differs from this, and most importantly, is in making clear that the testing of theoretical ideas is not the end point of the process of scientific inquiry but is generally only one step leading to further development and refinement of the theory. (Some accounts of the hypothetico-deductive method recognize this; see, for example, Hempel 1966.)

At the same time, however, we need to recognize what is presupposed by analytic induction. It assumes that social phenomena are governed by deterministic, albeit conditional, laws; such that if conditions X, Y, and Z occur, then event A will be produced in all circumstances. There are objections to this from several directions; and among ethnographers in particular the concept of deterministic laws is often rejected on the grounds that it denies the manifest capacity of people to make decisions about how to act. As we saw in Chapter 1, this is a key element of naturalism. In one of the most influential discussions of this issue, Matza (1969) argues that while people can behave in a manner that is predictable by laws, human life proper involves a transcendence of determining conditions. (For a discussion of the history and current status of analytic induction in the light of these problems, see Hammersley 1989b.)

TYPES OF THEORY

We have emphasized that by no means all ethnographic work is, or need be, concerned explicitly with the refinement and testing of theories. Equally, we should note the range of different types of theory with which ethnographers may be concerned. For example, in sociology there is a well-established, though by no means always clearly expressed, distinction between macro and micro levels of analysis.

'Macro' refers to theories that apply to large-scale systems of social relations. This may involve tracing linkages across the structure of a national society or even relations among different nation-states. Micro research, by contrast, is concerned with analysing more local forms of social organization, whether particular institutions or particular types of face-to-face encounter. What we have here, then, is a dimension along which the scale of the phenomena under study varies.

While in many respects ethnography is better suited to research on micro theory, it can play an important role in developing and testing macro theories (see, for example, Willis 1977 and 1981). Macro theories necessarily make claims about processes occurring in particular places and times that can be tested and developed through ethnographic inquiry. There have also been attempts to integrate macro and micro levels in various ways or to show that there is in fact only one level, not two. (See Knorr-Cetina and Cicourel 1981; also Hammersley 1984b.)

Cross-cutting the macro–micro dimension is the distinction that Glaser and Strauss (1967) make between substantive and formal theory. While macro–micro relates to variation in the scope of the cases under study, the substantive–formal dimension concerns the generality of the categories under which cases are subsumed. Formal categories subsume substantive categories. Thus, for example, the substantive study of taxi-drivers and their 'fares' can be placed under more formal categories such as 'service encounters' or 'fleeting relationships' (Davis 1959). Similarly, the study of a particular society can be used as an initial basis for theory about a general type of social formation; thus, Britain may be taken as an instance of capitalist, industrial, or even postmodern society.

Given these two dimensions, we can identify four broad types of theory, and, indeed, examples of all of these can be found in the work of ethnographers. Analyses of the structure, functioning, and development of societies in general, such as those of Radcliffe-Brown (1948b) and Harris (1979), are macro–formal.

Studies of particular societies, for instance Malinowski (1922) or Chagnon (1968), fall into the macro–substantive category. Micro–formal work consists of studies of more local forms of social organization. Examples would be Goffman on the 'presentation of self' (1959) and 'interaction ritual' (1972); Glaser and Strauss (1971) on 'status passage'; and Sacks on the organization of conversation (Sacks *et al.* 1974). Finally, there is micro–substantive research on particular types of organization or situation: for instance, Strong (1979) on 'doctor–patient interaction' or Piliavin and Briar (1964) on 'police encounters with juveniles'. All these types of theory are worthwhile, but it is important to keep clearly in mind the kind of theory one is dealing with, since each would require the research to be pursued in a different direction. (For a discussion of the development of formal as opposed to substantive theory, see Glaser and Strauss 1967; Glaser 1978.)

CONCLUSION

In this chapter we have looked at the process of analysis in ethnography, tracing it from foreshadowed problems and the initial examination of a body of data, through the generation of concepts of various kinds, to the development of typologies and theories. In addition, we examined the relationship between concepts and indicators in ethnographic research, and the testing of theoretical ideas by means of the comparative method. We stressed that there are different sorts of theory and that theories are not the only product of ethnographic work; equally common and important are descriptions and explanations. We must not forget, however, that typically all the various products of ethnographic work, whatever their other differences, take the form of texts: ethnographic analysis is not just a cognitive activity but a form of writing. This has some important implications, as we shall see in the next chapter.

Chapter 9

Writing ethnography

THE DISCIPLINES OF READING AND WRITING

One cannot ignore the work of reading and writing in the construction of ethnographic research. It is now widely recognized that 'the ethnography' is produced as much by how we write as by the processes of data collection and analysis; equally, how we write is linked directly to how we read.

The writing of ethnography – like any writing – demands discipline and work. There is no more damaging myth than the idea that there is a mysterious 'gift', or that writing is a matter of 'inspiration'. As Brodkey (1987) has pointed out, there is a pervasive romantic image of the writer as an essentially solitary figure struggling with a recalcitrant muse. Such views are dangerous and misleading. They inhibit systematic reflection on writing (and reading) as necessary aspects of the disciplinary or craft skills of social scientists. Given the reflexivity of social inquiry, it is vital to recognize that ethnographers construct the accounts of the social world to be found in ethnographic texts, rather than those accounts simply mirroring reality. And those accounts are constructed on the basis of particular purposes and presuppositions. Equally, one must recognize the significance of how those texts are read by social scientists, students, and others.

As more and more scholars have come to realize, then ethnography is inescapably a textual enterprise. It is not just a matter of writing, of course. When Clifford Geertz announces that 'ethnographers write' he offers a revealing half-truth: ethnographers do more than that. But writing is at the heart of the ethnographic enterprise. It is, therefore, important that a disciplined approach to ethnographic work should incorporate a critical awareness of writing itself. The discipline of writing is not just about the practical demands of getting words on paper; it requires the cultivation of a critical and theoretical orientation to textual practices.

Written language is an analytical tool, not a transparent medium of communication. We can never reduce writing to a simple set of 'skills' or prescriptions. What is needed is a rigorous understanding of texts as the products of readers' and writers' work. It thus calls for a widening of the ethnographer's traditional range of interests. One needs to think about more than 'research methods', as conventionally defined, or the substantive subject-matter. The contemporary ethnographer also needs to take some account of contributions from literary theory, rhetoric, text linguistics, and cognate fields. The aim is not to transform ethnography into yet another branch of 'cultural studies'. Rather, we need to cultivate an awareness of reading and writing as elementary features of ethnographic production.

At the same time, the discipline of writing implies embodied craft knowledge. It cannot be grasped and developed by pure reflection. While informed by reading and textual interpretation, it must be practised. Writing ethnography is intellectual *work*. In the course of that work, the ethnographer will recognize that there is no best way to 'write up' any given project. Indeed, the conventional rhetoric of 'writing up' has connotations that are quite inappropriate to the work of the reflexive ethnographer. There are many versions that can be constructed. There are different emphases, different theories, different audiences. Each way of constructing 'the ethnography' will bring out different emphases, and complementary – even contrasting – analyses. While our texts do not have an arbitrary relationship to 'the field', it is important to recognize as early as possible that there is no single best way to reconstruct and represent the social world.

The world does not arrange itself into chapters and subheadings for our convenience. There are many contrasting arrangements and 'literary' styles that we can impose, more or less legitimately, on the world. The author who fails to reflect on the processes of composition and compilation may find that a version has been constructed without adequate explicit understanding. The unthinking adoption of one or another textual arrangement is an abdication of control over one's material. Equally, the experience of writing – or at least considering – alternative versions or using different written styles can encourage greater mastery. Principled decisions about *how* to write are far better than drowning in a welter of data, or facing the paralysis of writer's block while waiting for inspiration to strike.

Our understanding of writing is inextricably linked to *reading*. We write in the light of what and how we read. For ethnographers (as for other scholars) the intellectual tradition of the discipline (anthropology, sociology, geography, folklore) 'writes itself' through their work. The individual scholar does not create his or her discipline afresh. The textual conventions of the past cannot be escaped entirely. The scholarly texts and the language, concepts, images, and metaphors of predecessors help to define the discursive space within which each new ethnography is produced and read. Hence it follows that the disciplines of writing are inextricable from the disciplines of reading. Ethnographers write, certainly; but their writing is shaped by what they have read.

The good ethnographer cannot hope to succeed without a habit of wide reading. The ethnographer ideally develops a broad, comparative perspective on the literature. Indeed, in their original formulation of 'grounded theory', Glaser and Strauss (1967) commended the creative use of written sources in the production and elaboration of concepts. It is the hallmark of creative work by interpretative social scientists that they approach 'the literature' in a catholic and creative fashion. One of the most important disciplines for the ethnographer developing craft skills is, therefore, to *read* the work of others. We need to cultivate the capacity to read for the rhetoric and forms of writing employed by others, rather than merely reading for content. That reading need not be confined to the work of other ethnographers, or other social scientists. There are, after all, many genres through which authors explore and express social worlds. The domains of fiction and non-fiction alike provide many sources and models for written representations. There is nothing which totally distinguishes fictional from non-fictional writing. There are differences, of course: non-fictional writing is committed to the accurate representation of some actual events, or the presentation of an abstract model that captures the essential features of the phenomena in question. Fictional writing is not committed and constrained in those ways. Nevertheless, there is no reason why the aspiring writer of anthropology or sociology should not learn from careful readings of many different genres. An acquaintance with the anatomy of a wide variety of texts will encourage an appreciation of how to make novel and insightful texts of one's own.

Wide and eclectic reading can also encourage the development of 'sensitizing concepts' (Blumer 1954). The creative ethnographer will not wish to wait until the 'writing-up' phase of the research before exploring possible sources and models. Indeed, the disciplines of reading should inform the research from its earliest phases: creative reading should ideally run through the entire process of research. The sources may be drawn from diverse origins. Many of our most successful sociological mentors have drawn on wide and eclectic reading. Erving Goffman's work was a prime example. His most successful studies generated highly original and productive insights on the basis of quite diverse written sources. Careful consideration of one of Goffman's major texts, such as *Asylums* (1961), will help illuminate just how adept he was at drawing together diverse ideas and observations, both 'fictional' and 'factual', 'serious' and 'popular'. For instance, in the essay 'The inmate world', in *Asylums*, Goffman's citations and quotations include: J. Kerkhoff, *How Thin the Veil: A Newspaperman's Story of His Own Mental Crack-Up and Recovery*; Ellie A. Cohen, *Human Behavior in the Concentration Camp*; Eugen Kogon, *The Theory and Practice of Hell*; Brendan Behan, *Borstal Boy*; Sara Harris, *The Wayward Ones: The Holy Rule of St Benedict*; Herman Melville, *White Jacket*; T.E. Gaddis, *Birdman of Alcatraz*; and a host of sociological, psychological, psychiatric, and other sources. There is no need for anyone to aspire to emulate Goffman's style in order to recognize and learn from his genius for using such resources in the construction of texts at once readerly and scholarly.

The general point was made by Davis (1974), who pointed to a number of thematic parallels between classic works of fiction and sociological classics. Davis noted that, like many other story-tellers, sociologists construct narratives of tragedy, irony, and humour. The important issue in Davis's analysis is to remind us that there is no absolute difference between the way a social scientist writes and the way a more 'literary' author tackles a similar topic. Further, both types of author have only the same fundamental resources – words on the page. All use the same sorts of recipes and materials in conveying arguments and persuading readers. Their readers bring to texts a common stock of understandings and assumptions. Equally, therefore, when we read *Asylums* and then turn to one of its literary analogues, such as *One Flew Over the Cuckoo's Nest*, we can start to recognize how each author uses the possibilities of written language to convey the experiences of inmates. Each author constructs a version of that sort of social world. Each does so under different auspices, for different purposes, and for different audiences. But if we wish to gain control over the resources of 'literary' style, then it will repay us to read critically both works, and others like them. Likewise, the ethnographer interested in everyday life in medical institutions will find plenty of productive themes, parallels, and contrasts within literary sources. It is an excellent intellectual exercise to read the literary and the sociological or anthropological together. That exercise makes one more aware of one's own work as a writer, as well as sharpening awareness of textual possibilities. There is a good deal to be learned from a comparative reading of, say, Thomas Mann's *Magic Mountain* and Betty MacDonald's *The Plague and I*, together with Julius Roth's ethnography of everyday life in a TB sanatorium (Roth 1963), and perhaps also Sontag (1979) on images of tuberculosis.

The point is not to argue that works of serious or popular fiction are to be read as if they were sources of 'data'. We do not assume that the work of a novelist – even when based on personal testimony or 'research' – is the equivalent of thoroughly researched, explicitly documented, and theoretically developed scholarship. Equally, we do not think that the ethnographer will necessarily wish to reproduce more overtly 'literary' styles of reportage. Rather, the reflective scholar will wish to be acquainted with a range of styles and conventions that are culturally available for the construction of descriptions and arguments. Neither the academic nor the writer of fiction has a monopoly over the relevant resources of written language. There is little point in the academic agonizing over epistemology and methodology, or suffering the slings and arrows of data collection, only to have no disciplined awareness of the means available to report those efforts.

In a similar vein various authors such as Pratt (1986a) have pointed out the textual parallels between ethnographic description and the conventions of 'travel' or explorers' accounts. The classic anthropological monograph incorporated elements characteristic of other genres that anthropologists would repudiate. The founding scholars of social and cultural anthropology did not just carve out a discipline; they adapted and incorporated literary conventions from other genres to produce a new textual format. The student of academic writing, and the writer of ethnography, can learn much about the ethnographic mode from careful comparisons of anthropology with the texts of travel writers, past and present. One may ask how different authors conjure up the spirit of a place, evoke its inhabitants, and construct the cultural forms. Then too there are various popularized and fictionalized accounts of ethnographic work (for example, Bowen 1954; Donner 1982). A reading of them and their reception by professional anthropologists again illuminates the commonalities and contrasts across the different bodies of writing (Pratt 1986b).

There are many genres and styles of both 'fact' and 'fiction'. The would-be ethnographic author will profitably explore their range and diversity. He or she will not necessarily remain content with following just one established sociological or anthropological exemplar. The sociologist of contemporary society or the 'anthropologist at home' may fruitfully explore the many ways in which modern industrial society has been represented: from realist novels to the 'new journalism' (Agar 1980). The ethnographer of a great city like London or Chicago will find many literary themes and images to explore, as will the student of small towns and rural 'communities'. The point has been made quite explicitly by Cappetti (1993) in relation to Chicago. She starts from the well-known affinities between the sociological representations of Chicago in the early decades of this century and the work of various literary figures. It was not an accident that the same Chicago fostered urban ethnography and realist fiction that often focused on similar subject-matter and shared similar values. There was direct overlap between the sociological and literary circles. James Farrell, author of the Studs Lonigan trilogy, read sociology at Chicago, while Chicago sociologists were encouraged to pay attention to realist fiction (cf. Atkinson 1982). Writing of those mutual influences, Cappetti remarks that

If one cannot properly understand the urban novels of James T. Farrell, Nelson Algren, and Richard Wright apart from the urban sociological studies that preceded and accompanied them, it would be equally a mistake to ignore the literary and, specifically, the novelistic influences that the Chicago sociologists themselves derived from the European and American urban literary tradition.

(Cappetti 1993:20)

An informed understanding of the genres and styles of literary or academic representation, therefore, forms a useful part of the ethnographer's craft knowledge. It is of crucial importance to recognize that crafting the ethnographic text is integral to the work of ethnography. 'Writing up' is not a mechanical exercise that can be performed routinely at the end of the 'real' research. The representation or reconstruction of a social world depends on how we write.

ETHNOGRAPHY AND RHETORIC

Whatever their chosen styles, then ethnographers need to have some awareness of the rhetorical devices that have been used in the production of ethnographic texts. In recent years there has been considerable scholarly interest in what conventions can be identified and how they are deployed in ethnographic writing. The discipline of anthropology has figured most prominently in this scrutiny of the ethnographic text, but this has reflected a much wider scholarly preoccupation with the 'rhetoric of inquiry' in both the natural sciences and the humane disciplines.

The ethnographer necessarily uses various figures of speech (tropes). These are used to construct recognizable and plausible reconstructions of social actors, actions, and settings. They are also used to convey many of the analytic themes as well. Very often, key concepts in sociology and anthropology are, in the broadest sense, metaphorical, in that they draw on imagery, analogy, and other devices. A physical and spatial image – transferred originally from other disciplinary contexts such as geology – is applied to social arrangements, giving the metaphor of 'social stratification', for example. In a similar way 'the market' is a metaphor, in that its usage in contemporary economics and social theory is extended well beyond its original designation of a 'market' as a local social institution. Indeed, such metaphors become so taken for granted in academic discourse that they lose the appearance of metaphorical usage.

Other well-established metaphors retain their 'as if' character. Goffman's well-known 'dramaturgical' metaphor – treating everyday social action in the guise of theatrical performances – may have lost its initial novelty, but it is still immediately recognized as a borrowing from one domain and an application to another. (This well-worn example also reminds us of the productive value of metaphorical usage. It prompts further analogies: the use of props, contrasts between backstage and front-of-house, the rehearsal of performances, and so on.) Whether overtly metaphorical or taken for granted, however, much of our thinking is organized by the use of metaphors. This is by no means confined to the ethnographic genre. McCloskey (1985) demonstrates the pervasiveness of metaphorical expression in modern economics, for example.

As an author of ethnography one's task is not to try to avoid metaphorical usage (and it is virtually impossible to do so anyway). The scholarly or scientific authenticity of a text is not enhanced by the elimination of analogy and simile. The graphic use of metaphorical descriptions must always be part of the ethnographer's repertoire. But equally this is no recommendation of absolute licence. A recognition of the power of figurative language should lead also to recognition of the need for disciplined and principled usage. If deployed without due reflection, metaphors may prove, like the apprentice sorcerer's accomplices, helpers that get out of hand, running away with and finally overwhelming their hapless originator. The reflective ethnographer, then, will need to try out figures of speech: testing them against the data, searching not just for their power to organize data under a single theme, but also for their extensions and limitations. They may be productive of new, often unanticipated, insights. The writer of ethnography will therefore need to try out and explore the values of various figures of speech, gauging their relevance to the issues at hand, sensing the range of connotations, allusions, and implications. Noblit and Hare (1988) usefully summarize a number of criteria that may be brought to bear on the choice and evaluation of metaphors. They include 'economy', 'cogency', and 'range'. Economy refers to the simplicity with which the concept summarizes; cogency to the efficiency of the metaphor, without 'redundancy, ambiguity and contradiction'; range refers to the capacity of the metaphor to draw together diverse domains (Noblit and Hare 1988:34).

Some features of the work of metaphor can be seen in Atkinson's work on the ethnography of medical education. In making sense of observations of bedside teaching it was apparent that the clinicians were able to use the hospital patients (whose diagnoses were often well known already) to produce displays of clinical wizardry and acumen to audiences of medical students. In various intermediate stages of writing and analysis Atkinson tried out various literary and other parallels, and at one point explored the metaphor of the medical teacher as 'thaumaturge', or wonder-worker. The term was chosen to be redolent of magical and religious 'mysteries', for there were connotations of the students being admitted to the mysteries of their craft (and hence of other ceremonials of admission, such as those found in Masonic ritual). Thaumaturgy would therefore capture and evoke potentially more than an unvarnished description of what the teachers and students did. Likewise, the metaphor implied its own extensions: the work of the hospital patient in such encounters could have been compared to that of the 'member of the audience' whose aid is solicited by the stage magician, for instance. In the published accounts this particular metaphor was not pursued, and its more florid connotations were not developed. There was a danger of glib sensationalism that was felt to be inappropriate. Many of the ideas were subsumed within a similar but different set of metaphors (Atkinson 1976 and 1981).

The productive exploration of ethnographic fieldwork and data, therefore, can involve experimentation and reflection on metaphorical usage, though the processes are not necessarily susceptible to conscious and rational control. They are often the products of our 'divergent' rather than 'convergent' thought processes. Nonetheless, the metaphorical can be facilitated. The ethnographic author should be willing to try out a range of possible concepts and analogies. The fruitful search is not for the 'best' set of ideas, but for a diversity of possible organizing themes and tropes. They can be assessed for the extent to which they capture the desired dimensions or categories; the appropriateness of connotations; their value in suggesting new lines of analysis and comparison. There is a direct continuity between metaphorical thought and the development of 'generic' concepts as advocated by Lofland and Lofland (1984). They link and juxtapose. They help to make the 'familiar' seem 'strange', and vice versa.

The master-trope of the metaphor is complemented by that of synecdoche. It is a form of representation in which the 'part' stands for the 'whole'. It is not, therefore, just a source of allusion; it is an inevitable feature of descriptions. In principle, it is not possible to provide a description of anything that will furnish a listing of every conceivable attribute and detail. In practice most descriptions do not even approximate to an exhaustive listing. Equally, what we treat as 'data' are necessarily synecdochal. We select particular features and instances, identify them as somehow characteristic or representative of places, persons, or events. We endow particular fragments of observed or reported life with significance, precisely in the way we choose and present them as 'examples', 'illustrations, 'cases', or 'vignettes'.

The criteria that may be brought to bear are varied. Aesthetic criteria undoubtedly interact with more logical issues. The principled use of synecdoche will almost certainly be regulated by craft judgments rather than by rigid formulae. Issues of economy and redundancy will always arise. The question of economy reflects the fact that we cannot include every detail and every scrap of knowledge. Not only are time and space at a premium in the production of any written account, so too is the reader's attention. Descriptions and exemplifications that are too dense, too detailed, or too protracted will not normally lead to a usable text. Comprehensiveness and comprehensibility compete to some extent. For the most part there is a trade-off between the two, and the ethnographer needs to construct accounts through partial, selective reporting. The relationship between the 'part' and the 'whole' needs to be a valid one, of course. The choice of exemplification or illustration must reflect adequate analysis of the data, in terms of concepts and indicators. The synecdoche is, therefore, the complement of the metaphor. Both use natural language to produce 'telling' accounts. The metaphor transforms and illuminates while the synecdoche describes and exemplifies. Each contrasts again with 'metonymy', the third of what are often referred to as the 'master-tropes'.

The metonymic in language exploits the dimensions of contiguity, causality, and sequence. The ethnographer uses metonymic language to organize the 'realist' descriptions of places and accounts of social action. Metonymy is the dominant mode through which ethnography narrates. The narrative is by no means the only style of ethnographic reportage, but it is of fundamental importance. Indeed, many scholarly accounts – not just ethnographies – tell 'stories'. Sometimes they are the 'grand narratives' of modern social theory (such as those of Marx) or of natural history (Darwin). Sometimes they are parables, such as the hypothetical morality tales propounded by economists (McCloskey 1985).

Richardson (1990a and b) and others have pointed out that the narrative mode is crucial to the organization of everyday life (in the form of mundane stories and accounts of personal experience) and of the organization of the ethnography itself. The ethnographer draws on and elicits narratives as 'data' and recasts them in the sociological or anthropological narratives of scholarly writing. The narrative mode is especially pertinent to the subject-matter of ethnographic inquiry. It furnishes meaning and reason to the reported events through contextual and processual presentations:

> Given the unavoidability of narrative within the social sciences, and given how human values, sensibilities, and ambiguities continuously reassert themselves in plain writing, we are propelled into taking seriously the relevance of narrative to the sociological enterprise. Narrative cannot be suppressed within the human sciences because it is ineluctably tied to the human experience; trying to suppress it undermines the very foundation of the human sciences.
>
> (Richardson 1990a:21)

Narrative creates particular kinds of order. It constructs accounts of intentions, and of unintended consequences. It reflects the fundamental importance of the temporal ordering of human experience (Adam 1990). In narrating events, we show how people act and react in particular social circumstances. In doing so we reveal and reconstruct those social actors as 'characters' or social 'types'. Equally, we can display the patterning of action and interaction, its predictable routines, and the unpredictable surprises or crises. We can 'show' the reader both the mundane and the exotic.

Further, the overall 'significance' of the ethnographic monograph may be conveyed through its narrative structures:

> Beyond the fragmentary narratives of persons and circumstances are the metanarratives that shape the ethnography overall. The ethnographic monograph, for instance, may be ordered in terms of large-scale narratives. It may take the form of a story of thwarted intentions; a display of order in chaos; or disorder in a rational organization. It can set up a reader's expectations only to deny them. It can transform the reported events of everyday life into the grand mythologies of human tragedy or triumph. The ethnography itself can become a morality tale; a high drama; a picaresque tale of low-life characters; a comedy of manners; a rural idyll. It may draw explicitly on literary parallels and archetypes.
>
> (Atkinson 1992b:13)

The transformation of 'the field' into 'the text' is partly achieved by means of the narrative construction of everyday life. The ethnographer needs to recognize the crafts of storytelling and learn to develop them critically. As Richardson argues, the narrative mode is to be valued as a basic tool in the ethnographer's craft:

> If we wish to understand the deepest and most universal of human experiences, if we wish our work to be faithful to the lived experiences of people, if we wish for a union between poetics and science, or if we wish to use our privileges and skills to empower the people we study, then we *should* value the narrative.
>
> (Richardson 1990b:133–4)

The point for the practising ethnographic author is, therefore, the need to recognize the analytic power of the narrative: to recognize and use narrative reconstructions in a disciplined manner.

The last of the master-tropes, irony, has been employed a great deal by social scientists – ethnographers among them – and it has been commented on quite widely. An ironic tone is highly characteristic of the social scientist's stance, and is most clearly marked when a perspectival, relativist point of view is adopted. The interpretative cultural scientist frequently trades in implicit or explicit contrasts. Ironic contrasts are frequently drawn on in the development of sociological or anthropological analyses. We trade in the complex and sometimes difficult contrasts between the 'familiar' and the 'strange', between the 'taken for granted' and the explicitly theorized, between intentions and 'unintended consequences' of social action. The ethnographer's insights are often produced out of the contrasts between competing frames of reference or rationality. Conventional morality may be contrasted with the situated moralities of particular cultures and subcultures. The constant dialectic between the Ethnographer, the Reader, and the Others (who are represented in the text) is replete with possibilities for irony.

The four 'master-tropes' we have just discussed are all intertwined within any given ethnographic monograph or similar text. We do not stop to decide to use one particular trope now, and turn to another later. We construct more or less successful accounts as we link large narrative themes with smaller narratives of instances. Those in turn stand in relationships of 'part-for-whole' for the general features of our chosen research settings and the social actors there. Likewise those general features and their analytic significance are often captured through our use of metaphoric figures.

Duneier's ethnography illustrates the deployment of the tropes of ethnographic composition in a highly readable and persuasive account (Duneier 1992). His is an ethnography based on a small number of black men in one particular neighbourhood of Chicago – a setting that is, of course, redolent of many earlier classics of ethnographic urban research. Duneier provides a number of vivid, graphically written accounts of his men and some social settings – most notably the restaurant that provides the concrete setting of much of the reported action, and that gives the monograph its title (*Slim's Table*). Embedded within his account are various narratives that are used to capture significant kinds of social interaction and that establish the various main characters who populate the ethnography. Likewise, the specific locale and the men who inhabit it, by the figure of synecdoche, stand for wider social types and processes. Duneier uses his own local ethnography to comment on broader social phenomena and to illustrate wider issues of sociological analysis. In particular, the men at Slim's Table display generic themes of 'race' and 'respectability' that Duneier claims have been poorly represented in previous research. In doing so he also draws ironic contrasts with sociological accounts and more popular stereotypes of the culture of black inhabitants of depressed inner-city neighbourhoods.

Before leaving this brief consideration of the rhetoric or poetics of ethnographic writing, we should note the place of *topoi* in ethnographic and other scholarly accounts. The *topos* in classical rhetoric may be translated as a 'commonplace'. It is a rhetorical device whereby the hearer's or reader's agreement or affiliation is solicited through the use of widely shared opinion or well-known instances. In scholarly writing the work of the *topos* is often accomplished by means of the 'taken-for-granted reference'. Such citations to the literature are part of the stock-in-trade of the academic author. They are not necessarily used to establish or falsify a specific finding or point of detail. Rather, they are used to establish standard reference-points. Indeed, they are sometimes recycled repeatedly in order to support a conventional assertion rather than for the specific content of the original work cited. They are used to endorse 'what everyone knows' in the discipline and become part of the encoding of scholarly credit. Ethnographic writing has many classic references that are used for such purposes. They are often cited by authors of ethnography: for instance, Geer (1964) on first days in the field, Becker (1967a) or Gouldner (1968) on partisanship, or Mills (1940) on vocabularies of motive.

The ethnographer may, of course, use the *topos* of the standard reference in order to demonstrate the comparative, generic and intertextual nature of the work. This helps construct the archetype. It keys the particular ethnographic text to a background of shared knowledge. It can create the appearance of universal frames of reference that transcend the local particularities of the ethnographic field. The *topoi* of the ethnographic genre must be treated with great care, however. The taken-for-granted reference may reproduce errors from text to text, from scholarly generation to generation. Secondly, an uncritical appeal to 'commonplace' wisdom (whether social-scientific or lay) may rob the ethnography of analytic cutting-edge and novelty. One should not resort to common sense and common knowledge as mere reflex. There needs to be a constant tension between novel insight and received wisdom. It is part of the ethnographic author's literary or rhetorical repertory. And like all the other resources, it is to be used in a disciplined manner.

WRITING AND AUTHORITY

The ways in which we write our ethnographies are, as we have seen, profoundly implicated in how we reconstruct the social worlds we report. The analysis of social life cannot be divorced from how we write about it. Equally, our construction of written texts is a value-relevant activity. In the construction of ethnographic texts we display implications of ethics and ideology. We display our implicit claims to authority. The recognition of the complex relationships between 'authority' and 'authorship' has given rise to some of the liveliest debate about the status and values of ethnographic work – most notably among cultural anthropologists.

In common with other cultural critics, some anthropologists have examined ethnographic texts for their ethical and moral implications. Here they parallel, for instance, the work of Said (1978) in his account of 'Orientalism' in European culture. It is argued that the ethnography has classically inscribed a radical distinction between the Observer and the Observed, who become the Author and the Other. Despite the overt commitments of ethnographers to cultural relativism and pluralism, it has been argued, the ethnographic monograph itself typically rests on quite other principles. Some critics – sometimes overstating the case, we believe – argue that, in its classic types in British, North American and continental European disciplines, the ethnography has presented 'a society' or 'a culture' from a single point of view. The author/ethnographer has implicitly claimed a position of omniscience and the authority to speak unequivocally of and for the people in question. Whatever the give-and-take of fieldwork itself, the ethnography has imposed a single, dominant and infallible format. As Boon (1983) has suggested, the standard contents of anthropological monographs functioned to subsume the variety of human societies under the rubric of a single analytic paradigm. Likewise, the characteristic style of the 'realist' sociological ethnography (van Maanen 1988) may reproduce a single, dominant 'voice' of the academic ethnographer. In the process, critics argue, the voices of the 'Others' become silenced: the researched exist only as the muted objects of the ethnographer's scrutiny. The ethnographic author thus reproduces the authority of the ethnographer as a dominating form of surveillance and reportage.

Similar arguments have also been entered by feminist critics of 'malestream' writing in the social sciences. As Devault (1990) and Stanley and Wise (1983) have argued, the feminist standpoint may subvert and transgress time-honoured modes of writing and representation that implicitly reproduce dominant modes of thought and discourse. As Devault summarizes the feminist problematic:

> Rhetorical processes – like all social interactions – are deeply gendered. Speakers and listeners produce and respond to statements on the basis of deep but usually unnoticed understandings of gender. In general, women's right to speak (or write) authoritatively is attenuated and circumscribed. For a woman to do scholarly work means speaking in the manner of the disciplinary tradition. They learn that, if they are to be heard, their texts must enter a discourse whose contours reflect male perceptions and concerns. The readers whose judgments are influential – the teachers, editors, reviewers, and colleagues who will incorporate and perhaps extend their work – have, in the past at least, mostly been men.
>
> (Devault 1990:98)

Devault herself discusses Krieger's 'stream-of-consciousness' ethnographic text on a women's community (Krieger 1983) as an example of a sociological work that self-consciously challenges some of the dominant conventions of ethnographic realist writing.

Such transgressions of conventional realism in ethnographic texts have been advocated by a number of authors in the pursuit of 'postmodern' aesthetics and ethics in ethnographic representation. The postmodern turn attempts to celebrate the paradoxes and complexities of field research and social life. Rather than subordinating the social world and social actors to the single narrative viewpoint of the realist text, the self-consciously postmodern abandons the single narrative and the dominant voice of the authoritative ethnographer (cf. Tyler 1986). Various postmodern ethnographies have been produced (for example, Dorst 1989; Rose 1989) that employ a striking variety of textual devices in a highly self-conscious way. Such avant-garde approaches need cautious appraisal. We certainly do not advocate gratuitous textual experimentation. Nevertheless, the contemporary ethnographer needs to be aware of such innovations, and to be able to evaluate their potential contributions to the genre.

WRITING AND RESPONSIBILITY

It is clear that the contemporary ethnographer, whatever his or her main discipline, cannot remain innocent about the conventions of ethnographic reporting. There is sufficient guidance available – of value to the novice and the old hand alike – to help in making principled decisions and choices (for example, Richardson 1990a; Wolcott 1990). A thorough awareness of the possibilities of writing is now an indispensable part of the ethnographer's methodological understanding. One cannot 'write up' an ethnography as if it were a mechanical exercise, or as if the written text were a transparently neutral medium of communication. *How* we write about the social world is of fundamental importance to our own and others' interpretations of it. To a considerable extent, the 'interpretations' of interpretative social science are couched in the poetics of ethnography itself. It is by no means novel, but illuminating nonetheless, to note that the very term 'ethnography' itself is used to describe the research process on the one hand, and its textual product on the other.

The well-informed ethnographer needs to recognize the reflexive relationship between the text and its subject-matter. A grasp of the rhetoric, or the 'poetics', of ethnographic writing is of fundamental importance. It would, however, be quite wrong to conclude that problems of rhetoric are the only issues involved. The relationship between the ethnographic text and its subject-matter may not be entirely straightforward. But it is not totally arbitrary. A recognition of the conventionality of writing does not entitle us to adopt a radically 'textual' approach. There are social actors and social life outside the text, and there are referential relationships between them. The ethnographer who engages in the arduous work of field research, data analysis, and scholarly writing will not be persuaded that the texts that constitute his or her 'data' and the texts of monographs, dissertations, papers, and the like are not referential. Indeed, it is a naive response to equate the recognition that our texts are conventional with the view that they are arbitrary.

Hammersley (1991a and 1993) suggests that the contemporary emphasis on rhetoric should not blind us to the more familiar preoccupations with scientific adequacy. We should certainly not privilege the rhetorical over the rational. There is no doubt that many ethnographies are successful (in terms of readers' critical response) by virtue of their style and persuasive use of rhetoric. On the other hand, persuasion is not the whole story. The critical reader of ethnography – as of any genre of scholarly writing – needs to be alert to the quality of the sociological or anthropological argument and the appropriate use of evidence in its support. In essence, therefore, Hammersley proposes that we should not, as readers, be unduly swayed or seduced by the readability of the ethnographic text. It is not enough that it prove 'evocative' or 'rich' in its descriptive detail, nor that it engage our sympathetic affiliation with the main characters, nor yet that it arouse our emotional responses to the reported scenes. It is equally important that the ethnography should display and demonstrate the adequacy of its methodological and empirical claims. It is important that the ethnography sustain its authoritative status as a work of scholarly research.

Although there is a complex relationship between rhetoric and science, the author of the ethnography cannot rely purely on the readability and plausibility of his or her writing. It is necessary to maintain a proper regard for the canons of evidence. The claims (for generalizability, for the robustness of the findings, etc.) need to be entered by the ethnography in a manner sufficiently explicit for the reader to be able to evaluate those claims. Indeed, prior to that, it is a requirement that the reader should be able to establish what claims are being made by the author in the first place. Moreover, the ethnography needs to establish what claims are being entered as to the originality of its findings; what analytical ideas are being developed; what the ethnographer treats as adequate support for his or her ideas; equally, what evidence would be treated as sufficient to falsify or at least modify those ideas.

In other words, we need to be able to recognize and evaluate the complex relationships between the various explicit and implicit messages that go into the whole ethnographic text. Some of these were identified by Lofland (1974) in his discussion of journal referees' criteria in evaluating qualitative research papers. First there is the criterion of the use of 'generic' conceptual frameworks. This reflects the extent to which the particular subject-matter of the ethnography is located in wider conceptual frameworks. It is not enough to report particular stories or events. The scholarly claim of the ethnography calls for a general analytic framework. Lofland's referees looked for the successful interweaving of the local and the general. Equally, there is the criterion of novelty. It is not necessary that the conceptual framework of the ethnography be totally new. Many are not. It is, however, important that the successful text demonstrate how existing ideas are being developed, tested, modified, or extended. Equally, the reader looks for how the evidence cited in the ethnography bears on such conceptual development. As Lofland suggests, the ethnographic text will not be evaluated positively if it achieves no more than a chronicle of events in a particular setting, and brings no new analytic framework to bear on it. It follows, therefore, that the analytic frame and the empirical evidence should be brought together in appropriate ways. In other words, as Lofland's discussion indicates, a successful textual arrangement should be adequately 'elaborated'. That is, it should be couched in a text that 'specifies constituent elements of the frame, draws out implications, shows major variations, and uses all these as the means by which the qualitative data are organized and presented'; further it should be 'eventful': endowed with 'concrete interactional events, incidents, occurrences, episodes, anecdotes, scenes and happenings someplace in the real world' (Lofland 1974:106,107). The analytic claims need to be 'grounded' or anchored in the particularities of observed social life. On the other hand, it should not be overburdened with the repetitious rehearsal of incidents and illustrations. Otherwise, it may topple over into the failing of being 'hyper-eventful'. Finally, Lofland suggests that critical readers wish to find the analytic frame and the illustrative data 'interpenetrated'. In other words, there should be a constant interplay between the concrete and the analytic, the empirical and the theoretical. It is part of the ethnographer's craft skill to try to strike a balance between the two, and that of the reader to evaluate the adequacy of the textual presentation. It is, however, the successful presentation of the local and the generic, the empirical and the abstract, that allows the reader to evaluate the ethnography's status and its claims.

There are no right and wrong ways of writing ethnography. The increasingly wide recognition of textual conventions will also encourage greater experimentation with textual forms. More and more anthropologists and sociologists will wish to use alternative modes of representation. The 'realist' text is not the only model that is available. It is important to recognize the value of such textual experimentation. Even if the ethnographer is not going to attempt the more extravagant exercises of some 'postmodern' authors, it is important to cultivate a critical awareness of the 'literary' conventions of scholarly writing, and to incorporate them as part of the craft or 'artisanal' knowledge of ethnography. It remains important to encourage novice and experienced ethnographers to understand their writing as part of their more general methodological expertise. We cannot continue to regard the 'writing up' of ethnographic work as innocent. On the contrary, a thorough recognition of the essential reflexivity of ethnographic work extends to the work of reading and writing as well. We must take responsibility for how we choose to represent ourselves and others in the texts we write.

AUDIENCES, STYLES, AND GENRES

A reflexive awareness of ethnographic writing should take account of the potential audiences for the finished textual products. Ethnographers are, after all, enjoined to pay close attention to the social contexts in which actors construct their everyday accounts. We note whether accounts are solicited or volunteered, to whom they are made, with what effect (intended or unintended), and so on. Ethnographers have not, however, always carried over such an attitude towards their own published accounts. There are potentially many audiences for social research: fellow research workers, hosts, students, and teachers in the social sciences; professionals and policy-makers; publishers, journal editors, and referees. There is too that amorphous audience the 'general public'. Audiences may expect and appreciate different forms and styles of writing: an academic monograph, a learned journal article, a popular magazine article, a polemical essay or pamphlet, a methodological or theoretical paper, or an autobiographical account of the research experience (see Schatzman and Strauss 1973).

Audiences differ in the background assumptions, knowledge, and expectations they bring to the ethnographic text. Some will be well versed in the particulars of the setting and may have particular interests deriving from that. Others will be more thoroughly conversant with sociological or anthropological perspectives, but have little or no knowledge of the field. Some readers will draw on theoretical and methodological perspectives that are in sympathy with the ethnography; some will start from a position of incomprehension or hostility, and may need to be won over by the author. Some readers address themselves directly to practical and evaluative considerations. Some will prove impatient with the details of 'the story', while others will read precisely for the details and the vignettes, skipping over the explicitly theoretical or methodological discussions.

We can never tailor our ethnographies to match the interests of all our potential audiences simultaneously. No single text can accomplish all things for all readers. A sense of audience and a sense of style or genre will guide the author towards multiple spoken and written accounts. And indeed such awareness may itself lead to new analytic insights. As Schatzman and Strauss put it:

> In preparing for any telling or writing, and in imagining the perspective of his specific audience, the researcher is apt to see his data in new ways: finding new analytic possibilities, or implications he has never before sensed. This process of late discovery is full of surprises, sometimes even major ones, which lead to serious reflection on what one has 'really' discovered. Thus, it is not simply a matter of the researcher writing down what is in his notes or in his head; writing or telling as activities exhibit their own properties which provide conditions for discovery.
>
> (Schatzman and Strauss 1973:132)

Just as the ethnographer has grappled with problems of strangeness, familiarity, and discovery 'in the field', so a consideration of audience and style can lead to parallel insights.

Richardson (1990a) provides an excellent account of audience and style for ethnographic work. She describes how a major piece of research she had conducted led to the production of various different versions, each aimed at a different kind of audience, and couched in a different style. Her work as an author included publications for academic sociologists on the one hand, and a popular book, aimed at the 'trade' market, on the other. Her spoken accounts of the research included appearances on chat-shows as a consequence of her popular writing. Each text implies a different version of the social phenomena it describes. In writing for different audiences, and in different styles, we are not simply describing 'the same thing' in different ways; we are subtly changing what we describe as well as how we do so. Wolf (1992) also describes and exemplifies alternative textual strategies in the production of her own research. She contrasts three different texts that she produced on the basis of her fieldwork in Taiwan. They had different styles, implied different readers, and took a different authorial point of view.

The majority of ethnographers will be thoroughly familiar with one dimension of stylistic contrast (usually aimed at the same sort of audience): that is, the contrast between 'realist' and 'confessional' accounts of the same project (van Maanen 1988). As van Maanen points out, it has been quite common for ethnographers to publish 'the ethnography' as a relatively impersonal, authoritative account, and then to produce one or more accounts of 'how I did it'. These latter autobiographical confessions are usually published 'elsewhere', separate from the realist account, either in collections of such essays, or safely tucked away in an appendix to the main monograph.

These are not the only issues of style and genre, however. The genre of, say, urban 'street' ethnography has tended to be different in style and tone from ethnographies of complex organizations. The 'classic' ethnographies of social or cultural anthropology differ from many of their contemporary counterparts. Morover, anthropology has developed genres that reflect the intellectual traditions associated with a particular geographical region (Fardon 1990). Van Maanen also goes on to identify a third variety of ethnographic writing (besides realist and confessional tales) – the 'impressionist' tale, in which the ethnographer employs more overtly literary devices in the evocation of scenes and actions.

The point is not to try to produce a definitive map of ethnographic styles, nor to suggest that each ethnography should be located within one or other genre. It is, however, important to recognize that how we write reflects directly on *what* we write about. The ethnographic text is part of the general process of reflexivity, in that it helps to construct the social world(s) it accounts for. It is, therefore, of profound importance that the ethnographer should recognize and understand what textual conventions he or she is using, and what receptions they invite on the part of readers.

Consideration of audience must also take account of the fact that our monographs, papers, and more popular texts may be read by our hosts or informants themselves. Neither the sociologist nor the anthropologist can assume that 'they' will never see the results of the research. If that was true of the non-literate cultures studied by many anthropologists once, it can no longer be assumed. One recent collection of autobiographical accounts by North American anthropologists (Brettell 1993) contains reflections on precisely that point. They document from geographically and socially diverse research settings the politics of readers' receptions, when they are themselves the 'subjects' of the research. As one of the authors describes, for instance, an awareness that her work would certainly be read by her elite intellectual informants in Ireland was present in the course of the fieldwork itself (Sheehan 1993):

> Inevitably, local suspicion of my discipline and research motives, combined with the fact of my informants' notoriety and influence, affected many of the decisions I made about how to write up my data, what information to include and to leave out, and how to connect the public lives and opinions of those I studied with the more private information about them I inevitably gained access to.
>
> (Sheehan 1993:77)

That sense of the 'audience' has been a recurrent theme in Sheehan's research, heightened by the knowledge that 'those I wrote about would also be, in some instances, the same people authorized to critique the publications resulting from my research' (1993:76). The response of key informants, such as 'Doc', to Whyte's *Street Corner Society* (1981), together with the politicized response when minority groups respond to their representation in ethnographic texts (Rosaldo 1986), sharpens our awareness of the complex relations of reading and writing that echo and amplify the social relations of 'fieldwork' itself.

Our actual or potential relations with readers of the ethnography are a particular case of a more general set of issues. The relationships of social research always have ethical implications, and the conduct of ethnographic work normally raises questions of research ethics. In the next chapter therefore we turn to a consideration of such issues.

Chapter 10

Ethics

In Chapter 1 we argued that, contrary to the views of some recent writers on qualitative research, the goal of ethnography should be the production of knowledge – not, say, the improvement of professional practice or the pursuit of political goals. In this sense for us social research is not necessarily, and should not be, political, though there are various other senses in which it could reasonably be described as such (see Hammersley 1994). Another way of putting this is to say that the only value which is central to research is truth: the aim should be to produce true accounts of social phenomena. And, indeed, that is our position. However, this does not mean that all other values can be ignored in the course of doing research. Clearly, there are ways of pursuing inquiry that are unacceptable. To say that the goal of research is the production of knowledge, then, is not to say that this goal should be pursued at all costs. There are ethical issues surrounding social research, just as there are with any other form of human activity. In this chapter we will look at these as they arise in ethnography, and at the variety of arguments deployed in relation to them. We will concentrate primarily on issues to do with the behaviour of the researcher and its consequences for the people studied, and for others belonging to the same or similar groups and organizations. (There are, of course, additional and equally important ethical matters, concerning relations with funding agencies – Willmott 1980; Pettigrew 1993 – and relationships within teams of researchers or between supervisors and research students – Bell 1977 – etc. For discussions of a wide range of ethical issues relating to social research generally, see Beals 1969; Diener and Crandall 1978; Barnes 1979; Punch 1986; Homan 1991.)

THE ISSUES

Most of the ethical issues we will discuss apply to social research generally, but the particular characteristics of ethnography give them a distinctive accent. We shall consider them under five headings: informed consent, privacy, harm, exploitation, and the consequences for future research.

Informed consent

It is often argued that the people to be studied by social researchers should be informed about the research in a comprehensive and accurate way, and should give their unconstrained consent. The most striking deviation from this principle in the context of ethnographic work is covert participant observation, where an ethnographer carries out research without most or all of the other participants being aware that research is taking place. Examples are Homan's work on old-time pentecostalists and Holdaway's study of the police (Homan 1978; Holdaway 1983; see also Bulmer 1982). Some commentators argue that such research is never, or hardly ever, justified, that it is analogous to infiltration by *agents provocateurs* or spies (Bulmer 1982:3). Such objections may arise from the belief that this kind of research contravenes human rights of autonomy and dignity, or from fears about its consequences. For instance, it has been suggested that 'social research involving deception and manipulation ultimately helps produce a society of cynics, liars and manipulators, and undermines the trust that is essential to a just social order' (Warwick 1982:58). Other writers take a contrary view. They point to the differences in purpose between covert research and spying; and they emphasize the extent to which we all restrict the disclosure of information about ourselves and our concerns in everyday life. It has also been suggested that the deception involved in covert participant observation 'is mild compared to that practised daily by official and business organizations' (Fielding 1982:94). On a more positive note, it seems likely that some settings would not be accessible to research, or at least not without a great deal of reactivity, if covert methods were not employed – though as we noted in Chapter 3 there is often some uncertainty surrounding this.

While the issue of informed consent is raised most sharply

by covert participant observation, it arises in other forms of ethnographic work too. Even when the fact that research is taking place is made explicit, it is not uncommon for participants quickly to forget this once they come to know the ethnographer as a person. Indeed, ethnographers seek to facilitate this by actively building rapport with them, in an attempt to minimize reactivity. Certainly, it would be disruptive continually to issue what Bell (1977:59) refers to as 'some sociological equivalent of the familiar police caution, like "Anything you say or do may be taken down and used as data ..." '.

Furthermore, even when operating in an overt manner, ethnographers rarely tell *all* the people they are studying *everything* about the research. There are various reasons for this. One is that, at the initial point of negotiating access, the ethnographer her- or himself often does not know the course the work will take, certainly not in any detail. But even later, once the research problem and strategy have been clarified, there are reasons why only limited information may be provided to participants. For one thing, the people being studied may not be very interested in the research, and an insistence on providing information could be very intrusive. Equally important, divulging some sorts of information might affect people's behaviour in ways that will invalidate the research. For instance, to tell teachers that one is interested in whether they normally talk as much to girls as to boys in the classroom could produce false results, since they may make an effort to equalize their interactions. (Of course, in action research this may not matter. Indeed, the aim may be to see how far behaviour can be changed. See Kelly's discussion of this aspect of the Girls into Science and Technology project: Kelly 1985.)

Besides often failing to provide all of the information that might be considered necessary for informed consent, even ethnographers whose research is overt sometimes engage in active deception. Participants may be given a false impression, for example that the ethnographer agrees with their views or finds their behaviour ethically acceptable when he or she does not. This will often be a matter of researchers not mentioning their own views; but sometimes it may even involve them indicating agreement or acceptance despite their real beliefs, as in the case of Fielding's research on an extreme right-wing organization or

Taylor's investigation of a ward in an institution for the 'mentally retarded' (Fielding 1982:86–7; Taylor 1991).

Roth has argued that all research falls on a continuum between the completely covert and the completely open (Roth 1962); and it is worth emphasizing that within the same piece of research the degree of openness may vary considerably across the different people in the field. For example, in his research on Bishop McGregor School, Burgess informed the teachers that he was doing research; but the students were only told that he was a new part-time teacher, though they found out about the research subsequently by asking him questions (Burgess 1985d:143ff).

The eliciting of free consent is no more straightforward and routinely achieved than the provision of full information. Ethnographers often try to give people the opportunity to decline to be observed or interviewed, but this is not always possible, at least not without making the research highly disruptive. For example, Atkinson's research on the bedside teaching of medical students in hospitals took place with the knowledge and consent of the specialists concerned, but not with that of either the students or the patients he observed (Atkinson 1981a and 1984). In the context of research on the police, Punch comments that 'In a large organization engaged in constant interaction with a considerable number of clients' it is physically impossible to seek consent from everyone and seeking it 'will kill many a research project stone dead' (Punch 1986:36). There are also difficulties raised by the fact that because ethnographers carry out research in natural settings their control over the research process is often limited: they simply do not have the power to ensure that all participants are fully informed and freely consent to be involved.

Above and beyond this, there is also the question of what constitutes free consent, of what amounts to a forcing of consent. For example, does an attempt to persuade someone to be interviewed or observed constitute a subtle form of coercion, or does this depend on what sorts of argument are used? It has also been proposed that some people, in some roles, for example those in public office, do not have the right to refuse to be researched, and therefore do not need to be asked for their consent (Rainwater and Pittman 1967).

Privacy

In everyday life we draw distinctions between public places (such as parks) and private places (like the bedroom), as well as between information that is for public consumption and that which is secret or confidential. A frequent concern about ethnographic research is that it involves making public things said and done for private consumption. And it is sometimes feared that this may have long-term consequences. For example, it has been suggested that all social research 'entails the possibility of destroying the privacy and autonomy of the individual, of providing more ammunition to those already in power, of laying the groundwork for an invincibly oppressive state' (Barnes 1979:22). Like informed consent, however, the concept of privacy is complex. What is public and what private is rarely clear-cut. Is the talk among people in a bar public or private? Does it make any difference if it is loud or *sotto voce*? Similarly, are religious ceremonies public events? It is not easy to answer these questions, and in part the answer depends on one's point of view.

We also seem to draw the distinction between public and private differently depending on who is involved. For instance, it is quite common for educational researchers to ask children about their friendships, but it is very rare for them to investigate friendship patterns among teachers; and, in part, this probably stems from the assumption that children's private lives are legitimately open to scrutiny in a way that those of adults are not, especially professional, middle-class adults. This is, of course, an assumption that is not beyond challenge. Also, privacy seems to be defined in terms of specific audiences that are or are not regarded as having legitimate access to information of particular kinds. (Not in front of the children; or not in front of the adults!) Sometimes, the invasion of privacy by researchers is justified on the grounds that since the account will be published for a specialized audience neither the people studied nor anyone else who knows them is likely to read it. But is this true? And, even if it is, does it excuse the invasion of privacy? Interestingly, some informants reacting to Scheper-Hughes's study of an Irish village, *Saints, Scholars and Schizophrenics*, complained that it had been written in a way that was accessible to them: 'Why couldn't you have left it a dusty dissertation on a library shelf that no one would read, or a scholarly book that only the "experts" would read?' (Scheper-Hughes 1982:vii).

Closely related to the issue of privacy is the idea advanced by some researchers that people have a right to control information relating to them, and that they must give their permission for particular uses of it by researchers (see, for example, Walker 1978; Lincoln and Guba 1989). Thus, Lincoln and Guba argue that 'when participants do not "own" the data they have furnished about themselves, they have been robbed of some essential element of dignity, in addition to having been abandoned in harm's way' (Lincoln and Guba 1989:236). The idea that participants own any data pertaining to them has its most obvious application in relation to interview data, but it could in principle at least be extended to observational data as well. It is suggested that by assigning such ownership rights to people they can be protected from the consequences of information they regard as confidential or damaging being disclosed publicly by the researcher. However, there has been criticism of this view: on the one hand, as opening up research to distortion of evidence by participants; on the other, as potentially forming part of a strategy used by researchers to put pressure on people to supply information that they would not otherwise divulge (Jenkins 1980).

Harm

While ethnographic research rarely involves the sorts of damaging consequences that may be involved in, say, medical experiments on patients or physicists' investigations of nuclear fission, it can sometimes have important consequences, both for the people studied and for others. These may arise as a result of the actual process of doing the research and/or through publication of the findings. At the very least, being researched can sometimes create anxiety or worsen it, and where people are already in stressful situations research may be judged to be unethical on these grounds alone. An example is research on terminal illness and how those who are dying, their relatives, friends, and relevant professionals deal with the situation. While there has been research in this area (for example, Glaser and Strauss 1968; Wright 1981), it clearly requires careful consideration of its likely effects on the people involved. The research process may also have wider ramifications, beyond immediate effects on the people actually studied, for larger categories of actor or for one or more social institutions. For example, Troyna and Carrington (1989) criticize several studies for the use of research techniques which, they believe, reinforce racism: techniques such as asking informants about the typical characteristics of members of different ethnic groups. This sort of criticism may also be extended to sins of omission as well as sins of commission. For example, is a researcher behaving unethically if he or she witnesses racist or sexist talk without challenging it? (For cases which raise these issues, see Hammersley 1980; Smart 1984:155–6; Gallmeier 1991: 227; Griffin 1991:116–18.)

Turning to the potentially harmful consequences of the *publication* of ethnographic accounts, these can come about in a variety of ways and may affect both the public reputations of individuals and their material circumstances. A well-known example is Vidich and Bensman's account of Springdale, a community in upper New York State (Vidich and Bensman 1958). Not only were some readers able to identify this community, but a few of the individuals described were recognizable too (notably those playing leading roles in local politics), and their behaviour was thereby opened up to public scrutiny. (For discussions of the ethical issues raised by this case, see Becker 1964; Vidich *et al.* 1964. And for a discussion of the advantages and disadvantages of giving pseudonyms to the people and places researched, see Homan 1991:142–8.)

In the case of Maurice Punch's study of Dartington Hall, a progressive private school in Devon, the problems surrounding publication dogged the later stages of the research. Initially, the Trust which financed the school, whose members included an eminent British sociologist, funded Punch to do a follow-up investigation of ex-students. At the same time, Punch was registered for a PhD and was on the look-out for a progressive boarding school to study, and it was agreed he could use Dartington for this purpose. However, the history of the research turned into a catalogue of conflicts and recriminations. Early on, despite being funded by the Trust, Punch was refused access to the school's files by the joint headteachers, even though these were his only means of tracing former students. The major battle arose, however, over the eventual publication of a book from his thesis. Rather foolishly, Punch had signed a document which stated that he would not publish anything arising from the research without the written consent of the chairman of the Trust. As a result, once he had completed his dissertation there was a lengthy struggle, with threats of legal action, before he managed to get agreement for publication. Opposition to publication seems to have arisen in large part from the trustees' judgment that the research showed Dartington in a bad light. Punch provides his own summary of the findings:

> First, it was argued that this type of 'anti-institution', with its nebulous guidelines for action, is difficult to operationalize at a day-to-day level because so many of its concepts are imprecise and because they conflict with institutional imperatives for cohesion and continuity. Second, I felt that the ideal of 'non-interference' by staff was often compromised by the staff's manipulation of the student society. But, in turn, the pupils could subvert the freedom offered to them with collective behaviour, and by powerfully enforced group norms and sanctions, that were the antithesis of the school's most cherished values. And third, there was evidence to suggest that some of the former pupils found it difficult to adjust to the wider society, remained dependent on the school and networks of former pupils, were somehow undermotivated in terms of conventional achievements, and rather than taking an active part in changing the world, seemed to opt out into a peripheral, artistic subculture.
>
> (Punch 1986:61–2)

It is not difficult to understand that the trustees might disagree with these findings, and why they wished that such a book not be published, especially given the increasingly hostile political environment in which the school found itself. And the trustees' fears were perhaps confirmed by the appearance in a national newspaper a week before the book's publication of the headline: 'An academic time-bomb in the form of a highly critical book is to explode under Dartington Hall progressive school next Thursday'. (Punch also found publication of an account of the story behind the research initially blocked by the British libel laws: Punch 1986:49–69.)

The reporting of research data or findings by the mass media has also been a significant factor in other studies. Morgan's research on women factory workers was picked up by national daily newspapers (Morgan 1972), and the Banbury restudy was described in a local newspaper under the headline: 'New probe into "snob town"' (Bell 1977:38). Clearly, such publicity can damage the reputations of individuals, organizations, and locations, as well as hurting the feelings of those involved.

What is significant in cases such as these, of course, is not just whether the information published and publicized is true, but what implications it carries, or what implications it may be taken to carry, about the people studied and others like them. And there is considerable potential for problems arising from these implications built into the very nature of social research, as Becker points out, drawing on the ideas of Everett Hughes:

> the sociological view of the world – abstract, relativistic, generalizing – necessarily deflates people's view of themselves and their organizations. Sociological analysis has this effect whether it consists of a detailed description of informal behavior or an abstract discussion of theoretical categories. The members of a church, for instance, may be no happier to learn that their behavior exhibits the influence of 'pattern variables' than to read a description of their everyday behavior which shows that it differs radically from what they profess on Sunday morning in church. In either case something precious to them is treated as merely an instance of a class.
>
> (Becker 1964:273)

The problem becomes even more serious, however, in the case of 'those who believe they possess the truth complete and undefiled', as Wallis (1977:149) points out, reflecting on his study of scientologists. He managed to publish his book and avoid being prosecuted for libel only through lengthy negotiation and some modification of the text. In a response to his work a representative of the Church of Scientology complained that faced 'with a social movement of phenomenal growth and increasing impingement on society in areas of social reform, yet he chose to paint, in dark tones, a small square in the lower left-hand corner of the canvas' (Gaiman 1977:169). It should be said, though, that responses to research reports on the part of those whose behaviour is described within them are not always negative, and are often minimal or non-existent.

The potential for damage caused by the publication of

research findings is not restricted to effects on what is publicly known or on the reputations of people or organizations. Also relevant is the use that may be made of the information. An extreme case is Condominas's anthropological account of Sar Luk, a mountain village in South Vietnam, published in French in 1957. This was subsequently translated illegally by the US government and used by its army in the Vietnam War as part of 'ethnographic intelligence'. The information produced by Condominas does not seem to have been directly implicated in the South Vietnamese army's destruction of Sar Luk, but it is clear that the publication of information about this village had at least potentially deadly consequences for the people living there, even though Condominas may not have been able to anticipate this (see Barnes 1979:155–6).

Even the existence of a PhD thesis in a university library can sometimes cause problems, as Wolf discovered in the case of his research on 'outlaw bikers':

> A few years . . . after I'd stopped riding with the Rebels, the Calgary police brought a member of the Rebels' Calgary chapter to court in an attempt to revoke his firearms acquisition certificate. A member of the Calgary police force claimed the status of 'expert witness' and acted as a witness for the crown prosecutor. 'Expert witness' means that the individual is considered capable of offering the court an 'informed opinion' on a judicial matter by virtue of his or her overall knowledge and familiarity with the situation. When the lawyer for the defendant asked on what grounds the police officer could claim any knowledge of the Rebels, the officer was able to justify his eligibility as an expert witness by virtue of having read my thesis. The Calgary Rebel eventually won his court case and retained his legal right to possess firearms; however, he came up to Edmonton to settle a score with me.
>
> (Wolf 1991:220)

While Wolf escaped retaliation, the Calgary Rebel and his associates made clear that they were against the publication of a book on the basis of his thesis: 'No way that you're going to publish that book!'. Wolf comments: 'it was an interesting ethical complication; it was a dangerous personal complication. However, these were not the brothers with whom I had made my original pact, and I have decided to go ahead and publish' (1991:221).

A more mundane example is Ditton's study of 'fiddling and pilferage' among bread salesmen. He opens the preface to his book in the following way:

> I am lucky enough to have a number of friends and colleagues. Probably not as many of the former, and perhaps more of the latter now that this book has been published. I don't expect that many of the men at Wellbread's will look too kindly on the cut in real wages that this work may mean to them, and my bakery self would agree with them.
>
> (Ditton 1977:vii)

It might be argued that Ditton's exposure of the 'fiddling and pilferage' among sales staff working for a particular bakery caused harm not only to the fortunes and reputations of those who worked for that bakery but perhaps also to those working for other bakeries as well.

Finch (1984) raises a more general issue about harm in relation to her own work on playgroups and clergymen's wives. She argues that it is difficult even for feminists 'to devise ways of ensuring that information given so readily in interviews will not be used ultimately against the collective interests of women' (1984:83). Of course, it is not always clear what is in whose interests, and some would argue that the value of scientific knowledge, or the public right to know, outweighs such considerations; but many ethnographers would insist on the importance of trying to ensure that the knowledge produced by research is used in pursuit of good, and not of bad, causes.

Exploitation

Sometimes it is claimed that research involves the exploitation of those studied: that the latter supply the information which is used by the researcher and get little or nothing in return. One of the teachers in the school that Beynon (1983:47) studied summed this up, commenting: 'When you first arrived we thought "Here's another bloke getting a degree on our backs!" We resented the idea that we were just fodder for research.' And it is suggested by some commentators that, typically, researchers investigate those who are less powerful than themselves, and for this reason are able to establish a research bargain that advantages them and disadvantages those they study. This is a problem that can even arise in those situations where the researcher has an intellectual and emotional commitment to the people being studied and seeks to establish a non-hierarchical relationship with them, as Finch makes clear in the case of feminists studying other women (Finch 1984).

Cannon found this to be an especially acute problem in her research on women with breast cancer. In dealing with it she encouraged the women themselves to reflect on the interview process, how and when it helped and did not help them, and left them substantially in control of the interviews (Cannon 1992:162–3) Nonetheless, she felt guilt that her research might make their situations worse:

> Most of the women I interviewed felt ill, or at least were experiencing a certain amount of discomfort at the time of the interview; they disliked being in the hospital and my clinic-based interviews meant that I asked them to stay longer than necessary; my questions required them to go way back to when they first found an abnormality in their breast, something which, to most women with secondary spread, seemed far away and hardly relevant to the more immediately life-threatening problems they now had.
>
> (1992:172)

At the same time, she was able to offer the women support, both physical and emotional, so much so that with some of them she became an important part of their social networks up to and including the point of death.

Here, as in many other cases, there were benefits as well as costs for those involved in the research, but these are never easy to assess. As a result, there are problems surrounding judgments about what exactly constitutes exploitation. The concept implies a comparison between what is given and received, and/or between what is contributed to the research, by each side. And yet, of course, most of the benefits and costs, and the relative contributions, cannot be measured, certainly not on any absolute scale. Whether or not exploitation is taking place is always a matter of judgment, and one that is open to substantial possible disagreement.

The argument about the exploitative potential of ethnographic research leads to a variety of recommendations: that researchers should give something back, in the way of services or payment;

that participants should be empowered by becoming part of the research process; or that research should be directed towards studying the powerful and not the powerless. Such proposed remedies do not always avoid the problem, however; and they are controversial in themselves.

Consequences for future research

Social researchers, and especially ethnographers, rely on being given access to settings. Research that is subsequently found objectionable by the people studied and/or by gatekeepers may have the effect that these and other people refuse access in the future. If this were to happen on a large scale, ethnographic research would become virtually impossible. This was one of the main arguments used by Fred Davis (1961b) in his criticism of Lofland and Lejeune's secret study of a branch of Alcoholics Anonymous (Lofland and Lejeune 1960; Lofland 1961); and by Erickson (1967) against the covert study of an apocalyptic religious group in *When Prophecy Fails* (Festinger *et al.* 1956). Of course, what is at issue here is the negative reaction of people to research and its findings, rather than ethics *per se*. And there may be good reasons routinely to expect such a negative reaction. Thus, Becker has claimed that there is an 'irreconcilable conflict between the interests of science and the interests of those studied', and that any good study is likely to provoke a hostile reaction (Becker 1964:276). This is an exaggeration, but it does point to the fallacy of assuming that the researcher and the people studied will see the research in the same way. As in life generally, there may well be conflicting interpretations and clashes of interest; and there are no simple general solutions to such conflicts. The upshot of this is that while the individual ethnographer may have an ethical obligation to colleagues not to 'spoil the field', it may not always be possible to meet this obligation; and sometimes the courses of action required to meet it may be undesirable on other grounds.

DIVERSE PERSPECTIVES

Clearly, these five ethical issues are subject to diverse points of view. However, there have been attempts by professional associations concerned with social research to develop ethical guidelines and codes of practice, outlining (with varying degrees of prescription and enforcement) rules that researchers ought to follow, or issues which they should consider, if they are to avoid unethical behaviour. (Many organizations have issued ethical guidelines for social research. For a useful discussion of ethical guidelines in the British context, see Homan 1991:ch.2.) Sometimes universities and research institutions themselves adopt codes of practice, and in the United States these are enforced in relation to some kinds of research by institutional review boards or committees which vet research proposals.

At the same time, the establishment and enforcement of guidelines have been challenged, on several grounds. Some criticize such guidelines for seeking to legislate where only practical judgment in context is appropriate. Others criticize them for trying to enforce ethical standards that are unrealistic, given the nature of the society in which research is to be done, and in particular the manipulation and perhaps unethical behaviour of some of those to be studied. The framing, and reframing, of ethical guidelines has sometimes sought to take account of both these sorts of criticism by recognizing conflicting considerations and exceptional circumstances. However, this opens them up to criticism from those who argue that the ethical standards embodied in professional ethical guidelines are too lax, and are over-concerned with the interests of their members. Thus, it may be claimed that while these guidelines usually require researchers to gain the informed consent of the people to be studied, the nature of the information that should be provided and the circumstances under which free consent can be assumed to have been given are not laid down with sufficient rigour, and that there are always loopholes allowing researchers to proceed without informed consent.

Building on our discussion so far, we can identify four contrasting positions which have had an impact on thinking about the ethical issues surrounding ethnographic research:

(a) First, there are those who argue that particular sorts of research strategy are illegitimate, and should never be employed by researchers. For example, deception is often proscribed, and the establishment of fully informed consent with participants insisted on. Similarly, strict rules are laid down by some about what constitutes invasion of privacy, and it is argued that researchers must take no action which infringes it. Warwick's criticism of Humphreys's study of homosexual encounters in public lavatories comes close to this position (Warwick 1982). Such views are usually justified by appeal to political or religious commitments and/or to the existence of certain inalienable human rights. Interestingly, though, Shils offers a version drawing on a sociological theory about the role of the sacred in modern societies (Shils 1959).

(b) Second, there are those who argue that what is and is not legitimate action on the part of researchers is necessarily a matter of judgment in context, and depends on assessment of the relative benefits and costs of pursuing research in various ways. This point of view usually places particular emphasis on the avoidance of serious harm to participants, and insists on the legitimacy of research and the likelihood that offence to *someone* cannot be avoided. It leaves open to judgment the issue of what the benefits and costs of particular research strategies are in particular cases, and how these should be weighed. No strategy is proscribed absolutely, though some may be seen as more difficult to justify than others. Becker seems close to this view (Becker 1964).

(c) A third position is ethical relativism. This implies that there is never a single determinate answer to the question of what is and is not legitimate behaviour on the part of a researcher. This is because judgments about the good and the bad are always dependent on commitment to a particular value perspective, and there is a plurality of values and cultures to which human beings can be committed. This position often leads to arguments to the effect that participants must be fully consulted or closely involved in the research, and that nothing must be done by the researcher that transgresses their moral principles. Lincoln and Guba (1989) adopt this position.

(d) Finally, there are those who seem to deny all relevance to ethical considerations, at least when carrying out certain sorts of research. A striking example of this is to be found in the writings of conflict methodologists. They argue that insistence on the establishment of informed consent would be counterproductive in the study of many large economic or state organizations, since those in control of them would have no scruples about manipulating the research for their own ends. It is suggested that in such contexts covert research may be essential (Lehman and Young 1974; Lundman and McFarlane 1976).

Douglas generalizes this argument, claiming that conventional views about the ethics of social research are based on a defective theory of society. On this basis he argues that deceptive methods are necessary to do good social science because the social world is characterized by evasiveness, deceitfulness, secrecy, and fundamental social conflicts (Douglas 1976). Douglas and the conflict methodologists argue, then, that researchers must be prepared to engage in unethical practices because this is often the only way that they will get the information they require. While those who pursue this line of argument may not believe that the end always justifies the means, they do believe that sometimes means which are ethically suspect from one point of view, such as deception, can be justified because they promise to produce a greater good, for example knowledge that can lead to social policies which will remedy social injustice.

The disagreements among these four positions are not just about values and their implications for action; they also relate to factual assumptions about the nature of the societies in which research is carried out, the sort of research that needs to be done and its relative value, etc. Questions are also raised about whether the same ethical standards should be applied to all those involved in research, or whether standards should vary. For instance, should the members of an extreme right-wing political organization which engages in racial harassment be accorded the same ethical consideration as members of a democratically elected government? And should either of these be treated in terms of the same ethical norms as patients on a cancer ward? These examples also highlight the fact that researchers do not operate in situations of complete freedom: those they study may not only have different needs and interests that should be taken into account, but will also have differential power to protect themselves and to pursue their interests in relation to researchers and others.

TAKING A VIEW

Our own position is closest to the second of the four views we outlined above, though we accept elements of all of them. In our judgment there are dangers in treating particular procedures as if they were intrinsically ethical and desirable, whether this is ensuring fully informed consent, giving people control over data relating to them, feeding back information about the research findings to them, or publishing information on the basis of 'the public's right to know'. What is appropriate and inappropriate depends on the context to a large extent, and sometimes actions that are motivated by ethical ideals can cause severe problems, not just for researchers but for the people they are studying as well.

Take the example of feeding back the findings of research to participants. This is now widely seen as an obligation on ethical grounds, because it is important to be open about one's research so that people can take a considered position in relation to it. The experience of Kelly in researching a city-centre youth work project illustrates such a commitment and its dangers. She engaged in overt participant observation, but because of the high turnover in clientele not all of the young people were aware that she was a researcher. Also, some of those who were aware of her role did not realize the sort of information she was collecting and would publish. As a result, when an interim report was circulated there was a strong negative reaction which affected not only the research itself but also relationships between staff and clients (Davies and Kelly 1976; Cox *et al.* 1978). What this case illustrates is that by being open in this way researchers may upset the informational economy of the groups and organizations they are studying: for instance, through making information previously known only to some available to all, or by making public and 'official' what had formerly only been private and informal. Underlying the treatment of any procedures as absolute ethical requirements are assumptions about how social settings *ought to be* that may neglect how they *actually are*.

In much the same way, the justification of research and of the publication of findings on the grounds of a public right to know can be dangerous if it is not tempered by other considerations. As Shils (1959) points out:

> good arguments can be made against continuous publicity about public institutions. It could be claimed that extreme publicity not only breaks the confidentiality which enhances the imaginativeness and reflectiveness necessary for the effective working of institutions but also destroys the respect in which they should at least tentatively be held by the citizenry.
> (Shils 1959:137)

Even Becker, whose views differ sharply from those of Shils, argues that one should refrain from publishing anything that will cause embarrassment or distress to the people studied if it is not central to the research or if its importance does not outweigh such consequences (Becker 1964:284). And, in fact, researchers frequently acquire confidential information that they do not use. In her study of gender and schooling in a rural English setting, Mason (1990:106) reports becoming 'aware of details of covert practices such as "moonlighting", "tax-dodging", and various details of "gossip" ', which she was asked to keep confidential. Sometimes, though, the researcher may decide that even data and/or findings that are centrally relevant to the research must be suppressed for ethical reasons. The anthropologist Evans-Pritchard provides an example of such self-censorship in his book *Witchcraft among the Azande*: he excluded information about a particular association devoted to the practice of magic, on the grounds of the consequences publication would have for its members: 'Europeans generally feel so strongly against this association and so fiercely punish its members that I refrain for the present from publishing an account of its rites, for some of them would offend European sentiments' (Evans-Pritchard 1937:511; quoted in Barnes 1979:40). Similarly, in their study of a college basketball team, Adler and Adler (1991:179) report practising 'a degree of self-censorship, avoiding discussing potentially discrediting aspects of the setting'.

It seems to us that there are values which most people, across most societies, would subscribe to in one form or another, and that these should guide researchers' judgments about what is and is not acceptable behaviour. And the values and feelings of those being studied must also be considered. However, it is important to recognize that it may not always be possible or desirable to avoid acting in ways that run contrary to these values. Values often conflict, and their implications for what is legitimate and illegitimate in particular situations is, potentially at least, always a matter for reasonable dispute. There is also the problem of the uncertain validity of our factual knowledge about what the consequences of different possible courses of action will and will not be, and thus about whether particular actions are likely to have undesirable effects.

For these reasons, what constitutes harm is a matter of judgment and may be contentious. A good illustration of this is provided by Homan's research on the prayer behaviour of old-time pentecostalists. In response to criticism of his covert research strategy, he argued that had he informed the congregations he was observing of his research he would have interfered with their worship in a way that was less justifiable than their being observed by a researcher without knowing it. Whether or not one agrees with him, it is clear that conflicting principles are involved here, and perhaps also disagreements about the consequences of adopting covert and overt research strategies (see Homan and Bulmer 1982). Similarly, in the case of Ditton's research on bakery staff, whether one regards the latter as having suffered harm as a result of his research is a matter for debate. On the one hand, their incomes may have been reduced as a result, and their reputations damaged, though it is not clear whether this actually happened. On the other hand, the behaviour they were engaged in could be described as unethical and as harming others. Given this, should they not take responsibility for their actions? But it might be asked why the particular people Ditton studied should have to face responsibility for their actions when others do not. After all, many businesses operate on the basis that there will be a certain level of theft on the part of employees. And one can raise questions about the levels of remuneration offered to bread workers compared to managing directors and shareholders of bakery firms. Moreover, the latter may also engage in criminal malpractice, perhaps on a greater financial scale, and without this being exposed to public scrutiny. Here too, then, there is plenty of scope for debate about whether the research caused harm, how serious this was, and whether it was legitimate.

The same potential indeterminacy surrounds other ethical issues. An example is the confidentiality of information:

> At times, in the course of conversations, teachers will say, 'and this is confidential'. But we might ask: what is actually held by the informant to be confidential – everything that is said, the name involved, or the occurrence of a particular episode? Further questions can also be raised: to whom is information confidential? To me and to the secretary who transcribes the tape? Or does it mean that sufficient

confidentiality has been observed if pseudonyms are used? . . .

There are, nevertheless, some materials that are always confidential to the researcher and permanently lost from view. For example, in the middle of a taped conversation with a teacher I was requested to 'shut that bloody machine off'. At this point the individual told me about something that he had not done. The teacher indicated that the information should never be used. . . . Such situations pose a major dilemma for me. If the informant did not intend the information to influence my interpretation why did he tell it at all? In some respects this appears to be an invitation to incorporate this material in some way, but if it is done without giving data and sources, the assertions may look ungrounded. This kind of situation also presents many other problems. First, the researcher colludes with the other person involved in the conversation if no material is used. Second, in this instance the data that are being witheld would dramatically change a public account of a situation, so in this sense the researcher is involved in some deception.

(Burgess 1988a and b:152)

Beynon (1983:42) recounts a similar experience, though a different response: ' "Shall I tell you the truth about this place and will you keep it to yourself?", queried Mr Jovial. I could hardly reply that even inconsequential chat constituted potentially usable data! "Please do," I replied, feeling thoroughly devious.'

As with confidentiality, so with honesty. The latter is certainly an important value, but this does not imply that we should always be absolutely honest. In everyday life most of us do not tell the whole truth and nothing but the truth in all circumstances. We are circumspect about whom we tell what, and we may even lie on occasion: not only to protect our own interests but to protect those of others too, sometimes even those to whom we are lying. What is at issue is not 'to deceive or not to deceive' in abstract, but what and how much to tell whom on what occasion. In research, as in everyday life, considerations about the likely effects of divulging various sorts of information and their desirability or undesirability arise and must be taken into account. In our view, an element of not telling the whole truth, even of active deception, may be justifiable so long as it is not designed to harm the people researched, and so long as there seems little chance that it will.

As we noted earlier, there is also scope for disagreement about whether a particular research project involves exploitation of the people studied. The demands made on participants by research can vary a good deal, but so also can assessments of the level and significance of those demands. In the case of ethnography the impact of the research may seem to be minimal, in the sense that often all that is required is that participants carry on much as normal. However, being observed or interviewed can itself be a source of considerable anxiety and strain. And while there are potential benefits from research for participants, for instance the chance to talk at length to someone about one's problems, how valuable these are found may vary considerably. Ultimately, it is the responsibility of ethnographers to ensure that they do not exploit the people they study, but this is necessarily a matter of judgment, and one that is open to challenge.

In this context, it is also important to remember that the possibility of dishonesty, manipulation, exploitation, and the causing of harm does not lie only on one side of the researcher-researched relationship. Wax (1952) notes how researchers may be seen as easy prey, as fair game whose sympathies and desire for information can be exploited for gifts and favours. Adler and Adler provide an example, describing how the drug dealers they were studying gradually began to take advantage of them:

> Money they gave us to hold, they knew they could always rely on having returned. Money we lent them in desperate times was never repaid, even when they were affluent again. Favors from us were expected by them, without any further reciprocation than openness about their activities.
>
> (Adler and Adler 1991:178)

A more extreme case is that of Wallis, who found himself subjected to retaliatory action. This involved

> the activities of a staff member of the Scientology organization who visited my university . . . presenting himself as a student wishing to undertake some study or research into Scottish religion. He asked to attend my classes and lectures and inquired whether I could put him up at my home for a

few days! This naturally aroused my suspicion, and I shortly recalled having seen him in a staff member's uniform when I had taken the Communication Course at the Scientology headquarters. However, I took no action at this stage, not knowing precisely how to react. During his short stay in Stirling he made visits to my home in my absence and, unknown to me at that time, presented himself to students and others as a friend of mine in order to make inquiries concerning whether or not I was involved in the 'drug scene'. After a couple of days I confronted him with my knowledge of his background.

At this point he changed his story, claiming now to be a defector from Scientology, come to sell me information. I informed him that I was not buying information and gave him to understand that I believed his present story as little as his earlier one. . . .

In the weeks following his visit a number of forged letters came to light, some of which were supposedly written by me. These letters, sent to my university employers, colleagues and others, implicated me in a variety of acts, from a homosexual love affair to spying for the drug squad. Because I had few enemies and because this attention followed so closely upon the receipt of my paper by the Scientology organisation, it did not seem too difficult to infer the source of these attempts to inconvenience me.

(Wallis 1977:157–8)

Scientologists also wrote to the body which was funding Wallis's research complaining of his unethical behaviour and threatening legal action.

So, ethnographers must weigh the importance and contribution of their research against the chances and scale of any harm that is likely to be caused (to the people involved, to others, or to future access), against the values of honesty and fairness, against any infringement of privacy involved, and against any likely consequences for themselves and other researchers. But there will be conflicting indications, difficult judgments, and probably disagreements. Ethical issues are not matters on which simple and consensual decisions can always be made. It is our view, however, that the most effective strategies for pursuing research should be adopted unless there is clear evidence that these are ethically unacceptable. In other words, indeterminacy and uncertainty should for the most part be resolved by ethnographers in favour of the interests of research, since that is their primary task.

CONCLUSION

We have identified a number of ethical issues surrounding ethnographic research, and outlined the rather different views about them to be found in the literature. We have also presented our own view that while ethical considerations are important they cannot be satisfactorily resolved by appeal to absolute rules, and that the effective pursuit of research should be the ethnographer's main concern. It is the responsibility of the ethnographer to try to act in ways that are ethically acceptable, taking due account of his or her goals, the situation in which the research is being carried out, and the values and interests of the people involved. In other words, as researchers, and as consumers of research, we must make judgments about what is and is not legitimate in particular cases. And we should be prepared to support our judgments with arguments if they are challenged. We must also recognize that others may disagree, even after we have presented our arguments, and not just because they have ulterior motives. It is important that the ethical issues surrounding research are discussed publicly, since this will feed into the deliberations of individual researchers and research teams.

Reflexivity carries an important message in the field of ethics as in other aspects of ethnography. Some discussions of the ethics of social research seem to be premised on the idea that social researchers can and should act in an ethically superior manner to ordinary people, that they have, or should have, a heightened ethical sensibility and responsibility. There is also a tendency to dramatize matters excessively, implying a level of likely harm or moral transgression that is far in excess of what is typically involved. (An example is Warwick's criticism of Laud Humphreys's study of homosexual activity in public lavatories as an infringement of the freedom of the men concerned: Warwick 1982:50.) Yet the ethical problems surrounding ethnographic research are, in fact, very similar to those surrounding other human activities. For example, what and how much to disclose of what one knows, believes, feels, etc., can be an issue for any sort of actor at any time. And what is judged to be appropriate or desirable can vary a good deal. Above all, in everyday life ethical issues are subject to the same uncertainties and disagreements, the same play of vested interest and dogmatic opinions, and the same range of reasonable but conflicting arguments. All that can be required of ethnographers is that they take due note of the ethical aspects of their work and make the best judgments they can in the circumstances. Like anyone else, they will have to live with the consequences of their actions; and, inevitably, so too will others. But then this is true of all of us in all aspects of our lives.

This is not quite the last word, however. What we have discussed up to now are the ethical considerations that should restrain researchers' actions in the pursuit of inquiry. But there can be exceptional occasions when a researcher should stop being a researcher and engage in action that is not directed towards the goal of producing knowledge. There is in fact always much action engaged in by ethnographers in the field that is not directly concerned with knowledge production. By its very nature, ethnography forces one into relationships with the people being studied, and one may do things because of those relationships, over and above any connection they have with the research. However, sometimes there will be actions that are needed because of those relationships, or because of obligations arising from other roles, which are not compatible with continuing as a resarcher, or at least which must be carried out at the expense of the research: an example might be taking action when one witnesses physical abuse of 'mentally retarded' residents by those employed to care for them (Taylor 1991:245–6).

Becoming a researcher does not mean, then, that one is no longer a citizen or a person, that one's primary commitment to research must be sustained at all costs. However, in our view situations where these other identities should override that of researcher are rather rare; and decisions to suspend or abandon the research role must arise from considerations that outweigh the value of the research very heavily. Account must also be taken of the usually very limited capacity of the researcher to help. A common example of this sort of action is the engagement of researchers in advocacy on the part of those they are studying.

And frequently associated with the commitment to advocacy, it seems to us, is an underestimation of the difficulties involved, an overestimation of the likelihood of success, and a neglect of the danger of making the situation worse (Hastrup and Elsass 1990).

Most of the time, in our view, then, the temptation to abandon the researcher role should be resisted. Certainly, we have little sympathy with attempts to redefine that role to make the researcher into some sort of political activist. Like absolutist conceptions of research ethics, this seems to be based on a conception of the researcher as in some sense above the world being studied, and thereby able to partake of god-like knowledge and powers. Against this, it is salutary to remind ourselves that the ethnographer is very much part of the social world he or she is studying, and is subject to distinctive purposes, constraints, limitations, and weaknesses like everyone else.

References

Abraham, J. (1989a) 'Testing Hargreaves' and Lacey's differentiation-polarisation theory in a setted comprehensive', *British Journal of Sociology*, 40, 1:46–81.
—— (1989b) 'Gender differences and anti-school boys', *Sociological Review*, 37, 1:65–88.
Adam, B. (1990) *Time and Social Theory*, Cambridge, Polity Press.
Adelman, C. (1977) 'On first hearing', in C. Adelman (ed.), *Uttering, Muttering: Collecting, Using and Reporting Talk for Social and Educational Research*, London, Grant McIntyre.
Adler, P.A. (1993) *Wheeling and Dealing*, New York, Columbia University Press, 2nd edn.
Adler, P.A. and Adler P. (1991) *Membership Roles in Field Research*, Newbury Park, Calif., Sage, 2nd edn.
Agar, M. (1973) *Ripping and Running: A Formal Ethnography of Urban Heroin Addicts*, New York, Seminar Press.
—— (1980) *Professional Stranger*, New York, Academic Press.
Aggleton, P. (1987) *Rebels Without a Cause: Middle-Class Youth and the Transition from School to Work*, London, Faber.
Altheide, D. (1976) *Creating Reality: How TV News Distorts Events*, Beverly Hills, Calif., Sage.
Arensberg, C.M. and Kimball, S.T. (1968) *Family and Community in Ireland*, Cambridge, Mass., Harvard University Press; first published 1940.
Atkinson, J.M. (1978) *Discovering Suicide: Studies in the Social Organisation of Sudden Death*, London, Macmillan.
Atkinson, P. (1976) 'The clinical experience: an ethnography of medical education', unpublished PhD thesis, University of Edinburgh.
—— (1981a) *The Clinical Experience*, Farnborough, Gower.
—— (1981b) 'Transition from school to working life', unpublished memorandum, Sociological Research Unit, University College, Cardiff.
—— (1982) 'Writing ethnography', in H.J. Helle (ed.), *Kultur und Institution*, Berlin, Dunker & Humblot.
—— (1984) 'Wards and deeds', in Burgess (ed.) (1984b).

—— (1985) 'Talk and identity', in S.N. Eisenstadt and H.J. Helle (eds), *Perspectives on Sociological Theory*, vol. 2, *Microsociology*, London, Sage.

—— (1988) 'Ethnomethodology: a critical review', *Annual Review of Sociology*, 14:441–65.

—— (1989) 'Goffman's poetics', *Human Studies*, 12:59–76

—— (1992a) 'The ethnography of a medical setting: reading, writing and rhetoric', *Qualitative Health Research*, 2, 4:451–74.

—— (1992b) *Understanding Ethnographic Texts*, Newbury Park, Calif., Sage.

Atkinson, P. and Heath, C. (eds) (1981) *Medical Work: Realities and Routines*, Farnborough, Gower.

Atkinson, P. and Weaver, A. (1994) 'From coding to hypertext', in R.G. Burgess (ed.), *Studies in Qualitative Methodology*, vol. 5, Greenwich, Conn. JAI.

Atkinson, P., Delamont, S., and Hammersley, M. (1988) 'Qualitative research traditions: a British response to Jacob', *Review of Educational Research*, 58, 2:231–50.

Bacon, F. (1960) *The New Organon or True Directions Concerning the Interpretation of Nature*, Indianapolis, Ind., Bobbs-Merrill; first published 1620.

Bales, R.F. (1966) 'Comment on Herbert Blumer's paper'. *American Journal of Sociology*, LXXI:545–7.

Ball, M.S. and Smith, G.W.H. (1992) *Analyzing Visual Data*, Newbury Park, Calif., Sage.

Ball, S.J. (1980) 'Initial encounters in the classroom and the process of establishment', in P. Woods (ed.), *Pupil Strategies*, London, Croom Helm.

—— (1981) *Beachside Comprehensive*, London, Cambridge, University Press.

—— (1983) 'Case study research in education: some notes and problems', in Hammersley (ed.) (1983a).

—— (1984) 'Beachside reconsidered: reflections on a methodological apprenticeship', in Burgess (ed.) (1984b).

—— (1994) 'Political interviews and the politics of interviewing', in Walford (ed.) (1994).

Barbera-Stein, L. (1979) 'Access negotiations: comments on the sociology of the sociologist's knowledge', paper presented at the Seventy-Fourth Annual Meeting of the American Sociological Association, August, Boston.

Barnes, J.A. (1979) *Who Should Know What? Social Science, Privacy and Ethics*, Harmondsworth, Penguin.

Barrett, R.A. (1974) *Benabarre: The Modernization of a Spanish Village*, New York, Holt, Rinehart & Winston.

Barzun, J. and Graff, H. (1970) *The Modern Researcher*, New York, Harcourt, Brace & World.

Beals, R. (1969) *Politics of Social Research: An Inquiry into the Ethics and Responsibilities of Social Scientists*, Chicago, Aldine.

Beattie, J. (1965) *Bunyoro: An African Kingdom*, New York, Holt, Rinehart & Winston.

Becker, H.S. (1953) 'Becoming a marihuana user', *American Journal of Sociology*, 59:41–58.

—— (1964) 'Problems in the publication of field studies', in Vidich, *et al.* (eds) (1964).

—— (1967) Comment reported in R.J. Hill and K. Stones Crittenden (eds) *Proceedings of the Purdue Symposium on Ethnomethodology*, Institute for the Study of Social Change, Department of Sociology, Purdue University.

—— (1968) 'Whose side are we on?'. *Social Problems*, 14:239–47.

—— (1970) 'Life history and the scientific mosaic', in H.S. Becker, *Sociological Work*, Chicago, Aldine.

—— (1971) Footnote to M. Wax and R. Wax, 'Great tradition, little tradition, and formal education', in M. Wax, S. Diamond, and F. Gearing (eds), *Anthropological Perspectives on Education*, New York, Basic Books.

—— (1974) 'Art as collective social action', *American Sociological Review*, 39:767–76.

—— (ed.) (1981) *Exploring Society Photographically*, Chicago, University of Chicago Press.

—— (1993) 'How I learned what a crock was', *Journal of Contemporary Ethnography*, 22, 1:28–35.

Becker, H.S. and Geer, B. (1957) 'Participant observation and interviewing: a comparison', *Human Organization*, XVI:28–34.

—— and —— (1960) 'Participant observation: the analysis of qualitative field data', in R.N. Adams and J.J. Preiss (eds), *Human Organization Research: Field Relations and Techniques*, Homewood, Ill., Dorsey Press.

Becker, H.S., Hughes, E.C., and Strauss, A.L. (1961) *Boys in White: Student Culture in Medical School*, Chicago, University of Chicago Press.

Bell, C. (1977) 'Reflections on the Banbury restudy', in Bell and Newby (eds) (1977).

Bell, C. and Newby, H. (eds) (1977) *Doing Sociological Research*, London, Allen & Unwin.

Bell, C. and Roberts, H. (eds) (1984) *Social Researching: Policies, Problems and Practice*, London, Routledge & Kegan Paul.

Belsey, C. (1980) *Critical Practice*, London, Methuen.

Bensman, J. and Vidich, A. (1960) 'Social theory in field research', *American Journal of Sociology*, 65:577–84.

Berger, P. and Luckmann, T. (1967) *The Social Construction of Reality*, London, Allen Lane.

Berlak, A.C., Berlak, H., Bagenstos, N.T., and Mikel, E.R. (1975) 'Teaching and learning in English primary schools', *School Review*, 83, 2:215–43.

Berreman, G. (1962) *Behind Many Masks: Ethnography and Impression Management in a Himalayan Village*, Monograph 4, Society for Applied Anthropology, Ithaca, NY, Cornell University Press.

Bertaux, D. (ed.) (1981) *Biography and Society: The Life History Approach in the Social Sciences*, Beverly Hills, Calif., Sage.

Bettelheim, B. (1970) *The Informed Heart*, London, Paladin.

Beynon, J. (1983) 'Ways-in and staying-in: fieldwork as problem solving', in Hammersley (ed.) (1983a).

Bloor, M. (1978) 'On the analysis of observational data: a discussion of the worth and uses of inductive techniques and respondent validation', *Sociology*, 12, 3:545–52.

Blumer, H. (1954) 'What is wrong with social theory?', *American Sociological Review* 19:3–10.

—— (1966) 'Reply to Bales', *American Journal of Sociology*, LXXI:545–7.

—— (1969) *Symbolic Interactionism*, Englewood Cliffs, NJ, Prentice-Hall.

Bogdan, R. and Taylor, S. (1975) *Introduction to Qualitative Research Methods*, New York, Wiley.

Bohannon, P. (1981) 'Unseen community: the natural history of a research project', in D.A. Messerschmidt (ed.), *Anthropologists at Home in North America: Methods and Issues in the Study of One's Own Society*, Cambridge, Cambridge University Press.

Boon, J. (1983) 'Functionalists write too: Frazer, Malinowski and the semiotics of the monograph', *Semiotica*, 46, 2–4:131–49.

Booth, C. (1902–3) *Life and Labour of the People in London*, London, Macmillan.

Borhek, J.T. and Curtis, R.F. (1975) *A Sociology of Belief*, New York, Wiley.

Bowen, E. (1954) *Return to Laughter*, London, Gollancz.

Brannen, J. (ed.) (1992) *Mixing Methods: Qualitative and Quantitative Research*, Aldershot, Avebury.

Brettell, C.B. (ed.) (1993) *When They Read What We Write: The Politics of Ethnography*, Westport, Conn., Bergin & Garvey.

Brewer, J. with Magee, K. (1991) *Inside the RUC: Routine Policing in a Divided Society*, Oxford, Clarendon Press.

Brodkey, L. (1987) *Academic Writing as Social Practice*, Philadelphia, Pa, Temple University Press.

Brown, P. (1987) *Schooling Ordinary Kids*, London, Methuen.

Brown, R.H. (1977) *A Poetic for Sociology: Toward a Logic of Discovery for the Human Sciences*, Cambridge, Cambridge University Press.

Bryman, A. (1988) *Quantity and Quality in Social Research*, London, Unwin Hyman.

Bryman, A. and Burgess, R.G. (eds) (1993) *Analyzing Qualitative Data*, London, Routledge.

Bulmer, M. (1979) 'Concepts in the analysis of qualitative data', *Sociological Review*, 27, 4:651–79.

—— (1980) 'Why don't sociologists make more use of official statistics?', *Sociology*, 14, 4:505–23.

—— (ed.) (1982) *Social Research Ethics: An Examination of the Merits of Covert Participant Observation*, London, Macmillan.

Bulmer, M. (1984) The Chicago School of Sociology, Chicago, University of Chicago Press.

Burgess, R.G. (1984a) *In the Field: An Introduction to Field Research*, London, Allen & Unwin.

—— (ed.) (1984b) *The Research Process in Educational Settings*, Lewes, Falmer.

Burgess, R.G. (ed.) (1985a) *Issues in Educational Research: Qualitative Methods*, Lewes, Falmer.
—— (ed.) (1985b) *Strategies of Educational Research: Qualitative Methods*, Lewes, Falmer.
—— (ed.) (1985c) *Field Methods in the Study of Education*, Lewes, Falmer.
—— (1985d) 'The whole truth? Some ethical problems of research in a comprehensive school', in Burgess (ed.) (1985c).
—— (1985e) 'In the company of teachers: Key informants and the study of a comprehensive school', in Burgess (ed.) (1985b).
—— (ed.) (1988a), *Studies in Qualitative Methodology*, vol. 1, *Conducting Qualitative Research*, Greenwich, Conn., JAI.
—— (1988b) 'Conversations with a purpose: the ethnographic interview in educational research', in Burgess (ed.) (1988a).
—— (ed.) (1989) *The Ethics of Educational Research*, Lewes, Falmer.
—— (ed.) (1990) *Studies in Qualitative Methodology*, vol. 2, *Reflections on Field Experience*, Greenwich, Conn., JAI.
—— (ed.) (1992) *Studies in Qualitative Methodology*, vol. 3, *Learning about Fieldwork*, Greenwich, Conn., JAI.
Burke, K. (1936) *Permanence and Change*, New York, New Republic.
—— (1964) *Perspectives by Incongruity*, Bloomington, Ind., Indiana University Press.
Campbell, J. (1992) 'Fieldwork among the Sarakatsani, 1954–5', in J. De Pina-Cabral and J. Campbell (eds), *Europe Observed*, London, Macmillan.
Cannon, S. (1992) 'Reflections on fieldwork in stressful situations', in Burgess (ed.) (1992).
Cappetti, C. (1993) *Writing Chicago: Modernism, Ethnography and the Novel*, New York, Columbia University Press.
Carey, J.T. (1972) 'Problems of access and risk in observing drug scenes', in J.D. Douglas (ed.), *Research on Deviance*, New York, Random House.
Carr, W. and Kemmis, S. (1986) *Becoming Critical*, Lewes, Falmer.
Cassell, J. (1988) 'The relationship of observer to observed when studying up', in Burgess (ed.) (1988a).
Chagnon, N.A. (1977) *Yanomamö: The Fierce People*, New York, Holt, Rinehart & Winston, 2nd edn.
Chambliss, W. (1975) 'On the paucity of original research on organized crime', *American Sociologist*, 10:36–9.
Chandler, J. (1990) 'Researching and the relevance of gender', in Burgess (ed.) (1990).
Chomsky, N. (1968) *Language and Mind*, New York, Harcourt, Brace & World.
Cicourel, Aaron (1967) *The Social Organization of Juvenile Justice*, London, Heinemann, 2nd edn.
Cicourel, A. and Kitsuse, J. (1963) *The Educational Decision Makers*, New York, Bobbs-Merrill.
Clifford, J. and Marcus, G. (eds) (1986) *Writing Culture: The Poetics and Politics of Ethnography*, Berkeley, Calif., University of California Press.
Coffey, A.J. (1993) 'Double entry: the professional and organizational

socialization of graduate accountants', unpublished PhD thesis, University of Wales College of Cardiff.

Cohen, P.S. (1980) 'Is positivism dead?' *Sociological Review* 28, 1:141–76.

Collier, J. and Collier, M. (1986) *Visual Anthropology: Photography as a Research Method*, Albuquerque, N.Mex., University of New Mexico Press, revised edn.

Corsaro, W.A. (1981) 'Entering the child's world – research strategies for field entry and data collection in a preschool setting', in J.L. Green and C. Wallat (eds), *Ethnography and Language in Educational Settings*, Norwood, NJ, Ablex.

Cox, A., Cox, G., Brandon, D., and Scott, D. (1978) 'The social worker, the client, the social anthropologist and the "new honesty"', occasional paper, Youth Development Trust, c/o Duncan Scott, Dept of Social Administration, University of Manchester.

Coxon, A.P.M. (1988) 'Something sensational . . . : the sexual diary as a tool for mapping detailed sexual behaviour', *Sociological Review*, 36, 2:353–67.

Crawford, P.I. and Turton, D. (eds) (1992) *Film as Ethnography*, Manchester, Manchester University Press.

Cressey, D. (1950) 'The criminal violation of financial trust', *American Sociological Review*, 15:738–43.

Currer, C. (1992) 'Strangers or sisters? An exploration of familiarity, strangeness, and power in research', in Burgess (ed.) (1992).

Curtis, J.E. and Petras, J.W. (eds) (1970) *The Sociology of Knowledge*, London, Duckworth.

Dalton, M. (1959) *Men Who Manage: Fusions of Feeling and Theory in Administration*, New York, Wiley.

Davies, R.M. and Atkinson, P.A. (1991) 'Students of midwifery: "Doing the obs" and other coping strategies', *Midwifery*, 7:113–21.

Davies, R.M. and Kelly, E. (1976) 'The social worker, the client, and the social anthropologist', *British Journal of Social Work*, 6, 2:213–31.

Davis, A. and Horobin, G. (eds) (1977) *Medical Encounters: The Experience of Illness and Treatment*, London, Croom Helm.

Davis, F. (1959) 'The cab-driver and his fare: facets of a fleeting relationship', *American Journal of Sociology*, 65, 2:158–65.

—— (1961a) 'Deviance disavowal: the management of strained interaction by the visibly handicapped', *Social Problems*, 1:120–32.

—— (1961b) Comment on 'Initial interactions of newcomers in Alcoholics Anonymous', *Social Problems*, 8:364–5.

—— (1963) *Passage through Crisis: Polio Victims and their Families*, Indianapolis, Ind., Bobbs-Merrill.

—— (1973) 'The martian and the convert: ontological polarities in sociological research', *Urban Life and Culture*, 2, 3:333–43.

—— (1974) 'Stories and sociology', *Urban Life and Culture*, 3, 3:310–16.

Davis, N.J. (1974) 'The abortion consumer: making it through the network', *Urban Life and Culture*, 2, 4:432–59.

Dean, J.P. and Whyte, W.F. (1958) 'How do you know if the informant is telling the truth?' *Human Organization*, 17:34–8.

Dean, J.P., Eichorn, R.L., and Dean, L.R. (1967) 'Fruitful informants for intensive interviewing', in J.T. Dolby (ed.), *An Introduction to Social Research*, New York, Appleton-Century-Crofts, 2nd edn.

Delamont, S. (1984) 'The old girl network: reflections on the fieldwork at St Luke's', in Burgess (ed.) (1984b).

Den Hollander, A.N.J. (1967) 'Social description: problems of reliability and validity', in D.G. Jongmans and P.C.W. Gutkind (eds), *Anthropologists in the Field*, Assen, Netherlands, Van Gorcum.

Denzin, N.K. (1971) 'The logic of naturalistic inquiry', *Social Forces*, 50:166–82.

—— (1978) *The Research Act: A Theoretical Introduction to Sociological Methods*, New York, McGraw-Hill, 2nd edn.

Deutscher, L. (1973) *What We Say/What We Do: Sentiments and Acts*, Glenview, Ill., Scott Foresman.

Devault, M.L. (1990) 'Women write sociology: rhetorical strategies', in A. Hunter (ed.), *The Rhetoric of Social Research: Understood and Believed*, New Brunswick, Rutgers University Press.

Dews, P. (1987) *Logics of Disintegration: Post-Structuralist Thought and the Claims of Critical Theory*, London, Verso.

Dexter, L. (1970) *Elite and Specialized Interviewing*, Evanston, Ill., Northwestern University Press.

Dey, I. (1993) *Qualitative Data Analysis: A User-Friendly Guide for Social Scientists*, London, Routledge.

Diener, E. and Crandall, R. (1978) *Ethics in Social and Behavioral Research*, Chicago, University of Chicago Press.

Diesing, P. (1972) *Patterns of Discovery in the Social Sciences*, London, Routledge & Kegan Paul.

Dingwall, R. (1977a) 'Atrocity stories and professional relationships', *Sociology of Work and Occupations*, 4, 4:371–96.

—— (1977b) *The Social Organization of Health Visitor Training*, London, Croom Helm.

—— (1981) 'Practical ethnography' in G. Payne, R. Dingwall, J.J. Payne, and M. Carter (eds), *Sociology and Social Research*, London, Routledge & Kegan Paul.

Ditton, J. (1977) *Part-Time Crime: An Ethnography of Fiddling and Pilferage*, London, Macmillan.

Dollard, J. (1957) *Caste and Class in a Southern Town*, New Haven, Conn., Yale University Press, 3rd edn; first published 1937.

Donner, F. (1982) *Shabono*, London, Bodley Head.

Dorst, J.D. (1989) *The Written Suburb: An Ethnographic Dilemma*, Philadelphia, Pa, University of Pennsylvania Press.

Douglas, J. (1967) *The Social Meanings of Suicide*, Princeton, NJ, Princeton University Press.

—— (1976) *Investigative Social Research*, Beverly Hills, Calif., Sage.

Duneier, M. (1992) *Slim's Table: Race, Responsibility and Masculinity*, Chicago, University of Chicago Press.

Easterday, L., Papademas, D., Schorr, L., and Valentine, C. (1977) 'The making of a female researcher', *Urban Life*, 6, 3:333–48.

Edgerton, R.B. (1965) 'Some dimensions of disillusionment in culture contact', *Southwestern Journal of Anthropology*, 21:231–43.

Erben, M. (1993) 'The problem of other lives: social perspectives on written biography', *Sociology*, 27, 1:15–25.

Erickson, K.T. (1967) 'A comment on disguised observation in sociology', *Social Problems*, 14, 4:366–7.

Evans, A.D. (1991) 'Maintaining relationships in a school for the deaf', in Shaffir and Stebbins (eds) (1991).

Evans, J. (1983) 'Criteria of validity in social research, exploring the relationship between ethnographic and quantitative approaches', in Hammersley (ed.) (1983a).

Evans, M. (1993) 'Reading lives: how the personal might be social', *Sociology*, 27, 1:5–13.

Evans-Pritchard, E.E. (1937) *Witchcraft, Oracles and Magic among the Azande*, Oxford, Clarendon Press.

Everhart, R.B. (1977) 'Between stranger and friend: some consequences of 'long term' fieldwork in schools', *American Educational Research Journal*, 14, 1:1–15.

Fardon, R. (ed.) (1990) *Localising Strategies: Regional Traditions of Ethnographic Writing*, Edinburgh, Scottish Academic Press.

Festinger, L. Riecken, H., and Schachter, S. (1956) *When Prophecy Fails*, St Paul, Minn., University of Minnesota Press; republished 1964, London, Harper & Row.

Fetterman, D. (ed.) (1984) *Ethnography in Educational Evaluation*, Beverly Hills, Calif., Sage.

Fetterman, D. and Pittman, M. (eds) (1986) *Educational Evaluation: Ethnography in Theory, Practice and Politics*, Beverly Hills, Calif., Sage.

Fielding, N.G. (1982) 'Observational research on the National Front', in Bulmer (ed.) (1982).

Fielding, N.G. and Fielding, J.L. (1986) *Linking Data*, Newbury Park, Calif., Sage.

Finch, J. (1984) ' "It's great to have someone to talk to": the ethics and politics of interviewing women', in Bell and Roberts (eds) (1984).

Fine, G.A. (1993) 'Ten lies of ethnographers: moral dilemmas in fieldwork', *Journal of Contemporary Ethnography*, 22, 3:267–94.

Finestone, H. (1967) 'Cats, kicks and colour', *Social Problems*, 5:3–13.

Fonow, M.M. and Cook, J.A. (eds) (1991) *Beyond Methodology: Feminist Scholarship as Lived Research*, Bloomington, Ind., Indiana University Press.

Fox, R.C. (1964) 'An American sociologist in the land of Belgian medical research', in Hammond (ed.) (1964).

Freilich, M. (1970a) 'Mohawk heroes and Trinidadian peasants', in Freilich (ed.) (1970b).

—— (ed.) (1970b) *Marginal Natives: Anthropologists at Work*, New York, Harper & Row.

Friedrichs, R.W. (1970) *A Sociology of Sociology*, New York, Free Press.

Gaiman, D. (1977) 'Appendix: a scientologist's comment', in Bell and Newby (eds) (1977).

Gallmeier, C.P. (1991) 'Leaving, revisiting, and staying in touch: neglected issues in field research', in Shaffir and Stebbins (eds) (1991).

Gamst, F.C. (1980) *The Hoghead: An Industrial Ethnology of the Locomotive Engineer*, New York, Holt, Rinehart & Winston.

Garfinkel, H. (1967) *Studies in Ethnomethodology*, Englewood Cliffs, NJ, Prentice-Hall.

Geer, B. (1964) 'First days in the field', in Hammond (ed.) (1964).

—— (1970) 'Studying a college', in R. Habenstein (ed.), *Pathways to Data*, Chicago, Aldine.

George, V. and Dundes, A. (1978) 'The gomer: a figure of American hospital folk speech', *Journal of American Folklore*, 91, 359:568–81.

Giallombardo, R. (1966) 'Social roles in a prison for women', *Social Problems* 13:268–88.

Giddens, A. (1979) 'Positivism and its critics', in T. Bottomore and R. Nisbet (eds), *A History of Sociological Analysis*, London, Heinemann.

Gitlin, A.D., Siegel, M., and Boru, K. (1989) 'The politics of method: from leftist ethnography to educative research', *Qualitative Studies in Education*, 2, 3:237–53.

Glaser, B. (1978) *Theoretical Sensitivity*, San Francisco, Sociology Press.

Glaser, B. and Strauss, A. (1964) 'Awareness contexts and social interaction', *American Sociological Review*, XXIX:669–79.

—— and —— (1967) *The Discovery of Grounded Theory*, Chicago, Aldine.

—— and —— (1968) *Time for Dying*, Chicago, Aldine.

—— and —— (1971) *Status Passage*, Chicago, Aldine.

Goffman, E. (1955) 'On face-work: an analysis of ritual elements in social interaction', *Psychiatry*, 18, 3:213–31.

—— (1959) *The Presentation of Self in Everyday Life*, New York, Doubleday.

—— (1961) *Asylums: Essays on the Social Situation of Mental Patients and Other Inmates*, New York, Doubleday.

—— (1963) *Behavior in Public Places*, Glencoe, Ill., Free Press.

—— (1971) *Relations in Public: Micro Studies of the Public Order*, New York, Basic Books.

—— (1972) *Interaction Ritual*, Harmondsworth, Penguin.

Gold, R.L. (1958) 'Roles in sociological fieldwork', *Social Forces*, 36: 217–23.

Golde, P. (ed.) (1986) *Women in the Field: Anthropological Experiences*, Berkeley, Calif., University of California Press, 2nd edn.

Goode, W.J. and Hatt, P.K. (1952) *Methods in Social Research*, New York, McGraw-Hill.

Goody, J. (ed.) (1968) *Literacy in Traditional Societies*, Cambridge, Cambridge University Press.

—— (1986) *The Logic of Writing and the Organisation of Society*, Cambridge, Cambridge University Press.

—— (1987) *The Interface between the Written and the Oral*, Cambridge, Cambridge University Press.

Gorbutt, D. (1972) 'The new sociology of education', *Education for Teaching*, 89, Autumn:3–11.

Gouldner, A.W. (1954) *Patterns of Industrial Bureaucracy*, New York, Free Press.

—— (1968) 'The sociologist as partisan', *American Sociologist*, May: 103–16.

—— (1970) *The Coming Crisis of Western Sociology*, New York, Basic Books.

Gregor, T. (1977) *Mehinaku: The Drama of Daily Life in a Brazilian Indian Village*, Chicago, University of Chicago Press.

Gregory, R. (1970) *The Intelligent Eye*, London, Weidenfeld & Nicolson.

Griffin, C. (1991) 'The researcher talks back: dealing with power relations in studies of young people's entry into the job market', in Shaffir and Stebbins (eds) (1991).

Guba, E. (1978) *Toward a Methodology of Naturalistic Inquiry in Educational Evaluation*, Los Angeles, Calif., Center for the Study of Evaluation, UCLA Graduate School of Education.

—— (ed.) (1990) *The Paradigm Dialog*, Newbury Park, Calif., Sage.

Gubrium, J. and Silverman, D. (eds) (1989) *The Politics of Field Research: Beyond Enlightenment*, Newbury Park, Calif., Sage.

Gurney, J.N. (1991) 'Female researchers in male-dominated settings: implications for short-term versus long-term research', in Shaffir and Stebbins (eds) (1991).

Hage, J. and Meeker, B.F. (1988) *Social Causality*, Boston, Mass., Unwin Hyman.

Hammersley, M. (1980) 'A peculiar world? Teaching and learning in an inner city school', unpublished PhD thesis, University of Manchester.

—— (1981) 'Ideology in the staffroom? A critique of false consciousness', in L. Barton and S. Walker (eds), *Schools, Teachers and Teaching*, Lewes, Falmer.

—— (ed.) (1983a) *The Ethnography of Schooling: Methodological Issues*, Driffield, Nafferton.

—— (1983b) 'Introduction: reflexivity and naturalism', in Hammersley (ed.) (1983a).

—— (1984a) 'The researcher exposed: a natural history', in Burgess (ed.) (1984b).

—— (1984b) 'Some reflections on the macro-micro problem in the sociology of education', *Sociological Review*, 32, 2:316–24.

—— (1985) 'From ethnography to theory: a programme and paradigm for case study research in the sociology of education', *Sociology*, 19, 2:244–59.

—— (1987a) 'Ethnography and the cumulative development of theory', *British Educational Research Journal*, 13, 3:73–81.

—— (1987b) 'Ethnography for survival?', *British Educational Research Journal*, 13, 3:283–95.

—— (1989a) 'The problem of the concept: Herbert Blumer on the relationship between concepts and data', *Journal of Contemporary Ethnography*, 18, 2:133–59.

—— (1989b) *The Dilemma of Qualitative Method: Herbert Blumer and the Chicago Tradition*, London, Routledge.

—— (1990) *Classroom Ethnography: Empirical and Methodological Essays*, Milton Keynes, Open University Press.

Hammersley, M. (1991a) *Reading Ethnographic Research: A Critical Guide*, London, Longman.

—— (1991b) 'Staffroom news', reprinted as appendix to Hammersley (1991a).

—— (1992) *What's Wrong with Ethnography?*, London, Routledge.

—— (1993) 'The rhetorical turn in ethnography', *Social Science Information*, 32, 1:23–37.

—— (1994) 'Is social research political?', in M. Hammersley, *The Politics of Social Research*, London, Sage.

Hammond, P.E. (ed.) (1964) *Sociologists at Work: Essays on the Craft of Social Research*, New York, Basic Books.

Hannerz, U. (1969) *Soulside*, New York, Columbia University Press.

Hansen, E.C. (1977) *Rural Catalonia under the Franco Regime*, Cambridge, Cambridge University Press.

Hanson, N.R. (1958) *Patterns of Discovery*, London, Cambridge University Press.

Hargreaves, A. (1981) 'Contrastive rhetoric and extremist talk: teachers, hegemony and the educationist context' in L. Barton and S. Walker (eds), *Schools, Teachers and Teaching*, Lewes, Falmer.

Hargreaves, D.H. (1967) *Social Relations in a Secondary School*, London, Routledge & Kegan Paul.

—— (1977) 'The process of typification in the classroom: models and methods', *British Journal of Educational Psychology*, 47:274–84.

Hargreaves, D.H., Hester, S., and Mellor, F. (1975) *Deviance in Classrooms*, London, Routledge & Kegan Paul.

Harré, R. and Secord, P.G. (1972) *The Explanation of Social Behaviour*, Oxford, Blackwell.

Harris, M. (1979) *Cultural Materialism: The Struggle for a Science of Culture*, New York, Random House.

Harvey, L. (1985) *Myths of the Chicago School*, Aldershot, Gower.

Hastrup, K. and Elsass, P. (1990) 'Anthropological advocacy: a contradiction in terms?', *Current Anthropology*, 31, 3:301–11.

Hawkes, T. (1977) *Structuralism and Semiotics*, London, Methuen.

Heath, C. (1981) 'The opening sequence in doctor–patient interaction', in P. Atkinson and C. Heath (eds) (1981).

Hempel, C.G. (1966) *Philosophy of Natural Science*, Englewood Cliffs, NJ, Prentice-Hall.

Henslin, J.M. (1990) 'It's not a lovely place to visit, and I wouldn't want to live there', in Burgess (ed.) (1990).

Hewitt, J.P. and Stokes, R. (1976) 'Aligning actions', *American Sociological Review*, 41:838–49.

Hitchcock, G. (1983) 'Fieldwork as practical activity: reflections on fieldwork and the social organization of an urban, open-plan primary school', in Hammersley (ed.) (1983a).

Hoffman, J.E. (1980) 'Problems of access in the study of social elites and boards of directors', in W.B. Shaffir, *et al.* (eds) (1980).

Holdaway, S. (1982) ' "An inside job": a case study of covert research on the police', in Bulmer (ed.) (1982).

—— (1983) *Inside the British Police: A Force at Work*, Oxford, Blackwell.

Holstein, J.A. and Miller, G. (eds) (1989) *Perspectives on Social Problems*, vol. 1, Greenwich, Conn., JAI Press.

—— and —— (eds) (1993) *Reconsidering Social Constructionism: Debates in Social Problems Theory*, New York, Aldine de Gruyter.

Homan, R. (1978) 'Interpersonal communications in pentecostal meetings', *Sociological Review*, 26, 3:499–518.

—— (1980) 'The ethics of covert methods', *British Journal of Sociology*, 31, 1:46–59.

—— (1991) *The Ethics of Social Research*, London, Longman.

Homan, R. and Bulmer, M. (1982) 'On the merits of covert methods: a dialogue', in Bulmer (ed.) (1982).

Humphreys, L. (1970) *Tearoom Trade*, Chicago, Aldine.

Hunt, L. (1984) 'The development of rapport through the negotiation of gender in fieldwork among the police', *Human Organization*, 43: 283–96.

Hunter, A. (1993) 'Local knowledge and local power: notes on the ethnography of local community elites', *Journal of Contemporary Ethnography*, 22, 1:36–58.

Hustler, D., Cassidy, A., and Cuff, E.C. (eds) (1986) *Action Research in Classrooms and Schools*, London, Allen & Unwin.

Jacob, E. (1987) 'Qualitative research traditions: a review', *Review of Educational Research*, 57, 1:1–50.

Jacobs, J.B. (1974) 'Participant observation in prison', *Urban Life and Culture*, 3, 2:221–40.

Jackson, J.F. (1990) 'Déjà entendu: the liminal quality of anthropological fieldnotes', *Journal of Contemporary Ethnography*, 19: 8–43.

Jahoda, M., Deutsch, M., and Cook, S.W. (1951) *Research Methods in Social Relations*, New York, Dryden.

Jeffrey, P. (1979) *Frogs in a Well: Indian Women in Purdah*, London, Zed Press.

Jenkins, D. (1980) 'An adversary's account of SAFARI's ethics of case study', in C. Richards (ed.), *Power in the Curriculum*, Driffield, Nafferton.

Johnson, J. (1975) *Doing Field Research*, New York, Free Press.

Jules-Rosette, B. (1978a) 'The veil of objectivity: prophecy, divination, and social inquiry', *American Anthropologist*, 80, 3:549–70.

—— (1978b) 'Towards a theory of ethnography', *Sociological Symposium*, 24:81–98.

Junker, B. (1960) *Field Work*, Chicago, University of Chicago Press.

Kaplan, A. (1964) *The Conduct of Inquiry: Methodology for Behavioural Science*, San Francisco, Chandler.

Kaplan, I.M. (1991) 'Gone fishing, be back later: ending and resuming research among fisherman', in Shaffir and Stebbins (eds) (1991).

Karp, D.A. (1980) 'Observing behavior in public places: problems and strategies', in Shaffir *et al.* (eds) (1980).

—— (1993) 'Taking anti-depressant medications: resistance, trial commitment, conversion and disenchantment', *Qualitative Sociology*, 16, 4: 337–59.

Keat, R. and Urry, J. (1975) *Social Theory as Science*, London: Routledge & Kegan Paul.

Keiser, R.L. (1970) 'Fieldwork among the Vice Lords of Chicago', in G.D. Spindler (ed.), *Being an Anthropologist*, New York, Holt, Rinehart & Winston.

Kelly, A. (1985) 'Action research: what it is and what it can do', in Burgess (ed.) (1985a).

Kemmis, S. (1988) 'Action research', in J.P. Keeves (ed.), *Educational Research Methodology and Measurement*, Oxford, Pergamon.

Klatch, R.E. (1988) 'The methodological problems of studying a politically resistant community', in Burgess (ed.) (1988a).

Knorr-Cetina, K.D. (1981) *The Manufacture of Knowledge: An Essay on the Constructivist and Contextual Nature of Science*, Oxford, Pergamon.

Knorr-Cetina, K.D. and Cicourel, A.V. (eds) (1981) *Advances in Social Theory and Methodology: Towards an Integration of Micro- and Macro-Sociologies*, Boston, Mass., Routledge & Kegan Paul.

Kolakowski, L. (1972) *Positivist Philosophy: From Hume to the Vienna Circle*, Harmondsworth, Penguin.

Kondo, D. (1990) *Crafting Selves*, Chicago, University of Chicago Press.

Kotarba, J.A. (1975) 'American acupuncturists: the new entrepreneurs of hope', *Urban Life*, 4, 2:149–77.

Krieger, S. (1979a) 'Research and the construction of a text', in N.K. Denzin (ed.), *Studies in Symbolic Interaction*, vol. 2, Greenwich, Conn., JAI Press.

—— (1979b) 'The KMPX strike (March–May 1968)', in N.K. Denzin (ed.), *Studies in Symbolic Interaction*, vol. 2, Greenwich, Conn., JAI Press.

—— (1983) *The Mirror Dance: Identity in a Women's Community*, Philadelphia, Pa, Temple University Press.

Krippendorff, K. (1980) *Content Analysis*, Beverly Hills, Calif., Sage.

Kuhn, T.S. (1970) *The Structure of Scientific Revolutions*, Chicago, University of Chicago Press, 2nd edn.

Labov, W. (1969) 'The logic of nonstandard English', *Georgetown Monographs on Language and Linguistics*, 22:1–31.

—— (1972) 'The transformation of experience in narrative syntax', in W. Labov (ed.), *Language in the Inner City*, Philadelphia, Pa: Pennsylvania University Press.

Labov, W. and Waletzky, J. (1967) 'Narrative analysis: oral versions of personal experience', in J. Holm (ed.), *Essays on the Verbal and Visual Arts*, Seattle, Wash., University of Washington Press.

Lacey, C. (1970) *Hightown Grammar*, Manchester, Manchester University Press.

—— (1976) 'Problems of sociological fieldwork: a review of the methodology of "Hightown Grammar" ', in M. Shipman (ed.), *The Organization and Impact of Social Research*, London: Routledge & Kegan Paul.

Landes, R. (1986) 'A woman anthropologist in Brazil', in Golde (ed.) (1986).

Lather, P. (1986) 'Issues of validity in openly ideological research', *Interchange*, 17, 4:63–84.

—— (1991) *Getting Smart: Feminist Research and Pedagogy with/in the Postmodern*, New York, Routledge.

Latour, B. and Woolgar, S. (1979) *Laboratory Life*, Beverly Hills, Calif., Sage; 2nd edn 1986, Princeton, NJ, Princeton University Press.

Lazarsfeld, P.P. and Barton, A. (1951) 'Qualitative measurement in the social sciences: classification, typologies and indices', in D.P. Lerner and H.D. Lasswell (eds), *The Policy Sciences*, Stanford, Calif., Stanford University Press.

Lee, R. (1992) 'Nobody said it had to be easy: postgraduate field research in Northern Ireland', in Burgess (ed.) (1992).

Lee, R. and Fielding, N. (eds) (1991) *Using Computers in Qualitative Research*, London, Sage.

Lehman, T. and Young, T.R. (1974) 'From conflict theory to conflict methodology: an emerging paradigm for sociology', *Sociological Quarterly*, 44, 1: 15–28.

Lepenies, W. (1988) *Between Literature and Sociology*, Cambridge, Cambridge University Press.

LePlay, F. (1879) *Les Ouvriers Européens*, Paris, Alfred Mame et Fils.

Lerner, D. (1957) 'The "hard-headed" Frenchman: on se défend, toujours', *Encounter*, 8, March:27–32.

Lever, J. (1981) 'Multiple methods of data collection: a note on divergence', *Urban Life*, 10, 2:199–213.

Liebow, E. (1967) *Tally's Corner*, London: Routledge & Kegan Paul.

Lincoln, Y.S. and Guba, E. (1985) *Naturalistic Inquiry*, Beverly Hills, Calif., Sage.

—— and —— (1989) 'Ethics: the failure of positivist science', *Review of Higher Education*, 12, 3:221–40.

Lindesmith, A. (1947) *Opiate Addiction*, Bloomington, Ind., Principia Press.

Lipset, D. (1980) *Gregory Bateson: The Legacy of a Scientist*, Englewood Cliffs, NJ, Prentice-Hall.

Llewellyn, M. (1980) 'Studying girls at school: the implications of confusion', in R. Deem (ed.), *Schooling for Women's Work*, London, Routledge & Kegan Paul.

Lodge, D. (1977) *The Modes of Modern Writing: Metaphor, Metonymy, and the Typology of Modern Literature*, London: Edward Arnold.

—— (1981) *Working with Structuralism*, London, Routledge & Kegan Paul.

Lofland, J. (1961) 'Comment on "Initial interactions of newcomers in AA" ', *Social Problems*, 8:365–7.

—— (1967) 'Notes on naturalism', *Kansas Journal of Sociology*, 3, 2:45–61.

—— (1970) 'Interactionist imagery and analytic interruptus', in T. Shibutani (ed.), *Human Nature and Collective Behaviour: Papers in Honour of Herbert Blumer*, Englewood Cliffs, NJ, Prentice-Hall.

—— (1971) *Analyzing Social Settings: A Guide to Qualitative Observation and Analysis*, Belmont, Calif., Wadsworth; for 2nd edition, see Lofland and Lofland (1984).

—— (1974) 'Styles of reporting qualitative field research', *American Sociologist*, 9, August:101–11.

Lofland, J. (1976) *Doing Social Life: The Qualitative Study of Human Interaction in Natural Settings*, New York, Wiley.

—— (1980) 'Early Goffman: style, structure, substance, soul', in J. Ditton (ed.), *The View from Goffman*, London: Macmillan.

Lofland, J. and Lejeune, R.A. (1960) 'Initial encounters of newcomers in Alcoholics Anonymous', *Social Problems*, 8:102–11.

Lofland, J. and Lofland, L.H. (1984) *Analysing Social Settings*, Belmont, Calif., Wadsworth, 2nd edn.

Lofland, L.H. (1966) *In the Presence of Strangers: A Study of Behaviour in Public Settings*, Working Paper 19, University of Michigan, Ann Arbor, Center for Research on Social Organization.

—— (1973) *A World of Strangers: Order and Action in Urban Public Space*, New York, Basic Books.

Loizos, P. (1975) *The Greek Gift: Politics in a Cypriot Village*, Oxford, Blackwell.

—— (1993) *Innovation in Ethnographic Film: From Innocence to Self-Consciousness 1955–1985*, Manchester, Manchester University Press.

Lundman, R.J. and McFarlane, P.T. (1976) 'Conflict methodology: an introduction and preliminary assessment', *Sociological Quarterly*, 17: 503–12.

Lyman, S.M. and Scott, M.B. (1970) *A Sociology of the Absurd*, New York, Appleton-Century-Crofts.

Lynch, M. and Woolgar, S. (eds) (1990) *Representation in Scientific Practice*, Cambridge, Mass., MIT Press.

Mac an Ghaill, M. (1991) '*Young, Gifted and Black: methodological reflections of a teacher/researcher*', in Walford (ed.) (1991a).

McCall, G.J. (1969) 'The problem of indicators in participant observation research', in G.J. McCall and J.L. Simmons (eds), *Issues in Participant Observation: A Text and Reader*, Reading, Mass., Addison-Wesley.

McCloskey, D. (1985) *The Rhetoric of Economics*, Madison, Wis., University of Wisconsin Press.

McCurdy, D.W. (1976) 'The medicine man', in M.A. Rynkiewich and J.P. Spradley (eds), *Ethics and Anthropology: Dilemmas in Fieldwork*, New York, Wiley.

McDermott, R. (1976) 'Kids make sense: an ethnographic account of the interactional management of success and failure in one first-grade classroom', unpublished PhD thesis, Stanford University, California.

MacDougall, D. (1992) 'Complicities of style', in Crawford and Turton (ed.) (1992).

MacIntyre, S. (1977) *Single and Pregnant*, London, Croom Helm.

McKeganey, N. and Cunningham-Burley, S. (eds) (1987) *Enter the Sociologist*, Aldershot, Avebury.

McPhail, C. and Rexroat, C. (1980) 'Ex cathedra Blumer or ex libris Mead?', *American Sociological Review*, 45:420–30.

Malinowski, B. (1922) *Argonauts of the Western Pacific*, London, Routledge & Kegan Paul.

—— (1967) *A Diary in the Strict Sense of the Term*, London, Routledge & Kegan Paul.

Manning, P.K. (1980) 'Goffman's framing order: style as structure', in J. Ditton (ed.), *The View from Goffman*, London, Macmillan.

Marshall, C. and Rossman, G. (1989) *Designing Qualitative Research*, Newbury Park, Calif., Sage.

Martin, J. (1981) 'A garbage can model of the psychological research process', *American Behavioral Scientists*, 25, 2:131–51.

Martinez, W. (1992) 'Who constructs anthropological knowledge? Toward a theory of ethnographic film spectatorships', in Crawford and Turton (ed.) (1992).

Mason, K. (1990) 'Not waving but bidding: reflections on research in a rural setting', in Burgess (ed.) (1990).

Matza, D. (1969) *Becoming Deviant*, Englewood Cliffs, NJ, Prentice-Hall.

Mayhew, H. (1861) *London Labour and the London Poor*, London, Griffin Bohn.

Mead, G.H. (1934) *Mind, Self and Society*, Chicago, University of Chicago Press.

Measor, L. (1983) 'Gender and the sciences: pupils' gender-based conceptions of school subjects', in M. Hammersley and A. Hargreaves (eds), *Curriculum Practice: Sociological Accounts*, Lewes, Falmer.

—— (1985) 'Interviewing: a strategy in qualitative research', in Burgess (ed.) (1985b).

Measor, L. and Woods, P. (1983) 'The interpretation of pupil myths', in Hammersley (ed.) (1983a).

Medawar, P. (1967) *The Art of the Soluble*, London, Methuen.

—— (1979) *Advice to a Young Scientist*, New York, Harper & Row.

Mehan, H. (1974) 'Assessing children's school performance', in H.P. Dreitzel (ed.), *Recent Sociology*, No. 5, *Childhood and Socialization*, London, Collier Macmillan.

Merton, R.K. (1959) 'Introduction: notes on problem-finding in sociology', in R.K. Merton, L. Broom, and L.S. Cottrell Jr (eds), *Sociology Today*, vol. 1, New York, Harper & Row.

Miller, S.M. (1952) 'The participant observer and "over-rapport"', *American Sociological Review*, 17, 2:97–9.

Mills, C.W. (1940) 'Situated actions and vocabularies of motive', *American Sociological Review* 5, 6:439–52.

Mitchell, R.G. (1991) 'Secrecy and disclosure in fieldwork', in Shaffir and Stebbins (eds) (1991).

Moffat, M. (1989) *Coming of Age in New Jersey*, New Brunswick, Rutgers University Press.

Morgan, D.H.J. (1972) 'The British Association Scandal: the effect of publicity on a sociological investigation', *Sociological Review*, 20, 2: 185–206.

Moser, C.A. and Kalton, G. (1971) *Survey Methods in Social Investigation*, London, Heinemann, 2nd edn.

Mungham, G. and Thomas P.A. (1981) 'Studying lawyers: aspects of the theory, method and politics of social research', *British Journal of Law and Society*, 8, 1:79–96.

Nadel, S.F. (1939) 'The interview technique in social anthropology', in

F.C. Bartlett, M. Ginsberg, E.J. Lindgren, and R.H. Thouless (eds), *The Study of Society*, London, Routledge & Kegan Paul.

Nader, L. (1986) 'From anguish to exultation', in Golde (ed.) (1986).

Noblit, G.W. and Hare, R.D. (1988) *Meta-Ethnography: Synthesizing Qualitative Studies*, Newbury Park, Calif., Sage.

Oakley, A. (1981) 'Interviewing women: a contradiction in terms', in Roberts (ed.) (1981).

Oboler, R.S. (1986) 'For better or worse: anthropologists and husbands in the field', in Whitehead and Conaway (eds) (1986).

Okely, J. (1983) *The Traveller-Gypsies*, London, Cambridge University Press.

Okely, J. and Gallaway, H. (eds) (1992) *Anthropology and Autobiography*, ASA Monographs 29, London, Routledge.

Olesen, V. (1990) 'Immersed, amorphous and episodic fieldwork: theory and policy in three contrasting contexts', in Burgess (ed.) (1990).

Olesen, V. and Whittaker, E. (1968) *The Silent Dialogue: A Study in the Social Psychology of Professional Socialization*, San Francisco, Jossey-Bass.

Ostrander, S.A. (1993) ' "Surely you're not in this just to be helpful?": access, rapport and interviews in three studies of elites', *Journal of Contemporary Ethnography*, 22, 1:7–27.

Papanek, H. (1964) 'The woman fieldworker in a purdah society', *Human Organization*, 23:160–3.

Parker, H.J. (1974) *View from the Boys: A Sociology of Downtown Adolescents*, London, David & Charles, 2nd edn.

Patrick, J. (1973) *A Glasgow Gang Observed*, London, Eyre Methuen.

Paul, B.D. (1953) 'Interviewing techniques and field relations', in A.C. Kroeber (ed.), *Anthropology Today: An Encyclopaedic Inventory*, Chicago, University of Chicago Press.

Pelto, P.J. and Pelto, G.H. (1978) 'Ethnography: the fieldwork enterprise', in J.J. Honigmann (ed.) *Handbook of Social and Cultural Anthropology*, Chicago, Rand McNally.

Perlman, M.L. (1970) 'Intensive fieldwork and scope sampling: methods for studying the same problem at different levels', in M. Freilich (ed.) (1970a).

Peshkin, A. (1985) 'Virtuous subjectivity: in the participant-observer's I's', in D.N. Berg and K.K. Smith (eds), *Exploring Clinical Methods for Social Research*, Beverly Hills, Calif., Sage.

Pettigrew, M. (1993) 'Coming to terms with research: the contract business', paper given at ESRC-sponsored seminar on Methodological and Ethical Issues Associated with Research into the Education Reform Act, University of Warwick.

Pettinari, C.J. (1988) *Task, Talk and Text in the Operating Room: A Study in Medical Discourse*, Norwood, NJ, Ablex.

Piliavin, I. and Briar, B. (1964) 'Police encounters with juveniles', *American Journal of Sociology*, 70:206–14.

Platt, J. (1981) 'On interviewing one's peers', *British Journal of Sociology*, 32, 1:75–91.

Plummer, K. (1975) *Sexual Stigma: An Interactionist Account*, London, Routledge & Kegan Paul.
—— (1983) *Documents of Life: An Introduction to the Problems and Literature of a Humanistic Method*, London, Allen & Unwin.
Pollard, A. (1985) 'Opportunities and difficulties of a teacher-ethnographer: a personal account', in Burgess (ed.) (1985c).
Pollert, A. (1981) *Girls, Wives, Factory Lives*, London, Macmillan.
Popper, K. (1972) *The Logic of Scientific Discovery*, London, Hutchinson.
Powdermaker, H. (1966) *Stranger and Friend: The Way of an Anthropologist*, New York, Norton.
Pratt, M.L. (1986a) 'Fieldwork in common places', in Clifford and Marcus (eds) (1986).
—— (1986b) 'Scratches on the face of the country: or, what Mr Barrow saw in the land of the Bushmen', in L. Gates Jr (ed.), *'Race', Writing and Difference*, Chicago, University of Chicago Press.
Prior, L. (1985) 'Making sense of mortality', *Sociology of Health and Illness*, 7, 2:167–90.
Prior, L. and Bloor, M. (1993) 'Why people die: social representations of death and its causes', *Science and Culture*, 3, 3:346–74.
Punch, M. (1979) *Policing the Inner City*, London, Macmillan.
—— (1986) *The Politics and Ethics of Fieldwork*, Beverly Hills, Calif., Sage.
Radcliffe-Brown, A.R. (1948a) *The Andaman Islanders*, Glencoe, Ill., Free Press.
—— (1948b) *A Natural Science of Society*, New York, Free Press.
Rainbird, H. (1990) 'Expectations and revelations: examining conflict in the Andes', in Burgess (ed.) (1990).
Rainwater, L. and Pittman, D.J. (1967) 'Ethical problems in studying a politically sensitive and deviant community', *Social Problems*, 14:357–66; reprinted 1969 in G.J. McCall and J.L. Simmons (eds), *Issues in Participant Observation: A Text and Reader*, Reading, Mass., Addison-Wesley.
Rawlings, B. (1988) 'Local knowledge: the analysis of transcribed audio materials for organizational ethnography', in Burgess (ed.) (1988a).
Rees, C. (1981) 'Records and hospital routine', in Atkinson and Heath (eds) (1981).
Reichenbach, H. (1938) *Experience and Prediction: An Analysis of the Foundations and the Structure of Knowledge*, Chicago, University of Chicago Press.
—— (1951) *The Rise of Scientific Philosophy*, Berkeley, Calif., University of California Press.
Richardson, L. (1990a) *Writing Strategies: Reaching Diverse Audiences*, Newbury Park, Calif., Sage.
—— (1990b) 'Narrative and sociology', *Journal of Contemporary Ethnography*, 19:116–35.
Riddell, S. (1992) *Gender and the Politics of the Curriculum*, London, Routledge.
Riemer, J.W. (1977) 'Varieties of opportunistic research', *Urban Life*, 5, 4:467–77.

Riesman, D. (1958) 'Interviews, elites, and academic freedom', *Social Problems* 6:115–26.

Robbins, T. (1988) *Cults, Converts and Charisma*, Newbury Park, Calif., Sage.

Roberts, H. (ed.) (1981) *Doing Feminist Research*, London, Routledge & Kegan Paul.

Robinson, D. (1971) *The Process of Becoming Ill*, London, Routledge & Kegan Paul.

Robinson, W.S. (1969) 'The logical structure of analytic induction', in G.J. McCall and J.L. Simmons (eds), *Issues in Participant Observation: A Text and Reader*, Reading, Mass., Addison-Wesley.

Rock, P. (1973) *Making People Pay*, London, Routledge & Kegan Paul.

—— (1979) *The Making of Symbolic Interactionism*, London, Macmillan.

Rohner, R. (1969) *The Ethnography of Franz Boas*, Chicago, University of Chicago Press.

Rosaldo, R. (1986) 'From the door of his tent', in Clifford and Marcus (eds) (1986).

Rose, D. (1989) *Patterns of American Culture: Ethnography and Estrangement*, Philadelphia, Pa, University of Pennsylvania Press.

Rosenhahn, D.L. (1973) 'On being sane in insane places', *Science*, 179: 250–8; reprinted in Bulmer (ed.) (1982).

Roth, J. (1962) 'Comments on "secret observation" ', *Social Problems*, 9, 3:283–4.

—— (1963) *Timetables*, New York, Bobbs-Merrill.

Sacks, H. (1972) 'On the analyzability of stories by children', in J.J. Gumperz and D. Hymes (eds), *Directions in Sociolinguistics: The Ethnography of Communication*, New York, Holt, Rinehart & Winston.

—— (1975) 'Everyone has to lie', in M. Sanches and B. Blount (eds), *Sociocultural Dimensions of Language Use*, London, Academic Press.

Sacks, H., Schegloff, E.A., and Jefferson, G. (1974) 'A simplest systematics for the organisation of turn-taking for conversation', *Language*, 50:696–735.

Sahlins, M.G. and Service, E.R. (eds) (1960) *Evolution and Culture*, Ann Arbor, Mich., University of Michigan Press.

Said, E. (1978) *Orientalism*, New York, Pantheon.

Sanjek, R. (ed.) (1990) *Fieldnotes: The Makings of Anthropology*, Ithaca, NY, Cornell University Press.

Scarth, J. (1986) 'The influence of examinations on whole-school curriculum decision-making: an ethnographic case study', unpublished PhD thesis, University of Lancaster.

Scarth, J. and Hammersley, M. (1988) 'Examinations and teaching: an exploratory study', *British Educational Research Journal*, 14, 3:231–49. Reprinted in Hammersley (1990).

Schatzman, L. and Strauss, A. (1955) 'Social class and modes of communication', *American Journal of Sociology*, 60:329–38.

—— and —— (1973) *Field Research: Strategies for a Natural Sociology*, Englewood Cliffs, NJ, Prentice-Hall.

Scheper-Hughes, N. (1982) *Saints, Scholars and Schizophrenics: Mental*

Illness in Rural Ireland, Berkeley, Calif., University of California Press, 2nd edn.

Schofield, J.W. (1990) 'Increasing the generalizability of qualitative research', in E.W. Eisner and A. Peshkin (eds), *Qualitative Inquiry in Education: The Continuing Debate*, New York, Teachers College Press.

Schuman, H. (1982) 'Artifacts are in the mind of the beholder', *American Sociologist*, 17, 1:21–8.

Schutz, A. (1964) 'The stranger: an essay in social psychology', in A. Schutz (ed.), *Collected Papers*, vol. II, The Hague, Martinus Nijhoff.

Schwartz, H. and Jacobs, J. (1979) *Qualitative Sociology: A Method to the Madness*, New York, Free Press.

Scott, G.G. (1983) *The Magicians: A Study of the Use of Power in a Black Magic Group*, New York, Irvington.

Scott, M.B. (1968) *The Racing Game*, Chicago, Aldine.

Scott, S. (1984) 'The personable and the powerful: gender and status in social research', in Bell and Roberts (eds) (1984).

Seaman, G. and Williams, H. (1992) 'Hypermedia in ethnography', in Crawford and Turton (eds). (1992)

Selltiz, C., Jahoda, M., Deutsch, M., and Cook, S. (1959) *Research Methods in Social Relations*, New York, Holt, Rinehart & Winston.

Sevigny, M.J. (1981) 'Triangulated inquiry – a methodology for the analysis of classroom interaction', in J.L. Green and C. Wallat (eds), *Ethnography and Language in Educational Settings*, Norwood, NJ, Ablex.

Shaffir, W.B. (1985) 'Some reflections on approaches to fieldwork in Hassidic communities', *Jewish Journal of Sociology*, 27, 2:115–34.

—— (1991) 'Managing a convincing self-presentation: some personal reflections on entering the field', in Shaffir and Stebbins (eds) (1991).

Shaffir, W.B. and Stebbins, R.A. (eds) (1991) *Experiencing Fieldwork: An Inside View of Qualitative Research*, Newbury Park, Calif., Sage.

Shaffir, W.B., Stebbins, R.A., and Turowetz, A. (eds) (1980) *Fieldwork Experience: Qualitative Approaches to Social Research*, New York, St. Martin's Press.

Shakespeare, P. (1994) 'Aspects of confused speech', unpublished manuscript, Open University.

Sharrock, W.W. and Anderson, R.J. (1980) 'On the demise of the native: some observations on and a proposal for ethnography', Occasional Paper 5, Department of Sociology, University of Manchester.

Sheehan, E.A. (1993) 'The student of culture and the ethnography of Irish intellectuals', in Brettel (ed.) (1993).

Sheridan, D. (1993) 'Writing to the archive: Mass Observation as autobiography', *Sociology*, 27, 1:27–40.

Shils, E. (1959) 'Social inquiry and the autonomy of the individual', in D.P. Lerner (ed.), *The Human Meaning of the Human Sciences*, New York, Meridian.

Silverman, D. (1973) 'Interview talk: bringing off a research instrument', *Sociology*, 7, 1:31–48.

—— (1993) *Interpreting Qualitative Data: Methods for Analysing Talk, Text and Interaction*, London, Sage.

Simons, H. (1981) 'Conversation piece: the practice of interviewing in case study research', in C. Adelman (ed.), *Uttering, Muttering: Collecting, Using and Reporting Talk for Social and Educational Research*, London, Grant McIntyre.

Sjoberg, G. and Nett, R. (1968) *A Methodology for Social Research*, New York, Harper & Row.

Skipper, J.K. and McCaghy, C.H. (1972) 'Respondents' intrusion upon the situation: the problem of interviewing subjects with special qualities', *Sociological Quarterly*, 13:237–43.

Skolnick, J. (1966) *Justice without Trial: Law Enforcement in Democratic Society*, New York, Wiley.

Smart, C. (1984) *The Ties that Bind: Law, Marriage and the Reproduction of Patriarchal Relations*, London, Routledge & Kegan Paul.

Smigel, E. (1958) 'Interviewing a legal elite: the Wall Street lawyer', *American Journal of Sociology*, 64:159–64.

Smith, D. (1987) *The Everyday World as Problematic: A Feminist Sociology*, Boston, Mass., Northeastern University Press.

—— (1993) ' "Literary" and business: "social problems" as social organization', in Holstein and Miller (eds) (1993).

Smith, J.K. (1989) *The Nature of Social and Educational Inquiry*, Norwood, NJ, Ablex.

Smith, J.K. and Heshusius, L. (1986) 'Closing down the conversation: the end of the quantitative-qualitative debate among educational inquirers', *Educational Researcher*, 15, 1:4–12.

Snow, D. (1980) 'The disengagement process: a neglected problem in participant observation research', *Qualitative Sociology*, 3, 2:100–22.

Sontag, S. (1979) *Illness as Metaphor*, London, Allen Lane.

Speier, M. (1973) *How to Observe Face-to-Face Communication: A Sociological Introduction*, Pacific Palisades, Calif., Goodyear.

Spradley, J.P. (1970) *You Owe Yourself a Drunk: An Ethnography of Urban Nomads*, Boston, Mass., Little, Brown.

—— (1979) *The Ethnographic Interview*, New York, Holt, Rinehart & Winston.

—— (1980) *Participant Observation*, New York, Holt, Rinehart & Winston.

Stanley, J. (1989) *Marks on the Memory*, Buckingham, Open University Press.

Stanley, L. (1992) *The Auto/Biographical I: Theory and Practice of Feminist Auto/Biography*, Manchester, Manchester University Press.

—— (1993) 'On auto/biography in sociology', *Sociology*, 27, 1:41–52.

Stanley, L. and Wise, S. (1983) *Breaking Out*, London, Routledge & Kegan Paul.

Stein, M.R. (1964) 'The eclipse of community: some glances at the education of a sociologist', in Vidich *et al.* (eds) (1964).

Stimson, G.V. and Webb, B. (1975) *Going to See the Doctor: The Consultation Process in General Practice*, London, Routledge & Kegan Paul.

Strauss, A. (1970) 'Discovering new theory from previous theory', in T. Shibutani (ed.), *Human Nature and Collective Behaviour: Essays in Honor of Herbert Blumer*, Englewood Cliffs, NJ, Prentice-Hall.

—— (1978) 'A social world perspective', in N.K. Denzin (ed.), *Studies in Symbolic Interaction*, vol. 1, Greenwich, Conn., JAI Press.

—— (1987) *Qualitative Analysis for Social Scientists*, Cambridge, Cambridge University Press.

—— (1993) *Continual Permutations of Action*, New York, Aldine de Gruyter.

Strauss, A. and Corbin, J. (1990) *Basics of Qualitative Research: Grounded Theory Procedures and Techniques*, Newbury Park, Calif., Sage.

Street, B.V. (1984) *Literacy in Theory and Practice*, Cambridge, Cambridge University Press.

Strong, P.M. (1979) *The Ceremonial Order of the Clinic: Parents, Doctors and Medical Bureaucracies*, London, Routledge & Kegan Paul.

—— (1982) 'The rivals: an essay on the sociological trades', in R. Dingwall and P. Lewis (eds), *The Sociology of the Professions: Medicine, Law and Others*, London, Macmillan.

Stryker, S. (1981) 'Symbolic interactionism: themes and variations', in M. Rosenberg and R.H. Turner (eds), *Social Psychology: Sociological Perspectives*, New York, Basic Books.

Styles, J. (1979) 'Outsider/insider: researching gay baths', *Urban Life*, 8, 2:135–52.

Sudarkasa, N. (1986) 'In a world of women: fieldwork in a Yoruba community', in Golde (ed.) (1986).

Sudnow, D. (1965) 'Normal crimes', *Social Problems*, 12:255–76.

—— (1967) *Passing On*, Englewood Cliffs, NJ, Prentice-Hall.

Sullivan, M.A., Queen, S.A., and Patrick, R.C. (1958) 'Participant observation as employed in the study of a military training program', *American Sociological Review*, 23, 6:660–7.

Suttles, G.D. (1968) *The Social Order of the Slum*, Chicago, University of Chicago Press.

Sykes, G. (1958) *The Society of Captives: A Study of a Maximum Security Prison*, Princeton, NJ, Princeton University Press.

Taylor, S.J. (1991) 'Leaving the field: research, relationships, and responsibilities', in Shaffir and Stebbins (eds) (1991).

Tesch, R. (1990) *Qualitative Research: Analysis Types and Software Tools*, London, Falmer.

Thomas, J. (1993) 'Catching up to the cyber age', *Writing Sociology*, 1, 2:1–3.

Thomas, R.J. (1993) 'Interviewing important people in big companies', *Journal of Contemporary Ethnography*, 22, 1:80–96.

Thomas, W.I. (1967) *The Unadjusted Girl*, New York, Harper & Row; first published 1923, Boston, Mass., Little, Brown.

Thomas, W.I. and Znaniecki, F. (1927) *The Polish Peasant in Europe and America*, New York, Knopf.

Thorne, B. (1983) 'Political activist as participant observer: conflicts of commitment in a study of the draft resistance movement of the 1960s', in R.M. Emerson (ed.), *Contemporary Field Research*, Boston, Mass., Little, Brown.

Tinbergen, N. (1972) *The Animal and its World*, vol. 1, London, Allen & Unwin.

Tobias, S. (1990) *They're Not Dumb, They're Different*, Tucson, Ariz., Research Corporation.

Toulmin, S. (1972) *Human Understanding*, Oxford, Clarendon Press.

Troustine, P. and Christensen, T. (1982) *Movers and Shakers: the study of community power*, New York, St Martin's Press.

Troyna, B. and Carrington, B. (1989) 'Whose side are we on? Ethical dilemmas in research on "race" and education', in Burgess (ed.) (1989).

Truzzi, M. (ed.) (1974) *Verstehen: Subjective Understanding in the Social Sciences*, Reading, Mass., Addison-Wesley.

Turnbull, C. (1973) *The Mountain People*, London, Cape.

Turner, R.H. (1962) 'Role-taking: process versus conformity', in A.M. Rose (ed.) *Human Behaviour and Social Processes*, London, Routledge & Kegan Paul.

Tyler, S.A. (ed.) (1969) *Cognitive Anthropology*, New York, Holt, Rinehart & Winston.

—— (1986) 'Post-modern ethnography: from document of the occult to occult document', in Clifford and Marcus (eds) (1986).

van Maanen, J. (1988) *Tales of the Field*, Chicago, University of Chicago Press.

—— (1991) 'Playing back the tape: early days in the field', in Shaffir and Stebbins (eds) (1991).

Vidich, A.J. and Bensman, J. (1958) *Small Town in Mass Society*, Princeton, NJ, Princeton University Press.

—— and —— (1964) 'The Springdale case: academic bureaucrats and sensitive townspeople', in Vidich *et al.* (eds) (1964).

Vidich, A.J., Bensman, J., and Stein, M.R. (eds) (1964) *Reflections on Community Studies* New York, Wiley

Von Wright, G.H. (1971) *Explanation and Understanding*, London, Routledge & Kegan Paul.

Walford, G. (ed.) (1987) *Doing Sociology of Education*, London, Falmer.

—— (1991a) 'Researching the City Technology College, Kingshurst', in Walford (ed.) (1991b).

—— (ed.) (1991b) *Doing Educational Research*, London, Routledge.

—— (ed.) (1994) *Researching the Powerful in Education*, London, UCL Press.

Walford, G. and Miller, H. (1991) *City Technology College*, Milton Keynes, Open University Press.

Walker, J.C. (1988) *Louts and Legends*, Sydney, Allen & Unwin.

Walker, R. (1978) 'The conduct of educational case studies: ethics, theories and procedures', in B. Dockerell and D. Hamilton (eds), *Rethinking Educational Research*, London, Hodder & Stoughton, 1978.

—— (1981) 'On the uses of fiction in educational research', in D. Smetherham (ed.), *Practising Evaluation*, Driffield, Nafferton.

Walker, R. and Adelman, C. (1972) *Towards a Sociography of Classrooms*, Final Report, SSRC Grants HR 996/1 'The analysis of classroom behaviour', and HR 1442/1 'The long-term observation of classroom events using stop-frame and cinematography', London, Centre for Science Education, Chelsea College.

Wallis, R. (1977) 'The moral career of a research project', in Bell and Newby (eds) (1977).

Warnke, G. (1987) *Gadamer: Hermeneutics, Tradition and Reason*, Cambridge, Polity Press.

Warren, C.A.B. (1972) 'Observing the gay community', in J.D. Douglas (ed.), *Research on Deviance*, New York, Random House.

—— (1974) *Identity and Community in the Gay World*, New York, Wiley.

—— (1988) *Gender Issues in Field Research*, Newbury Park, Calif., Sage.

Warren, C.A.B. and Rasmussen, P.K. (1977) 'Sex and gender in field research', *Urban Life*, 6, 3:349–69.

Warwick, D.P. (1982) *'Tearoom Trade*: means and ends in social research', in Bulmer (ed.) (1982).

Wax, M. (1952) 'Reciprocity as a field technique', *Human Organization*, 11:34–7.

—— (1982) 'Research reciprocity rather than informed consent in fieldwork', in J.E. Sieber (ed.), *The Ethics of Social Research: fieldwork, regulation and publication*, New York, Springer Verlag.

Wax, R. (1971) *Doing Fieldwork: Warnings and Advice*, Chicago, University of Chicago Press.

Weaver, A. and Atkinson, P.A. (1994) *Microcomputing and Qualitative Data Analysis*, Aldershot, Avebury.

Webb, E.J. and Salancik, J.R. (1966) 'The interview or the only wheel in town', *Journalism Monographs*, 2 November:1–49.

Webb, S. and Webb, B. (1932) *Methods of Social Study*, London, Longmans Green.

Werthman, C. (1963) 'Delinquents in schools: a test for the legitimacy of authority', *Berkeley Journal of Sociology*, 8, 1:39–60.

West, W.G. (1980) 'Access to adolescent deviants and deviance', in Shaffir *et al.* (eds) (1980).

Whitehead, T.L. (1986) 'Breakdown, resolution, and coherence: the fieldwork experiences of a big, brown, pretty-talking man in a West Indian community', in Whitehead and Conaway (eds) (1986).

Whitehead, T.L. and Conaway, M.E. (eds) (1986) *Self, Sex, and Gender in Cross-Cultural Fieldwork*, Urbana Ill., University of Illinois Press.

Whitten, N. (1970) 'Network analysis and processes of adaptation among Ecuadorian and Nova Scotian negroes', in M. Freilich (ed.) (1970a).

Whyte, W.F. (1953) 'Interviewing for organizational research', *Human Organization*, 12:15–22.

—— (1981) *Street Corner Society: The Social Structure of an Italian Slum*, Chicago, University of Chicago Press, 3rd edn.

Wieder, D. (1974a) *Language and Social Reality: The Case of Telling the Convict Code*, The Hague, Mouton.

—— (1974b) 'Telling the code', in R. Turner (ed.), *Ethnomethodology*, Harmondsworth, Penguin.

Willer, D. (1967) *Scientific Sociology*, Englewood Cliffs, NJ, Prentice-Hall.

Williams, R. (1976) 'Symbolic interactionism: fusion of theory and research', in D.C. Thorns (ed.), *New Directions in Sociology*, London, David & Charles.

Willis, P. (1977) *Learning to Labour: How Working Class Kids Get Working Class Jobs*, Farnborough, Saxon House.

—— (1981) 'Cultural production is different from cultural reproduction is different from social reproduction is different from reproduction', *Interchange*, 12, 2–3:48–67.

Willmott, P. (1980) 'A view from an independent research institute', in M. Cross (ed.), *Social Research and Public Policy: Three Perspectives*, London, Social Research Association.

Wilson, T.P. (1971) 'Normative and interpretive paradigms in sociology', in J.D. Douglas (ed.), *Understanding Everyday Life*, London, Routledge & Kegan Paul.

Wintrob, R.M. (1969) 'An inward focus: a consideration of psychological stress in fieldwork', in F. Henry and S. Saberwal (eds), *Stress and Response in Fieldwork*, New York, Holt, Rinehart & Winston.

Wolcott, H.F. (1990) *Writing Up Qualitative Research*, Newbury Park, Calif., Sage.

Wolf, D. (1991) 'High risk methodology: reflections on leaving an outlaw society', in Shaffir and Stebbins (eds) (1991).

Wolf, M. (1992) *A Thrice Told Tale: Feminism, Postmodernism and Ethnographic Responsibility*, Stanford, Calif., Stanford University Press.

Wolff, K.H. (1964) 'Surrender and community study: the study of Loma', in Vidich *et al.* (eds) (1964).

Woods, P. (1979) *The Divided School*, London, Routledge & Kegan Paul.

—— (1981) 'Understanding through talk', in C. Adelman (ed.), *Uttering, Muttering: Collecting, Using and Reporting Talk for Social and Educational Research*, London, Grant McIntyre.

—— (1985) 'Ethnography and theory construction in educational research', in Burgess (ed.) (1985c).

—— (1987) 'Ethnography at the crossroads: a reply to Hammersley', *British Educational Research Journal*, 13, 3:297–307.

Wright, M. (1981) 'Coming to terms with death: patient care in a hospice for the terminally ill', in Atkinson and Heath (eds) (1991).

Young, M. (1991) *An Inside Job: Policing and Police Culture in Britain*, Oxford, Clarendon Press.

Young, M.F.D. (ed.) (1971) *Knowledge and Control: New Directions in the Sociology of Education*, London, Collier-Macmillan.

Zelditch, M. (1962) 'Some methodological problems of field studies', *American Journal of Sociology* 67:566–76.

Zerubavel, E. (1979) *Patterns of Time in Hospital Life*, Chicago, University of Chicago Press.

Zimmerman, D.H. (1969) 'Record-keeping and the intake process in a public welfare agency', in S. Wheeler (ed.), *On Record: Files and Dossiers in American Life*, New York, Russell Sage Foundation.

Zimmerman, D.H. and Wieder, D.L. (1977) 'The diary: diary-interview method', *Urban Life*, 5, 4:479–98.

Znaniecki, F. (1934) *The Method of Sociology*, New York, Farrar & Rinehart.

Zorbaugh, H. (1929) *The Gold Coast and the Slum*, Chicago, University of Chicago Press.

Name Index

Abraham, J. 43
Adam, B. 249
Adelman, C. 230–1
Adler, P. 89, 280, 283
Adler, P. A. 9, 89, 280, 283
Agar, M. 128, 185, 244
Aggleton, P. 109
Atkinson, J. M. 169
Atkinson, P. 1, 33–5, 87, 126, 164, 188, 192, 199–200, 244, 247, 250, 266

Ball, M. S. 189
Ball, S. J. 43, 67, 138, 165, 225, 228, 230
Barbera-Stein, L. 54–5
Barnes, J. A. 263, 267, 272, 280
Barrett, R. A. 75–6, 78
Barton, A. 216
Beals, R. 263
Becker, H. S. 9, 20, 33, 103, 129, 189, 195, 211, 222, 232, 233, 252, 269, 271, 275, 280
Begenstoss, N. T. 46–7
Bell, C. 22, 263, 265, 271
Bensman, J. 214, 269
Berger, P. 125–6
Berlak, A. C. 46–7
Berlak, H. 36–7
Berreman, G. 74, 222
Bertaux, D. 131
Bettelheim, D. 104
Beynon, J. 89–91, 103, 273, 282
Bloor, M. 169, 228, 229

Blumer, H. 6–7, 11, 24, 160, 242
Bogdan, R. 66, 222
Bohannon, P. 206–7
Boon, J. 253
Booth, C. 3
Boru, K. 16
Bowen E. 101, 244
Brandon, D. 279
Brannen, J. 2
Brettell, C. B. 261
Brewer, J. 82–3, 96
Briar, B. 238
Brodkey, L. 239
Brown, P. 109
Bryman, A. 2
Bulmer, M. 169–70, 264, 281
Burgess, R. G. 22, 125, 133, 150, 152, 266, 281–2
Burke, K. 163

Campbell, J. 39
Cannon, S. 120, 122, 133, 151, 274
Cappetti, C. 161, 244–5
Carey, J. T. 178–9
Carr, W. 16
Carrington, B. 20, 269
Cassell, J. 60–1
Cassidy, A. 15
Chagnon, N. A. 238
Chambliss, W. 70–2
Chandler, J. 134–5, 143–4
Christensen, T. 155
Cicourel, A. 168, 169, 237
Coffey, A. J. 167–8

Subject Index

reflexivity 16–22, 227, 239–40, 285
and audiences 258–62
and political character of
research 20–1
and realism 17–19
relativism, ethical 277
research design 23–53
development of research
problems 29–36
forshadowed problems 24–9,
160
sampling within the case 45–53
selecting settings/cases 36–45
respondent validation 227–32
triangulation 230–2
responsibility, writing and 255–8
retrieval, data 193–203
rhetoric and ethnography 245–53
roles, field 99–109
acceptable incompetent 103–4
complete participant 104–7

Saints, Scholars and Schizophrenics
(Scheper-Hughes) 267–8
sampling 42–3, 45–53
context 51–3
people 50–1
time 46–9
schools studies 28, 36–7, 43–4, 67,
103, 133–4, 230, 281–2
deviant acts 32
emotionally disturbed children
54–5
fieldnotes 181–2
medical records 171–3
middle schools 147
nursery schools 98
private school 269–70
progressive schools 46–7, 181–2
protestant school 95–6
researching multiple audiences
85–6
school reports 170–2
secondary 132, 146
school reports 170–2
transfer to work 35
working-class boys 218–20
Scientology, study of 283–4
self-disclosure 91

settings/cases, selecting 36–45,
275
situated vocabularies 182–3
Slim's Table (Duneier) 251–2
social context 220–5
software, ethnographic 193–203
Computer Assisted Data
Analysis (CAQDAS) 197
Ethnograph 198, 199, 200
FY13000Plus 200
Golden Retriever 200
IZE 200
KWALITAN 100–1
NUDIST 201
Qualpro 198
Text Analysis Package 198
Textbase Alpha 198
solicited/unsolicited accounts
126–33
sources, documentary 159–65
sponsors 64
statistics, official 168–70
storage, data 193–203
strains/stresses of fieldwork
113–20
Street Corner Society (Whyte) 261
*Structure of Scientific Revolutions,
The* (Kuhn) 12
styles and genres 258–62
substantive analysis 31–2
symbolic interactionism 7
synecdoche, use of 248, 251–2

teachers 43–4
accounts 129–31
college 115–16
progressive school 181–2
researcher's relations with
89–91, 150
temporality 47, 161
concepts and indicators 225–6
importance of 46–9
Text Analysis Package software 198
Textbase Alpha software 198
thaumaturgy 247
theory 232–8
and comparative analysis 232–6
'grounded' 241
types of 236–8